Sick Enough turns the lights on for any
ing world of eating disorders—both th
professionals hoping to help them. Di........ ... ,..... .. ..ce treating all kinds of people with all kinds of eating disorders, Dr. Gaudiani
doesn't just give information, she inspires hope and paves a pathway to
recovery. Bottom line—*this book will save lives.*

Margo Maine, PhD, FAED, CEDS
Eating disorders specialist and author

Sick Enough is an incomparable contribution to a literature starving for an
embracing, social justice-informed perspective on the medical management of those with eating disorders. Impeccably and accessibly composed,
accentuated by case studies, metaphors and parables, this book validates
patients' diversity and lived experiences and comprehensively addresses
the vagaries of medical complications associated with disordered eating.
Dr. G.'s passionate and effective capacity for sharing the depth and range
of her clinical acumen ensures patients and professionals will equally
benefit.

Beth Hartman McGilley, PhD, FAED, CEDS
Licensed Clinical Psychologist in private practice

Dr. Gaudiani has created a work of great value that will not only educate
families, motivate sufferers, and inform clinicians, but also her voice of love
and human compassion, which all of us who know her deeply value, reso-
nates throughout the book. She has merged her unique depth of knowledge and experience with her huge heart and ability to compassionately
communicate. I am grateful for this invaluable resource. It will be a must-
have for all clinicians who treat eating disorders and a gift to all families
and sufferers as they understand and embrace their unique recoveries.

Sondra Kronberg, MS, RD, CDN, CEDRD-S
Executive Director, Eating Disorder Treatment Collaborative/
FEED of New York
Founder and Spokesperson, National Eating Disorders
Association (NEDA)

Dr. Gaudiani just wrote the book so many of us have been waiting for: fascinating, clear, and amazingly readable. Love and respect for the magic of
the doctor–patient relationship is center stage. Eating disorders are serious
and often deadly illnesses that take advantage of our cultural myth that
health can be read from body size. This is a map of how to pay attention to
what matters, ignore the distractions, and keep the faith.

Deb Burgard, PhD, FAED
Co-founder, Health at Every Size®

As an incredible resource for a wide range of medical problems encountered by those with eating disorders, this book provides an invaluable contribution to the field of eating disorders. Comprehensive in scope, it is written in language easily decipherable by patients, family members, and professionals from different disciplines. Dr. Gaudiani emphasizes that all individuals suffering from medical complications from eating disorders are sick enough to receive treatment and are deserving of recovery.

Anita Johnston, PhD
Author of *Eating in the Light of the Moon*

Sick Enough is a beautifully written medical guide for living with or caring for someone with an eating disorder. Dr. Gaudiani shares her wisdom in a discussion that is complete and practical. Metaphors, scientific studies and patient vignettes are offered as tools that will help those who are suffering to make sense of their experience. Her voice emerges from a loving respect and commitment, crafting a framework for care that supports emotional growth and wellbeing. This will be a go to resource for clinicians, patients and families alike.

Kimberli McCallum, MD, CEDS, FAPA
Founder and Chief Medical Officer McCallum Place Treatment Centers
Associate Professor Clinical Psychiatry, Washington University
School of Medicine

A rigorous medical guide to treating eating disorders, artfully weaving in the sociopolitical underpinnings, and as compassionate as it is captivating, *Sick Enough* is essential reading for clinicians and families. This book will be a game changer in eating disorder treatment.

Linda Bacon, PhD, Author of *Body Respect* and *Health at Every Size*

Knowledge is POWER. What might have been different if I had the power of knowledge when my daughter struggled with anorexia? I will never know but another mom who is desperately seeking knowledge to help her beloved child now has a resource written by Dr. Jennifer Gaudiani. *Sick Enough* provides a wealth of information that was specifically written to arm all those affected by eating disorders with the knowledge they need to fully recover.

Kitty Westin
Advocate

Sick Enough is a tremendous resource and a must-read for anyone in a position to influence the physical and emotional development of young men and women. Dr. Gaudiani's unique perspective as an internist and eating disorder specialist allows her to provide indispensable information on prevention, awareness, recognition, and treatment of the full continuum of eating disorders. A wealth of information and the best available go-to guide on DE and ED.

Caroline Silby, PhD
Sport Psychology Consultant to US Figure Skating and author of *Games Girls Play: Understanding and Guiding Young Female Athletes*

In *Sick Enough*, Jennifer Gaudiani's voice is one of guide, mentor, trusted companion, and sage. She tackles a complex and too-often deadly illness and transforms it—through a holistic perspective, metaphorical language and case studies—into a work worthy of breaking the secret code of eating disorders. Through compassion and respect, she is able to engage the authentic individual hiding beneath symptomology. This is not merely a book—it is a masterpiece.

Adrienne Ressler, LMSW, CEDS, F.iaedp
Vice President Professional Development, The Renfrew Center
Foundation Body Image Specialist

I have been waiting for a book like this to be written for my entire career. Dr. Gaudiani has written a book that is easy to digest while also being incredibly informative. There are wonderful case examples which illuminate the substantial medical issues facing people with eating disorders. This book is a necessary addition to anyone treating people with eating disorders.

Beth Mayer, LICSW
Former Executive Director of Multi-Service Eating Disorders
Association (MEDA)

Dr. Gaudiani weaves her knowledge, experience, skill, and care masterfully in this necessary book. She is one of those brilliant physicians who can present medically accurate information in an accessible way, and she provides us with meaningful information about bodies and eating disorders in a compassionate and ethical way. Written from a weight-inclusive lens, this book will be one I refer to often.

Carmen Cool, MA, LPC
Psychotherapist and educator

Sick Enough is a gift to the eating disorders field, addressing a significant need in the literature. Dr. Gaudiani provides a comprehensive discussion of the medical/nutritional concerns across eating disorder diagnoses in a manner that is accurate, easily understood, and respectful while addressing the stigma individuals with eating disorders often face. *Sick Enough* is a must-read for those with eating disorders, their families, all communities of support, as well as the professionals who care for these amazing individuals.

Leah L. Graves, RDN, LDN, CEDRD, FAED
Vice President of Nutrition and Culinary Services, Veritas
Collaborative, LLC

The field has very much needed a book written for and including everyone that suffers from eating disorders. Dr. Gaudiani in print, as in life, delivers passion, grace, intelligence and hope to those who seek to understand the impact of these illnesses on the human body. I unequivocally recommend this book to professionals and families alike.

Scott Moseman, MD, CEDS
Medical Director, Laureate Eating Disorders Program

The good medical care of an eating disorder patient is a real art. In her book, *Sick Enough*, Dr. Gaudiani's easy-to-understand explanations, case vignettes, and her own clinical experience are treasures for the eating disorder literature. This is a book I highly recommend for every single eating disorder specialist or any professional who takes care of eating disorders patients. I loved it! I give an enthusiastic standing ovation for this great addition to the literature of our field!

Eva Maria Trujillo Chi Vacuán, MD, FAED, CEDS, Fiaedp, FAAP
Past President, Academy for Eating Disorders
Medical Director and Founder of Comenzar de Nuevo, A.C.
Clinical Professor at Tecnológico de Monterrey School of Medicine

This year will be my 50th year as an academician and clinician taking care of patients with eating disorders. I read the book with great interest, admiring the blend of narrative medicine and up-to-date science leading to competent therapeutic advice. The old dictum was "He who knows syphilis knows medicine." It can now be replaced with "She who knows anorexia nervosa knows medicine." This book is a must-read for patients and their families ... and they would do well in buying one book for their primary practitioner.

Tomas Jose Silber, MD, MASS
Professor of Pediatrics, George Washington University
Medical Director, Donald Delaney Eating Disorders Program,
Division of Adolescent Medicine

If I or someone who I cared deeply about had an eating disorder, I would want to work with a physician who was competent, conscientious, caring, collaborative, courageous in advocating for patients, and coachable—humbly open to learning from research, patients, and herself. If you doubt such a physician exists, and, more important, if you are a person with an eating disorder, a family member, or a clinician who wants to learn a lot from a professional who integrates this level of expertise, character, and humility into a healing presence, then *Sick Enough* is an invaluable resource. Not only does "Dr. G." provide detailed and comprehensible information about a host of ways in which eating disorders compromise the human body, including the brain, she also deftly situates both illness and recovery in the context of intersecting psychological, interpersonal, cultural, and soul-full (or empty) dimensions.

Michael P. Levine, PhD, FAED
Emeritus Professor of Psychology, Kenyon College

Dr. G. shares her remarkable knowledge and style in a way that brings insight to a patient's experience with an eating disorder, awareness of the body's challenges and complications, and meaningful recommendations to patients, their families, and professionals. *Sick Enough* distinguishes itself as an essential read. Bravo to this comprehensive and timely volume!

Kathryn Cortese, LCSW, ACSW, CEDS
Editor-in-Chief, Gürze/Salucore

Get this book. It will make you an expert. Dr. Gaudiani is a superb physician with a healer's touch. Covering the full spectrum of eating disorders in diverse populations with all diagnoses, this is a guide to understand their experience, medical complications and treatment. Dispensing with the rumors, fads and social biases that surround these disorders, she has created a resource that is easy to read and absorb. Patents, families and providers will all benefit tremendously from this book.

Mark Warren, MD, MPH, FAED
Chief Medical Officer, Emily Program

Dr. Gaudiani communicates a basic love for this difficult work. Although "Dr. G." is a ferociously erudite scholar, there is a remarkable absence of jargon. The text is written in a lucid and intimate manner with both authenticity and humility. This inspired, compassionate book is a must-read for both the new and the seasoned provider. It is also a gift of knowledge and insight for patients and their loved ones.

Tamara Pryor, PhD, FAED
Executive Clinical Director, EDCare

Finally a comprehensive guide that covers the whole spectrum and depth of eating disorders in a way that is both scientific and poetic. This book serves practitioners with its rigorously highlighted evidence-based care for all the medical complications and serves patients and families with Dr. Gaudiani's innovative, "out of the box" use of unique metaphors. Lastly, Dr. Gaudiani's humanity shines through in the pages of this book as she offers glimpses into her own life.

Margherita Mascolo, MD, CEDS
Medical Director, ACUTE Center for Eating Disorders at Denver Health
Associate Professor of Medicine, University of Colorado Health
Sciences Center

Sick Enough

Patients with eating disorders frequently feel that they aren't "sick enough" to merit treatment, despite medical problems that are both measurable and unmeasurable. They may struggle to accept rest, nutrition, and a team to help them move toward recovery. *Sick Enough* offers patients, their families, and clinicians a comprehensive, accessible review of the medical issues that arise from eating disorders by bringing relatable case presentations and a scientifically sound, engaging style to the topic. Using metaphor and patient-centered language, Dr. Gaudiani aims to improve medical diagnosis and treatment, motivate recovery, and validate the lived experiences of individuals of all body shapes and sizes, while firmly rejecting dieting culture.

Jennifer L. Gaudiani, MD, CEDS, FAED is a Board-Certified internal medicine physician, known nationally and internationally for her work on the medical complications of eating disorders. Her outpatient medical practice, the Gaudiani Clinic, cares for individuals of all genders, shapes, and sizes, from around the United States.

Sick Enough

A Guide to the Medical Complications of Eating Disorders

Jennifer L. Gaudiani
MD, CEDS, FAED

Routledge
Taylor & Francis Group
NEW YORK AND LONDON

First published 2019
by Routledge
711 Third Avenue, New York, NY 10017

and by Routledge
2 Park Square, Milton Park, Abingdon, Oxon, OX14 4RN

Routledge is an imprint of the Taylor & Francis Group, an informa business

Library of Congress Cataloging-in-Publication Data
Names: Gaudiani, Jennifer L., author.
Title: Sick enough : a guide to the medical complications of eating
disorders / Jennifer L. Gaudiani.
Description: New York, NY : Routledge, 2019. | Includes
bibliographical references and index.
Identifiers: LCCN 2018025103 (print) | LCCN 2018025565 (ebook) |
ISBN 9781351184731 (Ebook) | ISBN 9780815382447 (hardback) |
ISBN 9780815382454 (pbk.) | ISBN 9781351184731 (ebk.)
Subjects: | MESH: Feeding and Eating Disorders–complications |
Case Reports
Classification: LCC RC552.E18 (ebook) | LCC RC552.E18 (print)
| NLM WM 175 | DDC 616.85/26–dc23
LC record available at https://lccn.loc.gov/2018025103

ISBN: 978-0-815-38244-7 (hbk)
ISBN: 978-0-815-38245-4 (pbk)
ISBN: 978-1-351-18473-1 (ebk)

Typeset in Baskerville
by Wearset Ltd, Boldon, Tyne and Wear

With infinite appreciation, I dedicate this book to my beloved husband, Bryan and daughters, Sydney and Skye; to my phenomenal team at the Gaudiani Clinic; to my immensely supportive parents; and to my patients, who have taught me so much.

Contents

PART V
Specific Populations · 173

Abbreviations

AAP	American Association of Pediatrics
ALT	alanine aminotransferase
ANBN	anorexia nervosa and bulimia nervosa
ARFID	avoidant restrictive food intake disorder
AST	aspartate aminotransferase
BED	binge eating disorder
BUN	blood urea nitrogen
CBC	complete blood count
CEDRD	Certified Eating Disorders Registered Dietitian
CEDS	Certified Eating Disorder Specialist
CPM	central pontine myelinolysis
CPR	cardiopulmonary resuscitation
Cr	creatinine
DEXA/DXA	Dual Energy X-Ray Absorptiometry
DI	diabetes insipidus
DKA	diabetic ketoacidosis
DMT1	type 1 diabetes mellitus
EDS	Ehlers Danlos Syndrome
FAED	Fellow of the Academy of Eating Disorders
FODMAP	fermentable oligo-, di-, mono-saccharides, and polyols
FSH	follicle stimulating hormone
GERD	gastroesophageal reflux disease
GI	gastrointestinal
GnRH	gonadotropin releasing hormone
HAES	Health At Every Size
iaedp	International Association of Eating Disorders Professionals
IBS	irritable bowel syndrome
IBS-C	IBS-constipation
IBS-D	IBS-diarrheal
IGF-1	insulin-like growth factor-1
IOC	International Olympic Committee
IOP	intensive outpatient program

ISCD	International Society for Clinical Densitometry
IUI	intrauterine insemination
IVF	in vitro fertilization
LH	luteinizing hormone
MCA	mast cell activation
MCD	mast cell dysfunction
NCGS	non-celiac gluten sensitivity
OSFED	other specified feeding and eating disorders
OT	occupational therapy
PCOS	polycystic ovarian syndrome
PEG	percutaneous endoscopic gastrostomy
PEJ	percutaneous endoscopic jejunostomy
PHP	partial hospitalization program
PICC	peripherally inserted central catheter
POTS	postural orthostatic tachycardia syndrome
PPIs	proton pump inhibitors
PT	physical therapy
PTH	parathyroid hormone
RAN	restrictive anorexia nervosa
RED-S	relative energy deficiency in sport
SE-AN	severe and enduring anorexia nervosa
SEED	severe and enduring eating disorders
SIADH	syndrome of inappropriate anti-diuretic hormone secretion
SIBO	small intestinal bacterial overgrowth
SLP	speech language pathologist
SMA	superior mesenteric artery
SPMI	severe persistent mental illness
TPN	total parenteral nutrition
TSH	thyroid stimulating hormone

Introduction

This is a book about the medical complications of eating disorders. I wrote it for patients and their loved ones as well as for clinicians who care for patients with eating disorders. You might be thinking, "Medical complications? Aren't these mental illnesses?" It turns out that eating less than the body needs, or purging by vomiting, laxative abuse, or various other means, can cause medical problems that range from mild to life threatening.

My Background

Let me give you a little background about myself. I was raised in Northern California, the oldest of three girls. When I left to attend Harvard at age 17, I knew two things about my future plans: I wanted to be an English major with a focus on poetry, and I wanted to be a doctor. I stayed true to these plans, in the process falling in love with the man who would one day become my husband. Having joyfully made college more of a time for growing up than for rigorous academics, I barely squeaked into just one of the 26 medical schools I applied to.

With relief, I started at Boston University School of Medicine. Two years later, my middle sister arrived for college. We had been having phone calls for months about her worries regarding food and body image. At the time, I knew nothing about eating disorders. All I could do was tell her I loved her and encourage her to eat enough and not punish her body. When she arrived to start college, it became clear that she had developed a full blown eating disorder. I recognized that my unconditional love probably wasn't going to be sufficient to help her, and I was grateful when she found a good therapist.

My sister suffered from bulimia nervosa for many years. Thankfully, she has been fully recovered since her mid 20s. Even though she never had to step up to a higher level of care, her recovery journey was hard, and it represented a formative and important time in her life. As her sister, I felt scared and powerless while she was in her illness. However, her journey inspired me to get into this field and take back power so that others might be helped. Illness in a family can bring surprising gifts and awaken opportunities to see the world in a new way. Supporting my sister gave me an immense appreciation for her courage. It also introduced me to the type of person susceptible to developing an eating disorder: intelligent, sensitive, hard working, and determined.

I decided at the end of medical school to specialize in internal medicine. Internists don't perform surgery or see children or pregnant women. They are trained to care for adults, concentrating on the inner workings of every organ system, essentially taking care of the whole person. Following my residency and chief residency at Yale, I decided not to subspecialize (which would have meant cardiology, gastroenterology, or endocrinology, for instance), but rather to remain a general internist. While my last name, Gaudiani (gow-dee-AH-nee), gets easier with time, I've always invited my patients and their families to call me "Dr. G."

My husband and I moved to Denver in 2007 with our then-toddler daughter. We love the outdoors, and the prospect of a work-life balance that favored weekend hikes and ski trips as a family sounded heavenly to a couple of Type A, intense professionals. I started working at the inner-city teaching hospital for the University of Colorado, called Denver Health. One year into my employment, the head physician of the hospital, who unbeknownst to me was also the world expert in the medical complications of eating disorders, wrote out an e-mail to my department asking if anyone wanted to help him grow and manage an inpatient medical unit dedicated to adults whose medical complications of anorexia nervosa had become so severe that they could not safely receive care anywhere else in the United States.

Pregnant at the time with my second daughter, and with my sister's experience in my heart, I immediately volunteered and in so doing changed the course of my career. I had the joy of being one of the leaders of the ACUTE Center for Eating Disorders at Denver Health for almost eight years. I learned on a daily basis from my remarkable patients and colleagues.

To my surprise, I discovered that while there are many superb therapists and dietitians who specialize in eating disorders, there are very few internists who do so, especially in outpatient settings. Patients and their families would tell me about their frustrations with the healthcare system during their years of illness: medical professionals who would miss physical signs of starvation and praise patients for weight loss, unwittingly reinforce patients' beliefs that they were "fine" and thus delay admission into needed higher levels of care, or focus narrowly on weight as a marker of health. This occurs in part because medical professionals receive almost no training in eating disorders. I, for instance, received zero hours of education on the topic. Patients with eating disorders come to be perceived as too mentally ill for the medical professionals and too medically compromised for the mental health professionals. They fall through the cracks.

At the bedsides of critically medically compromised patients with eating disorders, I became a listener and a storyteller. I simply adored my patients and relished the opportunity to care for the whole person and not just the numbers that quantified their malnutrition or the eating disorder behaviors that emerged from their emotional anguish. I learned how to diagnose and treat complicated, rare, and also common physical problems caused by malnutrition. In addition, I realized that Western medicine silos body and soul in ways that serve patients poorly, especially those with eating disorders. That is, mental illnesses are typically treated by one set of professionals, physical illnesses by another set, and the system keeps the two disciplines separate even though they are inextricably connected. Those with eating disorders show evidence of the mind-body connection in myriad ways. Emotional distress can trigger disordered behaviors, which negatively impact the ways the physical body functions, which in turn cause increased emotional distress. Good medical care must unite body and soul.

While at ACUTE, I would care for patients intensively for a few weeks and then help them transfer onwards to inpatient and residential eating disorder programs around the country. I missed experiencing the full arc of their stories. In 2016, I left ACUTE on warm terms in order to found my own outpatient medical clinic, the Gaudiani Clinic, where I can continue to follow my patients' lives over time, chapter by chapter. I founded my clinic to provide thoughtful, evidence-based medical care to individuals with eating disorders in the context of their everyday lives. I partner in a non-hierarchical manner with their existing outpatient eating disorder team (usually a therapist and a dietitian, sometimes others) in order to present a unified, thoughtful, individualized approach for outpatient recovery. After being fortunate enough to recruit a team of extraordinary professionals to the Gaudiani Clinic, we established the clinic's founding values of non-assumptiveness, open communication, non-binary perspectives, and honoring the whole person.

I now care for adolescents and adults of all shapes and sizes and all genders, both in person and with the help of a telemedicine platform, allowing me to see patients from around the country. I'm essentially a primary care provider for those with eating disorders, or where they have a great primary care doctor, I'm the specialist on the team. Overall, I work to use objective evidence of body suffering to break through patients' denial of disease and help motivate recovery work. In so doing, I try to ease physical symptoms that disrupt patients' ability to engage in the nutritional and therapeutic work needed for recovery. I'm now one of the few internists in the country who carries both the Certified Eating Disorder

Specialist (CEDS) and Fellow of the Academy of Eating Disorders (FAED) credentials.

It is important to share with you that, besides starting my own clinic, I have no financial disclosures to report with regards to what I write about in this book, no ownership stake or other financial relationship with any drug company.

Why Medical Complications Matter in Eating Disorders

Eating disorders are life-threatening mental illnesses, not choices. They affect people of all genders, ages, socioeconomic backgrounds, ethnicities, shapes, and sizes. I will review each disorder's formal diagnostic criteria throughout the book.

Anorexia nervosa carries the highest death rate of any mental illness, with patients experiencing six times the mortality rate of their healthy peers. Those with bulimia nervosa and those with atypical eating disorders (meaning not meeting all the diagnostic criteria, for instance not being formally underweight or not purging as often) have double the death rate of non-eating disordered peers.

Up to 20 percent of those who die from anorexia nervosa die by suicide.[1] Compared with gender- and age-matched groups, patients with anorexia nervosa are 18 times more likely to die by suicide, and those with bulimia nervosa are seven times more likely to die by suicide.[2] Eating disorders rank as the twelfth leading cause of disability in young women in industrialized countries.[3] These are intolerable diseases that cause untold suffering to patients and their families.

Despite these jaw-dropping statistics, the tragic and nearly universal reality for those with eating disorders is that they often believe they aren't sick enough to warrant changing their behaviors or seeking help. This is true for patients who come to my outpatient clinic, and it was true for the patients I saw at ACUTE. Denial of disease severity is one of the hallmarks of these mental illnesses. Patients may think their bloodwork isn't "that bad," or their weight isn't "that low," or they may point to the fact that they are still high achievers in school or at work.

In writing this book, I hope to establish that anyone with an eating disorder is sick enough to seek help. If you have even one of the medical issues detailed in the book, you are sick enough. If you have never had an eating disorder, but you have a disordered relationship with food and your body, you are at risk for the medical problems I describe. Sometimes it takes medical truths, challenging the false narrative of "I'm just being healthy," to make patients realize they are engaging in behaviors that are anything but healthy. Everyone has the potential for full recovery, and most medical problems will resolve with recovery.

Who Might Benefit from This Book?

Since joining the field, I have developed a passion for improving the quality of medical care for patients with eating disorders. I have lectured nationally and internationally about the medical complications of eating disorders, speaking most often to rooms of dedicated therapists and dietitians who are often put in the position of having to educate their patients' doctors. I have written blogs and developed webinar series to establish standards of care for diagnosis and treatment. I sat on the board of the International Association of Eating Disorders Professionals (iaedp) as its only internist, and I sit on the editorial board of the *International Journal of Eating Disorders*, a top peer-reviewed journal, reading and assessing the latest articles in the field. I am proud to have dedicated my career to patients with eating disorders.

However, I've never written a book. I realized I want to share my knowledge and perspective with more patients and families than I will ever be able to see one on one. I wrote this book for those who have an eating disorder or who have been on diets and want to know what might be happening in their bodies as a result. They might have been invalidated or even harmed by the medical system for years. They might have medical issues that are hard to measure and thus hard to diagnose and treat. They may not trust doctors one bit. I get it. I hope this book starts to heal some of this damage and validates patients' lived experiences.

This book is for families, too. Loved ones increasingly search online for information when the medical system fails them. Unfortunately, the internet is teeming with pseudoscientific information about bodies and nutrition, what's healthy and what's dangerous. I want to provide families with a source of information that's accurate (as far as the current state of the science, which is always evolving) and evidence based. When there aren't high quality journal articles to cite, I use trusted, expert recommendations. Families also need to be able to advocate for their loved one in the medical system. I encourage families to bring this book with them to medical settings, respectfully offering it up as a resource to open-minded, willing medical providers who simply haven't had sufficient experience with eating disorders.

This book is also for clinicians who work with individuals who have eating disorders: therapists, dietitians, social workers, physical and occupational therapists, speech language pathologists, nurses, advanced practitioners, and doctors. Clinicians who are drawn to this field have huge hearts, care deeply, and want the best for their clients. They often need to advocate for their clients and do so best when they know more about what is going on medically. This book will improve their knowledge base and help them develop ways to discuss these issues. In my own work with patients, I manage the medical aspects of their care so that dietitians and therapists can optimally deploy their expertise, undistracted by unaddressed medical issues. Where these clinicians do not have an experienced physician to partner with, I hope this book will help elevate everyone's level of medical knowledge and lead to better patient outcomes.

How the Book Will Unfold

The book is divided into five parts. Part I, "Not Enough Calories," offers a review of everything that goes wrong in the body from lack of sufficient nutrition. Part II, "Purging," describes the different types of purging and how each causes medical complications. Part III, "Patients in Larger Bodies," identifies the considerable harm caused by a medical system and society that inflict their size stigma and fat bias upon countless individuals. I firmly reject diet culture and suggest a different medical management style that honors body diversity. Part IV, "The Unmeasurables, a.k.a. The Very Real Medical Problems that Modern Medicine Can't Measure," examines medical problems that may not emerge directly from eating disorders but frequently co-occur and may impede recovery work. These are difficult to diagnose, and thus patients may receive inadequate medical care. Part V, "Specific Populations," comprises a series of shorter chapters that evaluate the relationship between specific patient groups and eating disorders. In the conclusion, I consider some ways in which we can each make a positive contribution to our loved ones' relationships with their bodies and food.

Each chapter opens with a fictional case designed to be representative of individuals with eating disorders, compiled from my lived experience as a physician working with this patient population. One of my intentions is to highlight various marginalized voices, and I may not get the language quite right, nor will my personal clinical experience allow me to represent all individuals and groups. I humbly acknowledge this. Drawing from years of teaching at the bedside, in the clinic, and in professional talks, I review the medical issues in each chapter just as I do in person with patients, families, and clinicians. I want these concepts to feel understandable and not "too medical." I make no mention of body weights so as to avoid triggering comparisons. Each chapter in Parts I through IV will end with a box in which I share a metaphor, story, or reflection that has been helpful to my patients over the years.

I cannot comment on therapeutic modalities (such as acceptance and commitment therapy or cognitive behavioral therapy) because these are outside of my scope of practice. Many outstanding books cover psychotherapeutic and sociological perspectives on eating disorder development and treatment. I do want to acknowledge that this book recommends best practices in "optimal," resource-neutral cases, ones in which insurance or personal finances allow appropriate diagnosis and full treatment. This by no means represents every family's situation.

I have immense compassion for the patients and families who are not insured, have inadequate health insurance for typical eating disorder care (such as governmental insurers or plans that lack out of network benefits) and inadequate financial resources, or experience institutional and systematic oppression and cannot advocate as successfully within the system. There are, it must be noted, serious ethical problems with recommending what care patients "should" receive, when in many cases there are inadequate resources to access this care. This is a devastating flaw in our healthcare system.

There are a few terms I will use throughout the book that should be clarified in advance. Standard grammar has historically required us to structure sentences in this way: "The patient wanted to see his/her results." The word "patient" is singular, so the pronoun is singular. However, I honor gender inclusivity. Gender is not binary, and I choose not to exclude anyone by arbitrarily sprinkling in the pronouns "hers" and "his" throughout. The alternative is called the "singular they,"[4] as in, "The patient wanted to see their results." I deliberately use this throughout the book. Along similar lines, the case vignettes categorize patients as "cisgender" when they identify with the sex that was assigned at birth, as opposed to transgender.

The concept of the "eating disorder voice" refers to the judgmental, unkind, relentless, comparison making, rule creating, never satisfied thoughts that can occupy people's minds. Everyone's eating disorder voice is unique, but certain themes appear over and over. I use the word "soul" to signify the psyche or emotional core. This is not meant to have any religious overtones. Finally, I mention the concept of "values" throughout the book. I invite each of my patients to share with me what really matters to them, what elements of their lives are most important, and what traits make them most fundamentally themselves. These concepts are all wrapped up into the word "values."

I welcome you to read this book either from cover to cover or to choose the chapters and topics most relevant to you. I hope you find it useful. If you are the one struggling with disordered eating or an eating disorder, please let me offer you these warm words of support: you can do this. I know it's scary, but you can recover. Right at this moment, you are sick enough.

Notes

1 Arcelus J, Mitchell AJ, Wales J, Nielsen S. Mortality rates in patients with anorexia nervosa and other eating disorders. A meta-analysis of 36 studies. *Arch Gen Psychiatry.* 2011 July; 68(7):724–731. doi: 10.1001/archgenpsychiatry.2011.74.
2 Smith AR, Zuromski KL, Dodd DR. Eating disorders and suicidality: what we know, what we don't know, and suggestions for future research. *Curr Opin Psychol.* 2017 August 12; 22:63–67. doi: 10.1016/j.copsyc.2017.08.023.
3 Hoek HW. Review of the worldwide epidemiology of eating disorders. *Curr Opin Psychiatry.* 2016 November; 29(6):336–339. doi: 10.1097/YCO.0000000000000282.
4 https://en.wikipedia.org/wiki/Singular_they. Accessed April 15, 2018.

Part I

Not Enough Calories

Let's start by talking about starvation. When I say starvation, I mean any situation in which not enough calories are consumed, over some period of time, to fulfil the body's needs. Starvation can occur in people of any body shape and size. It doesn't just happen in people with lower body weight, although society and the medical profession may not understand this fact. All too often, weight stigma causes patients in larger bodies to be praised for engaging in the same eating disordered behaviors that in an underweight person would cause great alarm. Low energy intake can occur during an eating disorder or disordered eating, but it can also happen when someone goes on a diet or participates in a fast or a "cleanse."

The *Diagnostic and Statistical Manual-5*, also called the DSM-5, published by the American Psychiatric Association and updated every decade or so, contains the official diagnostic criteria for mental illnesses.[1] All eating disorders are characterized by aspects of inadequate caloric intake with attendant risks of medical complications. Practically no one with an eating disorder stops eating and drinking altogether; that is a popular misconception. These are complicated illnesses that emerge from a combination of genetic, inherited temperamental traits and physiological, environmental, and sociological factors. I'll start by reviewing the definitions of the eating disorders most specifically tied to insufficient energy availability.

Anorexia nervosa is diagnosed when an individual persistently restricts caloric intake, leading either to significantly low body weight (related to what is minimally expected for age, sex, and health) or to arrested growth in children or adolescents. In addition, patients experience an intense fear of gaining weight or becoming fat, develop distortions in the way they perceive their bodies, and deny the severity of their behaviors and risks of low weight. Patients' sense of self-worth becomes unduly influenced by their body size and shape.

Anorexia nervosa comes in two subtypes: restricting and binge eating/purging. While both subtypes may manifest obsessive and compulsive over-exercise, those with restricting anorexia nervosa purely limit calories.

By contrast, those with purging anorexia nervosa may or may not engage in binge eating, but eating of any kind is frequently followed by compensatory behaviors such as vomiting, laxative abuse, or diuretic abuse (see Part II for further discussion of these behaviors). In both subtypes, patients by definition are significantly underweight. In general, anorexia nervosa has a prevalence of around 1 percent, with a ratio of females to males of 10:1.[2]

In atypical anorexia nervosa, which falls under the DSM-5 heading of other specified feeding and eating disorders (OSFED), patients engage in all the same behaviors and have equally severe body image distortions and fears as those with anorexia nervosa, but they are not formally underweight. Patients may lose a significant amount of weight and may be underweight relative to their typical body weight. Atypical anorexia nervosa is by far more prevalent than anorexia nervosa, occurring in up to 3 percent of the population in one large study.[3] The fact that these individuals receive the designation "atypical," despite representing by far the greatest number of patients with symptoms of anorexia nervosa, speaks to the ongoing problem of size stigma in medical and mental health communities.

In my clinical experience, many individuals with atypical anorexia nervosa don't believe they have an eating disorder because they aren't stereotypically emaciated. This is only reinforced by society and by medical providers who not only miss the eating disorder but praise such patients for their weight loss and presumed "health" when, in fact, the behaviors being used are the opposite of healthy. A recent study found that adolescents with atypical anorexia nervosa presenting to a specialized pediatric eating disorder unit were just as psychologically and medically ill as the patients with typical anorexia nervosa.[4]

In patients with atypical anorexia nervosa, if weight is checked during medical assessment, the calculation for "weight suppression" should be used. Weight suppression refers to the percentage of body weight lost, calculated as the highest recent body weight minus the current body weight, divided by the highest recent body weight. Weight suppression of even 5 percent, in the presence of anorexia nervosa symptoms, has been found to be clinically significant.[5] Of course, given that some individuals never lose weight, the whole person and their overall medical and psychological state must also be taken into account. Individuals with atypical anorexia nervosa, regardless of body shape and size, are unquestionably sick enough to seek treatment and recovery.

Patients with avoidant restrictive food intake disorder (ARFID), discussed in Chapter 14, also fail to take in enough calories, but without the focus on and distortions of body size and shape. The medical complications of starvation that will be discussed throughout Part I apply to them as well.

In Chapter 1, I will introduce the three main medical issues that emerge from starvation: slowed metabolism, organ dysfunction from insufficient energy intake, and treatment of malnutrition. These provide an organizing framework upon which we can understand most of what happens to the body when it receives inadequate calories. I will go into greater detail on each of these topics in Chapters 2, 3, 4, and 5.

Notes

1 American Psychiatric Association. *Diagnostic and statistical manual of mental disorders* (5th ed.) Arlington, VA: American Psychiatric Publishing; 2013.
2 Lindvall Dahlgren C, Wisting L, Rø Ø. Feeding and eating disorders in the DSM-5 era: a systematic review of prevalence rates in non-clinical male and female samples. *J Eat Disord.* 2017 December 28; 5:56. doi: 10.1186/s40337-017-0186-7.
3 Hay P, Mitchison D, Collado AEL, González-Chica DA, Stocks N, Touyz S. Burden and health-related quality of life of eating disorders, including Avoidant/Restrictive Food Intake Disorder (ARFID), in the Australian population. *J Eat Disord.* 2017 July 3; 5:21. doi: 10.1186/s40337-017-0149-z.
4 Sawyer SM, Whitelaw M, Le Grange D, Yeo M, Hughes EK. Physical and psychological morbidity in adolescents with atypical anorexia nervosa. *Pediatrics.* 2016 April; 137(4). pii: e20154080. doi: 10.1542/peds.2015-4080.
5 Forney KJ, Brown TA, Holland-Carter LA, Kennedy GA, Keel PK. Defining "significant weight loss" in atypical anorexia nervosa. *Int J Eat Disord.* 2017 August; 50(8):952–962. doi: 10.1002/eat.22717.

Chapter 1

30,000-Foot View

What Happens When You Starve Yourself?

Background

In clinic with patients and their families, when I discuss the topic of how starvation affects the body, I start by introducing the concept of the "cave person brain." The cave person brain refers to the part of our brain that manages the day-to-day functions of our bodies. It takes care of us as a mammal, rather than as a thinking, talking human being. It manages our temperature, digestion, heart rate, blood pressure, reproductive hormones, and to some extent, our animal reactions to the world, among others.

The Cave Person Brain and Metabolism

When our cave person brain senses it is not getting enough to eat, it has no insight that an eating disorder is enforcing food rules, that self-imposed or external bullying is driving a diet, or that everyone at work is doing a "cleanse" this week. It can only interpret, "We must be in a famine. We have to protect our person." Humans have survived as a species in part due to our exquisite ability to tolerate starvation. Our ancestors frequently faced food shortages. The cave person brain evolved to be highly responsive to this stressor.

When a person consumes too few calories, the cave person brain decreases their metabolic rate so that fewer calories are burned. As I will detail in Chapter 2, it does this by slowing down our heart rate, lowering our blood pressure, slowing our digestion, reducing blood flow to our hands and feet, and decreasing our feeling of energy to get things done, in order to make us hold still and conserve energy. This increases the likelihood that the person will survive until food is again available. In addition, the cave person brain fiercely strives to maintain our body weight.

What *is* metabolism, though? It's talked about all the time, and there is a lot of pseudoscience propagated about it. While "metabolism" refers to all biochemical processes that sustain life, I generally use the term "metabolism" to describe what is formally called "basal metabolic rate," which is the number of calories a body burns each day just by existing. Most of our daily caloric expenditure goes toward maintaining our body temperature at almost exactly 98.6 degrees Fahrenheit. We also burn calories for digestion, organ function, and hormone production. We use up far more calories to maintain a consistent temperature than we do going to the gym.

Exactly how the cave person brain responds to inadequate energy intake is highly variable from person to person, due to genetic factors. That is, if you have four people of similar age and body size who restrict calories similarly and move their bodies at a similar pace, they might have widely varying physiologic responses. One person might develop a slow heart rate but have normal digestion and energy. Another might have a normal heart rate but be plagued by slowed digestion. Yet another might lose lots of weight, while a fourth might lose almost no weight at all.

This variability poses a frustrating challenge for my patients. Many have been invalidated by medical providers and society at large. Despite severe mental illness that drives them to engage in serious eating disorder behaviors, they may "look normal" and thus don't generate appropriate concern or attention from some providers or others in their lives. Others suffer because, despite eating disorder behaviors, they have such protective genetics that they manifest almost no physical signs of malnutrition. Unfortunately, this further feeds into the eating disorder voice that tells them they must be fine since they look fine, that they need to push harder to lose weight.

Yet others can't believe how quickly they develop medical problems, even in the early days of an eating disorder or at a higher weight. They see an image online or a peer who looks "sicker" (i.e., usually meaning thinner), while they themselves hit a medical wall at a higher weight. All of these patients suffer from not feeling "sick enough."

The explanation for this variability probably lies in genetic subtleties that we cannot yet pinpoint. Bodies clearly have different genetic susceptibilities to what I broadly call "environmental exposures." When I talk with patients about this, I tend to remind them of a more familiar scenario. A 35-year-old man might die from liver failure after ten years of heavy drinking, while a 90-year-old man on his birthday might attribute his long life "to the whisky." What is the difference between these two heavy drinkers? All one can conclude is that they must have had different genetic sensitivities to environmental exposures.

Similarly, when my patients manifest few medical issues and a stable body weight despite eating disorder behaviors, I first validate that the behaviors themselves are worthy of care and treatment. I identify they must come from "survivor" genetic stock; their cave person brains are remarkably effective at defending their bodies from the effects of starvation. For others who develop medical problems early on in their eating disorder, I note they are genetically "sensitive." It's lucky they came to medical attention early before their eating disorder worsened. When examples of these differing clinical presentations arise, I will refer to them as "genetic variability."

Starvation and Hormones

There is another vital way in which the cave person brain reacts to starvation besides slowed metabolism. This is through radical changes in our hormones. When we starve ourselves, our brilliant cave person brain says, "Ah, I see we're in famine. This body is stressed out by too much activity and too little energy intake. Clearly it's not a safe time to produce a child." Accordingly, in adolescents and adults, the part of the brain called the hypothalamus essentially rolls hormone production back in time and produces preadolescent sex hormone levels, a condition called hypothalamic hypogonadism. As Chapter 3 will detail, this results in low estrogen levels and sometimes menstrual abnormalities for females and low testosterone levels for males. The complicated interplay of high stress hormones and low sex hormones in both sexes can lead to the one irreversible medical complication of prolonged malnutrition, one rarely anticipated by patients: bone density loss.

Starvation and the Brain

The last major way in which the cave person brain changes in response to starvation is to become vigilant and anxious. Remember back to when your pet last experienced a big thunderstorm. For some period of time after feeling threatened physically, your pet likely acted skittish. Maybe the cat got under the bed, eyes huge, tail puffy, claws ready. That is essentially what happens in the malnourished cave person brain too. The animal brain understands, "I'm at risk here. I'm vulnerable. I might not survive a dangerous encounter." So, it up-radars all of its risk monitors.

In a similar way, the malnourished person is constantly scanning the world for threats. That mental activity makes them much more rigid, resistant to change, and truly fearful much of the time. I have heard my patients say things like, "I'm terrified that it's almost lunchtime." I reassure them that much of this heightened animal anxiety is not fundamental to who they are and isn't even part of their eating disorder or anxiety disorder. It's their starved brain. I encourage my patients to have faith that as they renourish themselves, it will improve.

This same starved animal brain can make it very hard to sleep at night because again that brain thinks, "Stay a little alert in case something happens. Review the data. Are we safe?" This often results in a painfully repetitive process of reviewing what was eaten that day or how much movement was performed … ruminations not exactly conducive to sleep. I like to say that the starved person stays busy making "safety plans" all night long. This improves with nutritional rehabilitation.

So, in summary, the cave person brain is watching out for our animal body functions, the tasks we're not able consciously to alter. As people consider fad diets (like the so-called Paleo diet, supposedly designed to appeal to our inner cave person), they might remember we still carry our actual cave person brain with us to this day. It's got hundreds of thousands of years of trial and error to have figured out how best to save us from "famine." Our bodies don't like to be starved.

What Happens When Our Nutritional Gas Tank Becomes Empty?

Now let's turn to the broad concept of body dysfunction that occurs as a result of the nutritional gas tank being empty for too long, as I'll review further in Chapter 4. When our nutritional gas tank is empty, multiple organ systems run out of the energy they need to function normally. The most deadly example of this is hypoglycemia, meaning low blood sugar. Our bone marrow typically makes blood cells, but it stops doing so when malnourished. Our liver, which serves multiple purposes in our bodies, can malfunction. Our skin and hair can suffer immensely from starvation, making patients look far older than they are, with thin, brittle hair and fragile skin that easily bruises or tears and heals more slowly. Chapter 5 will cover extreme versions of body dysfunction due to malnutrition. These typically occur in patients who are profoundly underweight or who experience very rapid weight loss.

The good news is that nutritional rehabilitation will resolve all of these problems. Patients, providers, and caregivers must remember that the focus of diagnosis or treatment should never be on the malfunctioning organs themselves. These are nutritional problems which require nutritional solutions.

Nutritional Rehabilitation

The third major mechanism of medical complications in starvation actually has to do with nutritional rehabilitation: helping starving individuals begin to nourish themselves again. Experts in the eating disorder field have moved away from the term "refeeding" because it sounds somewhat condescending. The term "nutritional rehabilitation" is both accurate and more respectful. However, the concept of "refeeding syndrome" is still in use, and I will use the term when necessary.

Patients who need to restore body weight can become impressively hypermetabolic. Someone who has been restricting food, causing a slowed metabolism, may need far more calories than they would imagine to restore their organ systems and body weight. Chapter 6 considers how the body responds to the reintroduction of food.

Broadly speaking, reintroducing food can be a medically complicated and even deadly process itself. There are mechanical challenges with getting enough calories into a digestive system that has slowed to a near halt in order to spare calories. Critical electrolyte and fluid shifts can, if unmonitored, lead to death by low phosphorus levels or by congestive heart failure. These critical electrolyte and fluid shifts define what is called the "refeeding syndrome." Careful monitoring and medical management of these fluid and electrolyte shifts allows nutritional rehabilitation to proceed safely.

The "Perfect Child"

I frequently hear the question, "How did this eating disorder happen?" Of course, this is a really complicated question because eating disorders are immensely complex and require a multidisciplinary team to bring clarity to any individual's illness. Ultimately, the information that is currently available to us indicates that eating disorders likely emerge from a combination of inherited (genetic) temperamental traits and environmental and sociological factors. A diet or accidental weight loss often provides the "spark in the dry grass." Everyone's story about how their disorder developed is unique.

I am intensely interested in the ways that apparent medical problems actually originated from emotional distress and contributed to the development of an eating disorder. Over many years of listening to my patients' stories through this lens, I have developed a narrative that helps describe how such a situation can occur. Sometimes I use this story with my patients to validate their past experiences, especially the ways in which the medical system failed to meet their needs.

I'll tell the story as if I'm reading a storybook aloud, and in this case I will use female pronouns. There once was a little girl who from an early age was smart, intuitive, and sensitive. She could walk into a room and sense immediately how others were feeling. She also had a stronger than average reaction to external validation. That is, if someone praised her, she glowed. If someone criticized her, even a little bit, she closed down like a sea anemone.

This little girl might have grown up in an easygoing family, or she might have had a parent with a substance use disorder, an anger management problem, or anxiety. There might have been a sibling who was a wild child, or ill, who took up a lot of the family's attention.

Sometimes, if the girl herself had a problem, like a stomach ache, a well-meaning parent might try to reassure her by saying, "You're fine!" Maybe that parent looked up from their phone at that moment and those words just emerged. Maybe the parent had a hard time tolerating their child's distress, and this reaction soothed the parent. Maybe the parent, a little fatigued from their super-sensitive kid's reactions to the world, wanted to help her develop a tougher skin.

Whether or not it was ever explicitly spoken, this little girl inferred that it was preferable for her to be "fine." So she did her best. She was smart and a pleaser. She put a smile on her face and was sunny as often as possible, or at least quiet, and she was organized, driven, mature, and never a problem. Coaches, teachers, and family called her the "Perfect Child," words that made her glow.

However, she was still super-sensitive. She absorbed the world through her remarkable emotional radars, as numerous as the eyes of the Greek goddess Hera's multi-eyed guard Argus. And whether it was a classroom discussion about global warming or her awareness of arguments and conflict in her family or with her friends, she was absorbing everything and feeling extra worried, anxious, and burdened. She didn't seek a way to put words to these emotions because she was supposed to be fine.

But a sensitive soul can only absorb so much without any way of processing it. The little girl continued to grow, and she became more rigid in her routines, anxious around change, demanding of herself, and perfectionistic. Around middle school, hormones started to flow, her body started to change (which she didn't particularly welcome), and social dynamics became more complicated. Her sensitive self couldn't take this whirlwind of input without a way to identify, organize, and soothe her responses to it. So her stomach started to hurt. That emotional overflow appeared physically in the body, in particular during stressful times: on test days, when she'd have a fight with her friend, or any time that her worry level exceeded her ability to self-soothe.

Recurrent stomach aches got attention, because the Perfect Child now had something medically wrong with her. Her parents took her to the pediatrician, who examined her, maybe drew some blood, even sent her to a GI doctor, and of course you know what they told her: "You're fine." This really stung. She'd had a sense her whole life that maybe she wasn't actually fine emotionally, but she had managed that as best she could. Now she had actual pain, something wrong physically, and she was once again told she's fine? So frustrating and invalidating. The parents saw this, and as the symptoms persisted and maybe even escalated, they took her to a dietitian to see if the symptoms might be due to food intolerances.

The well-meaning dietitian said, "Well, let's try an elimination diet. Please avoid gluten, soy, sugar, and dairy." (This would never happen with a dietitian who has expertise in eating disorders.) And what did our rule-follower do? She followed that advice precisely.

Because she was doing something for herself, some part of her interpreted this dietary change as self-care. For a period of time, her tummy aches went away. She thought, "Wow, I really do have intolerances to those foods! And anyway, I want to be healthy, because there are so many bad foods out there."

Ultimately, this restrictive a diet couldn't meet her energy needs. The girl lost some weight, and people in our weight-obsessed society said, "You look great!" This positive reinforcement sealed the deal. She vowed to never go back to those old foods. The rigidity with which she adhered to her new regimen caused even more weight loss. That made her cave person brain kick in to slow her metabolism and raise her anxiety.

Her belly started to hurt again and now felt terribly full after just a few bites of food. She started running as a stress relief from all the pent-up tension. Unlike her peers, she actually felt less anxious when she was underfed, and the starvation numbed her sensitivity, which was a relief. Her food rules became more demanding, and she started actively fearing weight gain and believing that her body was unacceptably large. The obsessive focus on food and body size provided a welcome distraction from overwhelming life tasks.

Her bewildered family repeatedly said, "Wait, you've lost too much weight. You have to eat. Please." They watched their "Perfect Child" retreat, close off, snarl when challenged, and disconnect from the family. In a breathtakingly short time, the eating disorder voice had become more compelling than the voice of any loved one.

Chapter 2

Going into Hibernation

Case: Maddy

Maddy is a 19-year-old cisgender Caucasian female with anorexia nervosa. Her eating disorder started when she was 17, although she didn't even know she was developing one. She initially wanted to eat healthier and received praise from friends and coaches for her "healthy weight loss and eating." Over time, she became more and more rigid about food and exercise rules. Maddy has always been athletic, playing high school basketball and volleyball. Recently, she started feeling driven to run a few miles a day in addition to her athletic practices. Her coach became concerned as she acted more withdrawn and was not the outgoing team leader she had always been. Even after her coach took her aside and expressed concern, Maddy's weight loss continued to the point where she visibly looked underweight. The coach called Maddy's parents, who had also been worried. Maddy brushed them all aside politely, saying she was absolutely fine and pointing to the fact that she was getting great grades and just wanted to stay healthy.

When her parents push her to eat more at the dinner table, Maddy tells them that she gets full really quickly. She reminds them that she's always been able to listen to her body to know what it needs. As she prepares another big kale salad without dressing, she assures them she's getting good nutrients. She hopes these high fiber foods will finally help with her constipation, which has gotten worse and worse. Her parents note that she has started to wear multiple layers, even on warm spring days. She drinks a lot of hot tea. At last fall's pediatrician appointment, the doctor had noted a slow heart rate but agreed with Maddy that it must be because she's an athlete. The nurse that day had said to Maddy, "Wow, you've lost some weight! You look great."

Daily, Maddy is preoccupied with what she will eat. As she lies in bed at night, she can't get to sleep for hours as she mentally replays whether she ate too much and exercised enough. She's annoyed that it takes her longer to study than it used to, feeling like she'll read the same page five times without absorbing the information. She has blocked out her closest friends because she got tired of their nagging about food and weight, and it became too stressful to interact with them when they'd want to go out for meals. She's ambivalent about her college plans this fall. On the one hand, college will mean freedom, with no one to bug her about her weight and eating. On the other hand, she's always been a homebody, and she's really going to miss her family if she leaves for college. Online, Maddy sees photos of girls so much thinner than she is that she concludes she's okay and in no danger. If she's honest with herself, she sees those photos and feels like a failure because those girls are thinner. She resolves to tighten her rules just a little more the next day.

Maddy's parents bring her to a doctor with eating disorder expertise. On exam, her pulse is 45 when she's at rest. After she walks down the hall and back, her pulse is 95. Her blood pressure is 90/50 when lying down and doesn't change upon standing, and her temperature is 97.2 degrees. The exam is significant for a thin, somewhat withdrawn young woman with fine, pale hair growth on her cheeks, a regular, slow heart rate without any murmurs, normal lung and abdominal exam, and cool fingers and toes that have a reddish color. Labs drawn earlier in the week show normal results, and Maddy's electrocardiogram (EKG) is normal except for her resting heart rate of 45.

Maddy focuses on the fact that her labs are normal. She knows she's been right all along; there's nothing wrong with her. Sure, she realizes she's been less focused, angrier, and less engaged. And she doesn't always feel physically great, especially her digestive system. In light of her exam, though, she thinks to herself that she's not sick enough to be here or warrant everyone's concern.

Background

Let's talk about bears. Specifically, how they survive the long winter without any food.[1] Generally speaking, bears will emerge a little sluggishly from their dens in the spring, but they'll be remarkably strong and well for mammals that have neither eaten, urinated, defecated, nor moved much in almost half a year. After a slow start for a few months, during which they'll consume only 5000 calories a day, bears will eat like mad all summer, taking in 15,000 calories a day while drinking gallons of water. All summer, their heart rates will range from 60 beats per minute at night to 100 beats per minute during the day, and their temperature will run around 100 degrees Fahrenheit. In the fall, they start to slow down in preparation for hibernation.

Then comes the amazing part. All winter, while bears mostly sleep, their metabolic rate falls 75 percent.[2] Their heart rate drops to 10–20 beats a minute, and they breathe once every 45 seconds.[3] Scientists believe that this extraordinary heart slowing is achieved, among other mechanisms, by activation of the parasympathetic nervous system: a part of the autonomic nervous system, which are the nerves that control body function rather than sensory input. The parasympathetic nervous system controls what's called "vagal tone." While the sympathetic nervous system is responsible for "fight or flight," the parasympathetic nervous system is responsible for "rest and digest."

So, what about human "hibernators," whose cave person brain has registered that they are in a famine? We know from Chapter 1 that the cave person brain responds by slowing the metabolism across multiple organ systems. In this chapter, I'll discuss in detail how this manifests in terms of vital signs: the heart rate, temperature, and blood pressure, and gastrointestinal (GI) systems.

When I talk with my patients about hibernating bears and their own hibernating metabolisms, I remind them that humans are not bears and shouldn't ever go into metabolic hibernation. Also, when bears hibernate, they *sleep all winter*. They don't, while fasting, work a full time job, get a 4.0, raise children, connect with friends, keep up on social media, or go to the gym. They sleep.

Getting Started with a Patient

As a physician, I always start an initial consultation by inviting my patients to share their values and goals, both for the clinic and for life overall. This helps me operate in a non-assumptive manner. Rather than approach my patients from the hierarchal perspective of, "I'm the doctor. You're the patient. I'm healthy. You're not. You must do x/y/z to get well," I prefer to take a collaborative approach. Knowing what motivates them and what might impede their recovery allows me to help more effectively.

I then ask my patients to tell me their story, so that I can get to know them as a whole person. I want to hear not only the story of their eating disorder, but of salient life events, interests, and important relationships, so that I can begin to understand them holistically. I ask them to detail any medical concerns and choose the order in which they share these so that I know what their priorities are. When certain information isn't volunteered, I ask questions about symptoms that might be present but downplayed. In this way, patients can bring me their knowledge of themselves and what matters to them, and I can bring them my medical knowledge. Together we can set goals in a way that feels respectful, compassionate, and scientifically sound. Only at this point, after I have listened carefully and spent significant time with the patient, do I introduce the idea of the cave person brain. My goal is to use objective evidence of body suffering/ dysfunction to challenge patients' firmly held conviction that they are not sick enough to accept help.

The eating disorder voice is always going to try and tell my patients that they're fine because eating disorders are mental illnesses, not lifestyle choices. My patients often have great judgment when it comes to almost everything else in life … except food and their bodies. They are used to trusting their judgment and decision making, so they forget to question the ways in which this mental illness has taken over and distorted their perceptions of this one narrow set of topics. The problem is, when they have what I call their "eating disorder goggles" on, they end up with fun house distortions about what they need to eat, how their body looks, and where the dangers actually lie.

Conserving Heat

One of a mammal's most fundamental tasks is to maintain its body temperature precisely. To reduce the number of calories burned in the setting of inadequate energy intake, bodies radically change their temperature regulation. Patients may grow a soft, fine "pelt" of facial hair called lanugo, typically found on babies in utero, to prevent heat loss from the head. Lanugo goes away when patients restore weight.

In addition, the extremities become cool and reddish-blue colored. This is called acrocyanosis, literally "blue color pertaining to the end." As far as the cave person brain is concerned, fingers and toes aren't essential to survival. Why spend calories heating up blood and sending it where heat will be lost easily through the hands and feet? The body clamps down on the microcirculation of the end of our limbs.

Patients who restrict calories typically feel cold all the time, which makes them dress in layers and drink hot beverages. This is because their brain has become unwilling to do all the work of keeping them warm through shivering, instead pushing them to seek external sources of heat.

Orthostatic Vital Signs

Vital signs can be valuable sources of information when interpreted correctly. Some people have heard of orthostatic vital signs. The term "orthostatic changes" is frequently misapplied to those with restrictive eating disorders. True orthostatic vital signs occur in a person with low blood volume, typically either because they've just lost blood or because they are seriously volume depleted (in layperson's terms, dehydrated). Orthostatic changes also occur in response to some medicines, as well as in some people who have dysfunction of their autonomic nervous system, the nerves that control the inner workings of the body.

Orthostatic vital signs are checked by comparing readings from when the person is lying down with readings from after they have stood up for three minutes. If orthostatic, the systolic blood pressure (the top number) falls by at least 20 points, or the diastolic blood pressure (the bottom number) falls by 10, and the heart rate increases by 20 points. Normally, standing up causes blood to pool by gravity toward the legs. For the person with low blood volume, the usual mechanisms to prevent blood from pooling fail. The blood pressure falls, and the heart beats faster to try and make up for lower blood volume per squeeze.

Starving Heart vs. Athlete's Heart

However, the majority of patients who purely restrict calories, with a slow heart rate at rest and a faster heart rate with minimal exertion, do *not* have orthostatic vital signs. The key is that their blood pressures do not change significantly. It's very common for patients to assume that their heart rate is low during a restricting eating disorder in which they are also exercising because, "Dr. G, I'm an athlete." This is often accepted without question in medical settings.

In an athlete's heart, cardiac and skeletal muscles are strong and beautifully conditioned. As a result of regular use, rest, and appropriate caloric refueling, the body needs less oxygen and less energy to do any given task. Thus, when an athlete is at rest, their efficient and strong heart needs only to beat perhaps 55 times a minute. Studies have proven that it's actually rare for an athlete's resting heart rate to fall below 50.[4] Furthermore, when an athlete gets up and walks across the room, the heart rate barely budges. That relatively minimal amount of physical movement represents no exertion for a nourished, strong body.

By contrast, in a starving person's heart, the pulse is slow at rest because of high vagal tone, like that of the hibernating bear. The body doesn't want to burn any more calories than necessary on extra heartbeats at rest. When the starving person walks across the room, their cave person brain recognizes that this body has lost skeletal muscle mass from restriction. In addition, the heart muscle itself can lose mass.[5] Even if patients have continued to work out every day while malnourished, that activity only breaks down muscles even faster, so that patients in reality are weakened and deconditioned. As a result, their heart rate rises—sometimes dramatically—upon minimal exertion.

To distinguish between the starving person's heart and the athlete's heart, I use the "walk across the room test." I check the patient's pulse at rest and then again after asking them to walk down the hall and back. Bradycardia refers to a heart rate below 60 beats per minute, while tachycardia formally refers to heart rates above 100. When the resting pulse and the ambulatory pulse are quite different, but the blood pressure remains about the same, then we know that this heart is not an athlete's, but instead a starving person's heart. In my experience, a difference from resting to walking of around 75 percent or more is significant, for instance, from 50 to 88. It's important to note that some people won't have heart rate changes as distinctly. That doesn't mean they are "fine," but rather that the survival genes of their genetic variability happen to preserve their cardiac function.

Starved Thinking

Starvation often makes a person more rigid, fearful, and anxious, with difficulty falling asleep. In the 1940s, a landmark study was the first to document the symptoms of a starving brain. A group of young men who were conscientious objectors to serving in war zones signed up to serve their country at home through a groundbreaking science experiment. Ancel Keys, a physiologist fascinated by the relationship between nutrition and physical function, gathered 36 of these young men at the University of Minnesota to study how prisoners of war and concentration camp captives would weather restricted calories, high energy output, and then, once rescued, nutritional rehabilitation.

Dubbed the Minnesota Starvation Experiment,[6] the study started by feeding the young men 3200 calories a day for three months, with the goal of starting the starvation investigation with men who were fit, at "ideal" weights, and rested. Subsequently, for the next six months, the men were fed around 1500 calories a day, with foods reflecting what was commonly available in wartime Europe. They were required to perform intensive exercise, mimicking conditions of work camps or of migrations of refugees from the war. The goal was to make them lose 25 percent of their body weight. Careful psychological and physiological testing was performed throughout. Following this phase, for the next 12 weeks, the men were divided into separate groups for different types of rehabilitation diets. Ultimately, for the final eight weeks, they were allowed to consume what they wished but were still closely monitored.

The results were remarkable. Physically, the men showed all the signs of cave person brain reactions to starvation that I have discussed above. Their metabolic rate fell dramatically, with reduced body temperatures, blood pressures, and heart rate. What was unexpected, though, was the psychological impact on these men. Remember, these men didn't have the inherited temperamental traits that we associated with those who develop eating disorders: intelligent, highly sensitive, anxious, and self-judgmental. And the study didn't take place in a society where people are awash every day in overvaluation of the thin ideal, constant diet and body size talk, and social media images.

Nonetheless, after a mere six-month stretch of low calorie intake, high energy output, and substantial weight loss, the men almost universally reported high levels of depression and emotional distress. They scored high on symptoms of hysteria and hypochondria, and some of the men began self-harming. They felt preoccupied with food, both during the starvation and rehabilitation phases, and reported viewing others who ate normally with a fascinated, judgmental disgust. As they became socially withdrawn and isolated, they felt like their concentration and judgment were impaired. Sound familiar?

After discussing the Minnesota Starvation Experiment, I reassure my patients that at least some portion of the mood dysregulation and even despair they can feel during prolonged restriction comes from their starved brain. Something profound changes in our brains when we are malnourished. It's physical, and it gets better with nutritional rehabilitation. I can't tell you how many patients I see even two weeks into regular, adequate food intake who report a major improvement in their anxiety and hopelessness.

Patients who feel desperate body image dissatisfaction while underweight often look at themselves in the mirror months later, after full weight restoration, and realize, "Oh, I look good." These examples inform my strong recommendation that individuals swiftly begin taking in adequate calories and, when underweight, fully restore weight during the recovery process. Failing to fully renourish the brain and body bears the risk of trapping patients in a purgatory of starved brain perceptions. Nutritional rehabilitation, discussed in detail in Chapter 6, is good for the brain.

Gastroparesis

Patients who restrict calories can feel unusually full after eating. This can be a source of frustration for loved ones, who assume it's one of the symptoms of the eating disorder and insist they "just eat." In general, my patients have been able to rely their whole lives on signals from their bodies to tell them how much to eat and when to stop. Within the eating disorder, it becomes easy to think, "Everyone says to listen to my body, and it's saying I'm full now after a small amount of food, so I'm listening to my body and eating very little." The anorexia likes that logic. However, if we look at this phenomenon through the lens of cave person brain, we will see that something medical is occurring.

Gastroparesis is the official diagnosis for this symptom, from *gastro* (stomach) + *paresis* (paralysis). Gastroparesis has nothing to do with moving the bowels and everything to do with the stomach organ itself. Typically, when someone eats a meal, their stomach gets to work digesting the food, using wave-like movements of its smooth muscle, called peristalsis, to move the food around and eventually into the small intestine. However, in starvation the cave person brain doesn't want to spend a single extra calorie on a wriggle of that smooth muscle because normal digestion isn't necessary for survival. Gastroparesis is practically universal in the setting of significant weight loss, in patients of all body sizes.[7]

This can make a person feel "Thanksgiving dinner" full after just half a sandwich. Even more challenging, the nausea, fullness, and bloating of gastroparesis creates a two-fold trigger. One, the person feels uncomfortably full, and two, the belly looks distended. Fullness is a very complicated symptom for those who restrict. I defer unpacking the "why" of that point to therapists, but I compassionately acknowledge it as a fact with my patients. And for many, the appearance of the stomach is a major part of body image distress, so a visibly distended stomach can really challenge the recovery mindset. As always, there are some patients whose digestion never becomes abnormal. They are the rare and lucky ones, at least in terms of enduring the digestive challenges of recovery.

For the first few months of recovery, patients have to resist their intuitions about what their body needs, nutritionally, until they are well into nutritional rehabilitation. Following the intuitions of a starved body keeps people malnourished, making the symptoms worse and the recovery that much harder. For some period of time, nutrition has to be prescriptive, not intuitive.

From a diagnostic perspective, as a physician, I rarely need to perform any studies to verify gastroparesis. The clinical presentation of weight loss, caloric restriction and symptoms of early fullness or nausea, with or without clinical underweight, are sufficient to make the diagnosis of gastroparesis. Those with diabetes, stroke, dysfunction of the autonomic nervous system, and others without a known cause (called "idiopathic") can also experience gastroparesis, unrelated to nutritional status.

When symptoms persist beyond the anticipated timeline or are atypical, I order a gastric emptying study. This nuclear medicine study is performed at a radiology center, where the patient is required to eat a scrambled egg/egg-substitute or small portion of oatmeal that has been mixed with a small, harmless amount of radioactive material that emits photons. Over the course of the next four hours, the patient gets scanned briefly by a gamma camera at regular intervals. The more egg that remains in the stomach, the more radiation signal is picked up by the camera. Normal gastric emptying in adults shows about 10 percent of food gone at one hour, 60 percent of food gone at two hours, and 90 percent of food gone at four hours.[8] Gastroparesis will be diagnosed when food persists beyond this normal time range.

Gastroparesis Treatment

Gastroparesis is one of the most important conditions to diagnose in my patients because there are so many "tools in the medical toolbox" that can markedly improve symptoms. There are enough emotional roadblocks on the eating disorder recovery highway that I'm happy to be able to clear away as many of the medical roadblocks as possible. That said, gastroparesis can be a very intrusive, difficult condition to manage. I like to lay out all the options, give patients my recommendation for where to start treatment, and then together we see how they respond and go from there. In the grand scheme of things, almost everyone's gastroparesis of malnutrition will fully resolve with consistent food intake and, in those who are underweight, complete weight restoration.

There are important pharmacologic tools for gastroparesis treatment. The main one is metoclopramide (met-uh-CLOW-pram-ide). Metoclopramide is a medicine that acts on the stomach to speed up its emptying time. It doesn't work on the bowels, so it isn't a medicine for constipation. I prescribe half of a 5 mg tablet, or 2.5 mg, by mouth up to four times a day. It must be taken fully 30–45 minutes before each meal, or it won't work. The majority of patients take metoclopramide for a few months, cutting back on the frequency of dosing as able. It can radically improve the symptoms of gastroparesis, and it does not cause weight gain (an important point for many of my patients).

The most common negative effect of metoclopramide is fatigue in the first two weeks of taking it, which usually subsides on its own. Metoclopramide does have a serious negative effect to watch out for, though, as it can be permanent. Tardive dyskinesia refers to twitching of the lips and tongue, and dystonia refers to involuntary muscle contractions in general. A typical adult dose of metoclopramide is 5–10 mg four times a day, so the dose I put my patients on is much smaller, however some psychiatric medicines increase the risk. I tell my patients if they have any twitches to stop metoclopramide immediately and never take it again. That can sound scary, but ultimately, it's about the balance of risk and benefit. When the only way to recover from an eating disorder is to consume sufficient food every day, and painful abdominal fullness and nausea interferes with that process, the benefit of medication typically outweighs the risk.

For those who yearn to recover as "naturally" as possible and feel uneasy about taking a medicine, I like to make the following point: nothing is more unnatural than a stomach whose emptying has been slowed 500 percent from normal due to starvation. Metoclopramide only speeds up stomach emptying back toward normal. However, my patients are certainly free to see if they can make progress in nutritional rehabilitation without medications.

For those who cannot take metoclopramide due to allergic or muscle reactions, two other medicines, both antibiotics, can stimulate stomach emptying. Liquid erythromycin ethylsuccinate 200 mg by mouth twice a day will either really help someone's gastroparesis, or it will make them vomit and have diarrhea. It is a reasonable option to try if metoclopramide isn't an option. Alternatively, in severe gastroparesis where metoclopramide is helpful, but not sufficient, erythromycin can be added twice a day.

The other antibiotic is azithromycin.[9] Azithromycin is easy to take at one 250 mg tablet daily, and a study has shown that it is non-inferior to erythromycin for gastric emptying.[10] However, for multiple reasons, I don't love putting patients on long term antibiotics, even for a couple months.

There are risks of killing off the good bacteria we all have in our gut or of promoting antibiotic resistance. In addition, both medicines can prolong a key measure on the EKG, called the QT interval. When taking either of these, an EKG should be checked every week for the first few weeks, and then intermittently thereafter.[11]

Constipation

Let's turn to a problem that's related to gastroparesis: constipation. The cave person brain doesn't want to waste an extra calorie on a wriggle of *any* of the digestive system. As a result, the colon, or large intestine, slows down considerably. As with gastroparesis, constipation is almost universal in those with with caloric restriction and weight loss, regardless of body weight.

Constipation is officially defined as a patient having two or more of the following symptoms during at least 25 percent of bowel movements, over the past three months: straining, having lumpy or hard stools, feeling the sensation of incomplete evacuation or the sensation of stool obstruction (sometimes called an impaction), needing to assist stool removal with a finger or put manual pressure on the pelvic floor, or having fewer than three bowel movements a week.[12]

Some patients who don't focus much on their bowel habits might one day suddenly realize they feel nauseated or have pain in one quadrant of their abdomen. These can be symptoms of constipation. Other patients develop an obsessive focus, such that that their entire life is tethered to their bowel habits.

Diagnosing constipation can be a challenge because while doctors want patients to have a reasonable number of bowel movements each week, they don't want to inadvertently prescribe a bowel regimen (meaning medicine to treat constipation) that causes diarrhea. I use plain radiography—a one-view x-ray of the abdomen—as a good objective tool to determine retained stool volume. There is no reason to check an x-ray in a patient who has been restricting calories and has developed classic constipation symptoms. I would initiate a treatment regimen that seems reasonable and adjust it over time. However, in the case of patients already on a reasonable regimen who feel they have inadequate emptying, I would order a plain film.

A plain film exposes a patient to very little radiation. Because all of us get exposed to some radiation every day in our lives, from radon in our homes to cosmic rays that are stronger at higher altitudes, it's estimated that a person experiences about 3–5 mSv of radiation a year just living on the planet. An abdominal x-ray exposes one to an additional 0.7 mSv, a very small amount.[13] The x-ray will tell me if the patient's colon is full of retained stool or not. If not, I'll let them know that it appears, despite what they perceive about inadequacy of bowel movements, that they are actually keeping up with their body's needs. However, if the x-ray shows lots of stool, I will know we have to push higher on medication doses.

Treatment of Constipation

What are the best ways to manage constipation caused by slowed metabolism? First of all, there are nutritional considerations. Drinking plenty of water (2–4 liters/64–108 ounces a day) definitely helps. Doctors typically recommend high fiber diets for general constipation. Interestingly, though, it turns out that in constipation of slowed metabolism, as with gastroparesis, *high fiber diets don't help, they only cause bloating*. Once again, this is the rare time when a doctor will ask a patient to eat a low fiber diet. Remedies like fiber supplements, or prune juice will just make the tummy bloated and uncomfortable. Ultimately, though, as nutritional rehabilitation progresses, and the metabolism speeds up and constipation becomes less of an issue, fiber can be reintroduced.

The best first-line medication for constipation of slowed metabolism is polyethylene glycol. The best first-line medication for constipation of slowed metabolism is polyethylene glycol, an osmotic laxative. That means it helps draw water into the intestines, allowing stools to soften and move more easily. Polyethylene glycol is safe from toddler age on up. Some patients tell me that polyethylene glycol doesn't work for them or causes bloating, and in those cases I have other management options. However, some of these patients haven't tried a high enough dose. Where 17 grams a day mixed in eight ounces of water is the recommended adult dose, many of my patients need to take a double dose (34 grams/two packets) in a big glass of water twice a day.

Some make the mistake of taking polyethylene glycol in as small an amount of water as possible, because they don't like the taste. In my clinical experience, this can cause a "glue effect." The dry, powdery medicine turns into a paste that sticks. Polyethylene glycol is not a stimulant laxative, unlike senokot or bisacodyl, which can potentially damage the colon and are medications of abuse in purging eating disorders. Nor does it cause the intestinal tract to form any dependency.

It's worth mentioning a couple of the other common bowel medications that are used by many patients. Docusate sodium is a stool softener. It's harmless but also probably not helpful in constipation of slowed metabolism. Magnesium hydroxide and magnesium citrate are osmotic laxatives like polyethylene glycol and perfectly fine to use.

Glycerin suppositories can be used in situations where patients have developed very hard stools that are difficult to pass. The glycerin melts in the rectum and lubricates the passage of the hard stool. Enemas, typically phosphate enemas, are also osmotic laxatives. When high doses of oral medicines are insufficient, a phosphate enema can be administered as directed. However, enemas are invasive and should be avoided when possible.

Normal Blood Tests

Finally, let's talk about normal blood laboratory values in those who restrict calories. I have heard countless times, "But Dr. G, my labs are fine! That means I'm fine too." As should now be clear, patients who restrict calories can have many medical problems that do not cause the blood tests to become abnormal. Insurance companies, with their lack of eating disorder expertise, point to normal lab work as a reason not to authorize someone for a needed higher level of care. Doctors' offices and staff members may believe they are being positive and reassuring in announcing the bloodwork is normal. Yet this may erroneously plant the message that the patient is therefore fine. Emergency department staff see normal labs and send patients home rather than admitting them medically. Small wonder that patients learn to point to normal labs in the belief they are about to be released back into the wilderness of their eating disorders again.

It turns out that nearly every patient who purely restricts—that is, does not purge—has normal labs. There are, of course, exceptions to this. I'll discuss these in Chapter 4 when I review organ systems that become dysfunctional due to the nutritional "empty tank." However, even in those cases, the electrolytes almost always remain normal in those who purely restrict. Electrolytes refer to most of the numbers on the basic metabolic panel: the potassium, sodium, bicarbonate, calcium, phosphorus, and magnesium.

How can this be? How can a patient who has regrown fetal facial hair, has cold hands and feet, a hibernating heart, slowed digestion, and anxiety and obsessiveness from a starved brain possibly have normal bloodwork? The answer once again lies in our amazing cave person brain, which evolved to keep us safe during famine. Virtually no patient with anorexia nervosa stops eating altogether. Some of my patients have said to me, "I'm not sick, Dr. G. I mean, I'm eating something every day." Even in those who eat very little, the body fiercely defends its electrolyte homeostasis, carefully balancing out electrolytes to keep the body on an even keel.

This is a great reminder that our cave person brain is far smarter than we are when it comes to managing our bodies, especially as the modern internet encourages us daily to adopt some new set of food rules. There is simply no chance that our thinking brain can come up with diet strategies to "fool" the body into anything. Our bodies are constantly working for our survival in complicated and remarkable ways, regardless of the silly new fads to which we expose them. Viewing the body in this appreciative way, rather than as some enemy to be vanquished or disappointment to be fixed, is much more productive ... and scientifically sound.

Case Resolution: Maddy

Maddy's eating disorder doctor learns that her values and motivations in life include connection and kindness with her family and friends as well as being productive and engaged in school and sports. A long conversation reveals Maddy's life story and illuminates her medical symptoms. The doctor reviews with her the concepts covered in this chapter, while also gently pointing out the ways in which her eating disorder has pulled her in the exact opposite direction of her values. Maddy sees that she's out of connection with her family and friends, all of whom have been distanced by the demands of her anorexia nervosa. School has become increasingly stressful because her starved brain lacks the ability to absorb and remember information. She has always prided herself on her intelligence, and she can see that the starvation has diminished her thinking abilities. Athletically, she's been benched for the rest of her sports season, with her coach naming her eating disorder as the cause. And as for kindness ... she hasn't been showing a lot of that to herself lately, nor does she have extra energy to spare so that she can share it with anyone else.

As the doctor starts to lay out an overall treatment plan, Maddy is willing for her parents to join the conversation, which is always optimal. The doctor tells the three of them that Maddy has two options. One, she can choose to try recovery as an outpatient, in the context of her home, friends, family, and everyday life. To choose outpatient treatment, she will need to see a multidisciplinary outpatient team, comprised of the doctor, a dietitian, and a therapist. A meal plan will be created by her dietitian, and she has to be able to follow it fully even when she doesn't feel like it. While this approach will be scary and uncomfortable physically and emotionally, it's absolutely necessary.

The doctor tells her that to stay outpatient, she has to let her dietitian be her dietitian. Her anorexia is not allowed to play this role. That means if her dietitian asks her to eat a serving of rice, six ounces of chicken and a cup of milk at dinner, her anorexia is not allowed to override and decide, "Actually, four ounces of chicken is enough." What's more, Maddy will have to restore a certain amount of weight each week. Because her metabolism will speed up in the first few weeks of increased food, she may not start gaining right away. She and her therapist will work through pragmatic skills to help her when she's wavering and provide support during this difficult time.

The other option is for Maddy to admit to a higher level of care, such as an intensive outpatient program (IOP, with several hours of programming and meal support a few days a week) or a partial hospitalization program (PHP, with full day treatment but home at night). Most patients want to start as outpatients. The doctor reminds Maddy that in either case, she will have to eat more than she has in a long time and deal with body changes. What she can control is the setting: outpatient or higher level of care. Either way, her anorexia nervosa must go.

Medically, Maddy doesn't have a temperature problem, a heart problem, or a digestive problem. She has a starvation problem. This will therefore have a nutritional solution. Every single one of Maddy's medical issues will resolve with full weight restoration. Maddy wonders who will know she's suffering when she's no longer in an obviously suffering body. This is where the support of her treatment team and parents will be essential.

In the meantime, Maddy's doctor can use medical tools to help clear medical roadblocks from her journey toward recovery. If needed, the doctor will prescribe her metoclopramide 2.5 mg, 30 minutes before breakfast, lunch, and dinner, and before bed. She might need to be on the medicine for a few months, over time only taking it before the meals that make her most full. Finally, for her constipation, she can start with one dose (17 grams) of polyethylene glycol a day in eight ounces of water. If that's insufficient, the dose can be increased.

While acknowledging that recovery is going to be hard, the doctor encourages Maddy to remember who she really is and to keep her values at the forefront of her thoughts when she's struggling. She can go to college as planned in the fall, if in recovery, or she can take a year off, be with her family, and get a job. What she will not be allowed to do is live secretly with her eating disorder. Her parents and the treatment team will insist that she make consistent progress in recovery. If she cannot do this in the outpatient setting, everyone will make sure she gets to a higher level of care.

As Maddy's case exemplifies, the anorexia nervosa voice is insidious and pervasive. It uses Maddy's intelligence for its own means. It's like anorexia is a terrorist who has wrested control of the cockpit from Maddy, holding her body as a hostage. If only she had been given the intellectual equivalent of a toy airplane, her anorexia would be a lot less powerful. Fortunately (and unfortunately), she has the brain equivalent of a fighter jet. Thus, when anorexia is at the controls, it really sounds convincing. In this scenario, everyone will be working to give the controls back to Maddy.

The House on Fire, a.k.a. Combatting "I'm Fine"

Very often, patients will try and convince me that they are actually fine. (I view the word "fine" as the four-letter f-word of our field.) They feel they are not sick enough for a higher level of care, to eat the full meal plan their dietitian has prescribed them, to warrant my concern, or to change anything they are doing in their disorder, etc. They say, "But Dr. G, I get a 4.0/I'm a star employee/I can still run every day/I'm a good mom/my potassium is normal/my weight is normal. I'm fine!" This line of reasoning can sound convincing.

An eating disorder will passionately defend itself. Like an abusive partner, it can push all other close connections away. When anything threatens it, it will lash out and become remarkably cruel to the person threatening it (the therapist, the parent, the partner) and even meaner to the patient. Eating disorders scathingly whisper that patients are nothing without their eating disorder.

What's so hard about eating disorders is that patients retain their intellectual capacity and many aspects of their emotional capacity. We would never urge someone with schizophrenia, in the midst of a psychotic episode, "Use your inner wisdom here. Are there *really* little green men in the room?" The psychotic person can't access the real world. The little green men are their reality.

We all have to keep in mind that for someone with anorexia nervosa, the beliefs that food and rest will cause devastating harm to their bodies, and their perception that their bodies are wretchedly inadequate and revolting, are their reality as well. And yet reminding patients to access their inner wisdom is a key element nearly every practitioner uses in their treatment of anorexia nervosa. Where the person with schizophrenia is fully incapacitated during a psychotic episode, the patient with anorexia nervosa can competently navigate the rest of the world, at least initially. This bizarre fact easily leads family members and friends to misjudge the severity and cruelty of this mental illness.

To combat the delusion that a patient is fine, I use a metaphorical story called "The House on Fire." Imagine that a young woman is standing outside her burning house, and the fire department rushes up. The firefighter jumps out and says, "We're here to put out your fire!" She says, "What fire?" He looks concerned and says, "Well, your fire. I smell the smoke. I feel the heat. I see the flames." She smiles and says, "Oh no. If my house were on fire, it would be so hot that my sidewalk would be bubbling. And because my sidewalk isn't bubbling, I couldn't possibly have a house fire." The firefighters understand her to be mentally ill, and they go put out her fire.

I go on to remind my patients that there is no single marker of illness that I look at to determine whether they are sick enough to proceed with recovery efforts. Saying, "My blood work is fine" is like saying, "My sidewalk's not bubbling." This is an extremely important point because someone who is fine can comfortably reject what all these people are telling them about how concerned they are and can proceed with restricting and exercising. The concept of "fine" stalls recoveries.

I try to introduce these concepts the first time I hear my patient trying to convince me how fine they are, so that the next time it happens, I can simply say in shorthand and with kindness, "House on fire." I remind them of all the objective evidence of hibernation physiology they possess, medical signs that they aren't fine at all.

Notes

1 Berg von Linde M, Arevström L, Fröbert O. Insights from the den: how hibernating bears may help us understand and treat human disease. *Clin Transl Sci.* 2015 October; 8(5):601–605. doi: 10.1111/cts.12279.
2 http://content.time.com/time/health/article/0,8599,2052118,00.html. Accessed January 4, 2018.

3 www.bear.org/website/bear-pages/black-bear/hibernation/191-5-stages-of-activity-and-hibernation.html. Accessed January 4, 2018.

4 Bjørnstad H, Storstein L, Meen HD, Hals O. Electrocardiographic findings in athletic students and sedentary controls. *Cardiology.* 1991; 79(4):290–305. Review. PubMed PMID: 1782647.

5 Oflaz S, Yucel B, Oz F, Sahin D, Ozturk N, Yaci O, Polat N, Gurdal A, Cizgici AY, Dursun M, Oflaz H. Assessment of myocardial damage by cardiac MRI in patients with anorexia nervosa. *Int J Eat Disord.* 2013 December; 46(8):862–866. doi: 10.1002/eat.22170.

6 Keys A, Brozek J, Henshel A, Mickelson O, Taylor, HL (1950). *The biology of human starvation, (Vols. 1–2).* Minneapolis, MN: University of Minnesota Press.

7 Mascolo M, Geer B, Feuerstein J, Mehler PS. Gastrointestinal comorbidities which complicate the treatment of anorexia nervosa. *Eat Disord.* 2017 March–April; 25(2):122–133. doi: 10.1080/10640266.2016.1255108.

8 Seok JW. How to interpret gastric emptying scintigraphy. *J Neurogastroenterol Motil.* 2011 April; 17(2):189–191. doi: 10.5056/jnm.2011.17.2.189.

9 Chini P, Toskes PP, Waseem S, Hou W, McDonald R, Moshiree B. Effect of azithromycin on small bowel motility in patients with gastrointestinal dysmotility. *Scand J Gastroenterol.* 2012 April; 47(4):422–427. doi: 10.3109/00365521.2012.654402.

10 Moshiree B, McDonald R, Hou W, Toskes PP. Comparison of the effect of azithromycin versus erythromycin on antroduodenal pressure profiles of patients with chronic functional gastrointestinal pain and gastroparesis. *Dig Dis Sci.* 2010 March; 55(3):675–683. doi: 10.1007/s10620-009-1038-3.

11 I cannot fully discuss the pros and cons of another medicine called domperidone, a medicine that has been banned in the US by the FDA because of studies that showed a 70 percent increase in sudden cardiac death by prolonged QT interval. (Leelakanok N, Holcombe A, Schweizer ML. Domperidone and Risk of Ventricular Arrhythmia and Cardiac Death: A Systematic Review and Meta-analysis. *Clin Drug Investig.* 2016;36(2):97–107.) Because I currently am unable to prescribe it, I don't feel qualified to comment upon it. It remains available in countries with superb medical systems. Practitioners there feel that perhaps those initial studies weren't performed optimally and may have overstated the risks.

12 Simren M, Palsson OS, Whitehead WE. Update on Rome IV criteria for colorectal disorders: implications for clinical practice. *Curr Gastroenterol Rep.* 2017 April; 19(4):15. doi: 10.1007/s11894-017-0554-0.

13 Kwon H, Jung JY. Effectiveness of a radiation reduction campaign targeting children with gastrointestinal symptoms in a pediatric emergency department. *Medicine (Baltimore).* 2017 January; 96(3):e5907. doi: 10.1097/MD.0000000000005907.

Chapter 3

Hormones and Bones

Case 1: Josh

Josh is a 26-year-old cisgender Caucasian male graduate student. He developed anorexia nervosa at age 17. After one residential treatment episode a year ago, he's been maintaining a low, but improved, body weight. An avid cyclist, he continues to ride with a cycling group five days a week. He lifts weights one day a week and hikes or plays Frisbee with his friends the other day.

Josh's left shin has begun to hurt after he cycles, and massage hasn't helped. Four weeks later, an MRI confirms a tibial stress fracture. Faced with the prospect of backing off on his normal exercise routines, Josh finds himself thinking more than usual about restriction. As he teeters on the brink of acting on disordered behaviors, he decides to step up his visits with his outpatient therapist and dietitian to twice a week.

Josh's intensive work reminds him that he does not want to relapse and go back to treatment, missing out on school and the social connections he's come to value so much. He also realizes that the focus on leanness and "healthy eating" in his cycling group are contributing to his unwillingness to finish restoring weight. Josh sees a sports medicine doctor who advises him to see a specialist in eating disorders. He has never had a bone density scan, so the sports medicine doctor orders one.

Josh notes that his sex drive disappeared during the most intense years of his anorexia nervosa and hasn't fully returned. He wakes with spontaneous erections less often than when he was a teenager and had been ascribing this to "getting older." His bone scan shows Z-scores of -2.6 in the spine, -2.2 at the femoral neck, and -2.0 at the total hip (normal greater than -1.0). His morning total testosterone level on two occasions, prior to his specialist visit, was found to be 225 and 219 ng/dL respectively (normal 280–1100 ng/dL).

Case 2: Aniya

Aniya is a 30-year-old cisgender Middle Eastern American female who works in finance. Aniya's anorexia nervosa started, and menstrual periods stopped, when she was 18, and she received long term outpatient treatment at that time. She felt she *had achieved into a good recovery by age 27. However, despite now being at the same weight as when she was 18, her periods have never restarted. She exercises moderately and mindfully, mostly doing yoga or going on walks with friends. Her gynecologist has offered to put her on the Pill to "jump start" her period. A bone density scan five years ago was read as normal.*

Aniya sees an eating disorder physician for a thorough evaluation. Her estradiol levels come back at 15 ng/mL (normal levels vary by day of the menstrual cycle but are usually greater than 30 ng/mL). A repeat bone density scan shows Z-scores of −1.8 in the spine, −1.6 at the femoral neck and −1.5 at the total hip. The official read says "within the expected range for age." A pelvic ultrasound reveals that her uterus and ovaries are small, with sizes more commonly seen in a 12 year old.

Case 3: Aidan

Aidan is a 17-year-old cisgender Caucasian male who developed anorexia nervosa, restricting subtype, when he was 12. He's been in and out of treatment programs, where he consistently feels isolated as one of two or three male patients in a sea of females. He doesn't get much out of sitting in body group and hearing his peers talk about their periods. In fact, he feels like he somehow has to apologize when girls talk about male-inflicted traumas they've experienced. Aidan feels further isolated from his peers since he has absolutely no interest in dating and no sex drive whatsoever. The idea of relationships or intimacy feels overwhelming and unimaginable to him.

Although Aidan's father is 6' and his mother is 5' 7", Aidan is 5' 2" and has restored weight fully twice, briefly, only to relapse again after residential treatment. He has not grown much since his eating disorder started and has delayed puberty. His family wonders if he should be started on growth hormone or testosterone now that he's finishing residential treatment again and is nearing his target body weight.

One day, Aidan trips over a curb and falls. After a week of intense foot pain, he learns he's broken his foot in two places. Concerned, the urgent care doctor asks about his bone density. No one has ever checked it.

Background

Hormones and bones are topics that bring a lot of patients with eating disorders into my clinic. For some patients, going through puberty is the initial trigger for disordered eating. As puberty launches, girls who fear change and feel highly perfectionistic see their bodies start to transform in ways that feel alien. They begin to become feminized in a world where being female can come with a lot of expectations and burdens. Rightly enough, they might learn in science class that one must have a certain amount of body fat in order to begin menstruating. In some cases, this scientific truth leads preteens to think that the arrival of their period means they're "fat."

In fact, it is normal for girls to gain 30 pounds or more during adolescence. That can happen gradually or rapidly depending on growth patterns. Possibly no one tells these girls how wonderfully normal and healthy this is. In our thin-focused society where models can be shaped like tall, lanky 11 year olds with breasts, parents and kids can overreact to absolutely appropriate body changes, including typical growth and concomitant weight changes. Adolescent weight gain may start with kids looking generally heavier or thicker around the middle, which is normal. Children don't typically spring, fully formed, into their adult proportions.

Given the sensitivity of adolescents generally, wayward comments from family members like, "Whoa, I think you've had enough mashed potatoes," or "Maybe you need to get out and run a little more," can have a painful impact. Families want the best for their kids, and their comments about eating and activity may intend to foster health, but families too need education about necessary weight gain and body changes. Teenagers barraged by commercial and social messages about their inadequacies and faults deserve to feel safe and accepted in their bodies at home. It may be the only safe space in which they can do so.

Normally, girls acquire up to 90 percent of peak bone mass by age 18, and boys acquire this same percentage by age 20.[1] By one's early 20s, the window shuts for further significant deposition of bone density. This is the skeleton that the person will have for the rest of their life. Bone then continually remodels itself throughout our lives, as small amounts are constantly being formed and resorbed. In general, this balance remains neutral, and our bone density remains normal until later life. However, bone density loss can occur early and rapidly in malnutrition, even while the body weight is still normal. Of all the medical complications of malnutrition, bone density loss is the only one that is not fully reversible.

The Science of Bone Density Loss and Hypothalamic Hypogonadism

During starvation, our clever cave person brain surveys the situation and understands that now is not a safe time for making babies. Sex drive, pursuing a partner, losing menstrual blood monthly, and carrying a pregnancy would take up too many calories and body resources. So, the cave person brain begins an intricate hormonal alteration to protect our body during this low resource time. It shuts down the part of the brain responsible for initiating sex hormone production, the hypothalamus. The term for this process is hypothalamic hypogonadism.

During starvation, the hypothalamus resets its hormonal production to preadolescent levels by altering how gonadotropin-releasing hormone (GnRH) is released. Abnormal GnRH pulses cause low levels of luteinizing hormone (LH) and follicle stimulating hormone (FSH) to be released from the anterior pituitary. Low LH and FSH lead to low estrogen and testosterone synthesis in the ovaries and testicles, respectively. In addition, the cave person brain induces growth hormone resistance and decreases insulin-like growth factor-1 (IGF-1) concentrations. Our stress hormone, the natural steroid cortisol, rises to help us manage the physiologic stress of malnutrition and underweight.[2] All of these changes, and more, occur relatively rapidly during starvation.

In response, bone density begins to fall. The bone microarchitecture becomes impaired, bone strength decreases, and fracture risk rises. Both cortical rich (long bone) and trabecular rich (spinal bone) sites are affected. However, trabecular rich spinal bone is particularly influenced because it is more metabolically active and has a higher turnover rate.[3]

Bone density is often discussed as it pertains to women following menopause, but there are key differences between bone density loss in postmenopausal women and in malnourished people. After menopause, women's estrogen levels fall, which means that more bone is resorbed than previously in their lives. However, if she is otherwise healthy, she will continue to make new bone. Bone density declines rapidly right after menopause and then slowly declines thereafter, as a little more bone is resorbed than is newly made.

In some ways similarly, in starvation, estrogen levels are also low and thus bone is resorbed. However, due to all the other hormonal changes, from growth hormone resistance to low IGF-1 levels to high cortisol levels, *the starving person reduces new bone production.* As a result, bone density loss can be remarkably rapid. Indeed, the bone density loss from anorexia nervosa looks physiologically and biochemically similar to bone density loss in individuals who have to take high doses of steroids for inflammatory conditions. Presumably, our own high levels of cortisol, our stress steroid, cause similar changes to patients on chronic pharmaceutical steroids.

An important study found that girls and young women with anorexia nervosa have a 60 percent increase in fracture risk compared with age-matched controls, even before bone scans showed reduced bone mineral density. This higher risk for fracture was observed as early as one year into the diagnosis of a patient's anorexia nervosa, and the results were independent of the amount of exercise being done.[4] Fracture is the biggest concern in bone density loss, and notably, patients with any history of anorexia nervosa have a 200–300 percent increase in fracture risk.[5,6]

Some of my patients might think, "What's the big deal? Fine, I won't trip over the cat and break something." First, as in Josh's case, stress fractures can sideline athletes for weeks or months. The consequences of stress fracture range from pain and disability, to frustration at not being able to participate in one's sport, to threatened loss of scholarship funding for elite collegiate athletes.

Second, one can develop permanent kyphosis, a permanently hunched upper back. Our spine is made up of vertebral bodies like building blocks, one on top of the other. When the vertebral bodies become too fragile, they can start to lose height and crunch down on themselves, like a sponge cake that flattens. These are called compression fractures. Furthermore, spinal bones often don't compress down evenly, but rather crunch forward because of our body mechanics, so that a person's upper spine is permanently curved forward. No amount of posture work or yoga can fully fix this curvature once the bone is altered. I have seen patients even in their 20s and 30s with kyphosis.

Third, patients can end up with chronic bony pain from compression fractures. It's a sad and powerful sight to witness a young person relegated permanently to a walker, on strong pain medicines that cause dependency, constipation, and heightened pain sensitivity.

Diagnosis of Bone Density Loss

Bone density loss is typically diagnosed with a Dual Energy X-Ray Absorptiometry (DEXA, or DXA) scan. In adults, images are taken of the lumbar spine, femoral neck, total hip, and sometimes the forearm. Results are then reported as either a T-score for post-menopausal women and men 50 or older, or a Z-score for children, premenopausal women, and men under 50. While some controversy exists about how exactly to evaluate children's and adolescents' bone density results, consensus exists that only spinal measurements should be measured, with the results reported out as a Z-score.[7]

The International Society for Clinical Densitometry (ISCD) has established how to interpret DXA scores. These vary by age groups and are important for patients and families to know about. This is because we must always view "standard results" through the lens of eating disorder physiology. A bone density result that shows clinically significant bone density loss in someone with anorexia nervosa may be interpreted by the radiologist as "normal" by ISCD standards.

Below, I explain the ISCD's methodology for interpreting DXA findings (Table 3.1). The lowest score determines the overall diagnosis. It is not medically sound to say, "I have osteoporosis in my spine but osteopenia in my hips." If there is osteoporosis anywhere, the diagnosis is osteoporosis.

Individual patients' information about the clinical presence of fracture or secondary cause of bone density loss is not included on a DXA scan report. Many of my patients have been told their DXA is normal when in fact they actually meet full criteria for osteoporosis once all the information is taken into account. Additionally, we have to pay attention not just to the official read on the radiology report but to what results are expected.

Table 3.1 Official ISCD Interpretation of DXA Findings

Score	Clinical Presentation	Interpretation
Children and adolescents[1]		
Z-score greater than −2.0	No recurrent fractures	Within the expected range for age
Z-score less than −2.0	No recurrent fractures	Below the expected range for age
Z-score less than −2.0	Vertebral compression fracture	Osteoporosis
	Or two long bone fractures by age 10	
	Or 3+ long bone fractures by age 19	
Young people (20–50 years old)[2]		
Z-score greater than −2.0	No recurrent fractures	Within the expected range for age
Z-score less than −2.0	No recurrent fractures	Below the expected range for age
Z-score less than −2.0	Fracture of any kind or secondary cause of osteoporosis[3]	Osteoporosis
Any score	Fracture (except for digits) from fall of standing height or less, without major trauma such as a motor vehicle accident	Osteoporosis
Adults over 50		
T-score greater than −1.0	(See below)	Normal
T-score between −1 and −2.5	(See below)	Osteopenia
T-score less than or equal to −2.5	(See below)	Osteoporosis
Any score	Fracture (except for digits) from fall of standing height or less, without major trauma such as a motor vehicle accident	Osteoporosis

Notes
1 Lewiecki EM, Gordon CM, Baim S, Leonard MB, Bishop NJ, Bianchi ML, Kalkwarf HJ, Langman CB, Plotkin H, Rauch F, Zemel BS, Binkley N, Bilezikian JP, Kendler DL, Hans DB, Silverman S. International Society for Clinical Densitometry 2007 adult and pediatric official positions. *Bone.* 2008 December; 43(6):1115–1121. doi: 10.1016/j.bone.2008. 08.106.
2 Cohen A, Shane E. Evaluation and management of the premenopausal woman with low BMD. *Curr Osteoporos Rep.* 2013 December; 11(4):276–285. doi: 10.1007/s11914-013-0161-4.
3 Secondary causes of osteoporosis include estrogen deficiency, glucocorticoid exposure, hyperparathyroidism, and anorexia nervosa).

Athletes, for instance, should have 5–15 percent higher bone density than non-athletes because they expose their bodies to bone-loading exercise on a regular basis.[8] Such exercise gives an electrical signal to the bone to thicken and become stronger. For instance, the bones in a pitcher's throwing arm are stronger than in his non-throwing arm.[9] The American College of Sports Medicine and International Olympic Committee define normal bone density in athletes participating in weight-bearing sports as −1 or better.[10] However, if the DXA scan shows a Z-score of anything higher than −2.0, the official read will say, "Within the expected range for age." Doctors must, therefore, appropriately interpret the results for the patient. Otherwise, we miss the opportunity to highlight pathology emerging from the eating disorder, to diagnose and treat fragile bones, and to prevent future problems and motivate recovery.

When a female patient loses her period, a DXA should be performed within a year, either in the context of anorexia nervosa or athletics. For those women who don't lose their periods, the DXA should be checked within a year or so of restrictive behaviors having started. In children and adolescents with anorexia nervosa, the timing is less clear. Certainly, if they have had any long bone fractures, a DXA should be checked. However, since fracture risk is already increased by 60 percent after one year of anorexia nervosa, patients and parents should be informed of this risk and promptly pursue treatment. Males often get missed by the medical system on this issue; within a year of anorexia nervosa diagnosis or behaviors, they too need a baseline bone density evaluation.

Treatment

As a physician, I want to ensure that patients and families are aware of the current state of the art diagnosis and treatment of bone density loss due to eating disorders, hoping that this empowers them to bring the evidence without delay to their practitioners. I have seen many cases of delayed diagnosis and improper treatment of patients with regard to their bones over the years. It's critical to get the message to the person who matters most: the one whose body is being affected. I will also note that the science constantly evolves. These are the evidence-based treatments at the time of this writing.

Perhaps not surprisingly, the gold standard of treatment for bone density loss due to anorexia nervosa is full weight restoration, which in females may be accompanied by the return of a regular menstrual period.[11] Every study on the topic has shown that patients who restore their weight fully can regain some bone density. As will be discussed further below, many restart their period while still underweight; this does not mean they are done restoring weight.

Unfortunately, complete normalization of bone mineral density after anorexia nervosa is rare. It is the one medical complication of anorexia nervosa that may never fully resolve. Every single day that someone is underweight from malnutrition, they lose skeletal strength. In adolescents with anorexia nervosa, every day that passes still underweight is another day they are not mineralizing their bones to last the rest of their lives.

Adequate calcium and vitamin D intake makes sense, but these alone do not make a difference in improving bone density. In pill form, a person can only absorb 500 mg of calcium at a time. The vitamin D-OH level should be kept above 30 ng/UL.[12] I always believe food sources are best for one's vitamins and minerals, but over the counter calcium and vitamin D tablets are fine as well. Some people find that taking calcium supplements causes constipation or nausea.

Well-designed trials have now given us good data on the pharmaceutical treatment of bone density loss from malnutrition. That said, each patient is an individual, and treatment must be offered accordingly. I will discuss the oral contraceptive pill more in the menstrual function section at the end of this chapter. The key takeaway with regards to the Pill is this: oral contraceptive pills *do not work* for bone density loss, as proven over and over again among adolescents, athletes, and adults.[13,14,15,16] Despite this, oral contraceptives continue to be prescribed inappropriately because practitioners were taught that the Pill "protects your bones and jump starts your period." This is incorrect.

That said, transdermal estrogen, also called the "estrogen patch," is emerging as a terrific treatment option for amenorrheic women with either anorexia nervosa or exercise-induced bone density loss/poor bone accrual. The low dose estrogen patch, which is not a contraceptive, is thought to be effective because it delivers estrogen, a bone anti-resorptive, to the body, without having a negative "first-pass effect" at the liver. "First-pass metabolism" refers to a process by which medicines taken by mouth are processed and eliminated by the gut and liver before ever reaching the rest of the body.[17] Unlike the oral contraceptive pill, which does have a "first-pass effect" and down-regulates IGF-1 production at the liver, transdermal estrogen doesn't down regulate IGF-1, an important bone-building hormone.

Low dose patch estrogen has been shown to improve bone density when used as a bridge to the gold standard of weight restoration.[18,19] It may take months for someone with bone density loss and amenorrhea to restore sufficient weight and maintain it for enough time to correct the low estrogen/high stress hormone state that contributes to bone density loss. Even imagining that the weight restoration process is smooth and continuous, which is by no means always the case, the individual will still be losing bone density daily.

Thus, use of a transdermal estrogen patch helps boost bone density until the person can naturally support bone health. The patch may not allow full catch up of bone density levels, but it still helps. Studies have even showed that the estrogen patch helps with memory and cognition in young athletes with irregular or absent periods.[20] The dose is typically a 100 μg 17-β-estradiol patch applied to the skin twice weekly. Once a month for ten consecutive days, the woman must also take a form of progesterone so that the uterus is not exposed to unopposed estrogen. This is best taken at night when our natural progesterone peaks and causes mild sleepiness, as 10 mg of medroxyprogesterone or 200 mg of micronized progesterone. This regimen should be started as soon as low bone density is diagnosed in a woman under 50 who loses her period in the setting of inadequate calorie intake.

Presently, there are a number of other evidence-based prescription treatments for anorexia-mediated bone density loss. All of them have significant drawbacks, but they are still vital tools in the toolbox. The class of medicines called the bisphosphonates are anti-resorptive medications. That is, they help keep bone from being broken down. A randomized controlled trial in 2011 showed for the first time that bisphosphonates do improve bone density loss in young women with anorexia nervosa more than placebo, as measured by DXA one year later.[21] They are not hard to take; the dose is usually one pill once a week in the morning on an empty stomach. Sitting up for half an hour after taking this medication helps prevent heartburn.

However, bisphosphonates stay in the system for a long time, well beyond the period of actively taking the medicine. They also cross the placenta, and animal studies have shown harm to fetuses, although limited human observational studies of pregnant women taking bisphosphonates have not demonstrated harm to the baby.[22,23] There is also a rare but meaningful risk of jaw osteonecrosis, meaning bone breakdown, from bisphosphonates.

The decision to use a bisphosphonate or not then becomes an individualized one in females, taking into account risk of harm from bone density loss versus risk of harm from a pharmaceutical. For women of current or future child bearing age with amenorrhea and bone density loss, I almost always start with transdermal estrogen and weight restoration. For a young woman who has fully weight restored, has her period back, and has progressive and significant osteoporosis, especially with fracture history, I will consider a bisphosphonate only if I am convinced she has neither the interest nor the ability to get pregnant in the immediate future. This might apply to a 19-year-old college student with severe bone density loss and an intrauterine device (IUD) in place. For recovered women who are ready to partner and have kids in the next few years, and who don't have any fractures or deformities arising from their bone density, I would hold off on bisphosphonates for the time being. In these patients I recommend weight maintenance, mindful weight-bearing exercise, and adequate calcium and vitamin D intake.

The last pharmaceutical to discuss that is currently evidence based for patients with eating disorders is teriparatide. Teriparatide is, by contrast with the bisphosphonates, an anabolic agent. That means it promotes bone formation. A well-designed study showed that it may be significantly more effective than the bisphosphonates in adults with anorexia nervosa.[24] However, teriparatide is harder to take. It is administered via a daily, subcutaneous (that is, shallow) injection and must be refrigerated at all times. It is also enormously expensive, and it's often a complicated dance to get insurance to cover it.

There is a black box warning that comes with teriparatide about a risk of it causing bone cancer (osteosarcoma). This emerges from rat studies, wherein rats given 3–60 times the relative human dose of teriparatide had such bone growth stimulation that it turned cancerous. In 15 years of subsequent studies, not a single human case of attributable bone cancer has been reported.[25] This medicine cannot be used in those who have not attained their full adult height. I reserve its use for adult patients who have severe bone density loss and/or a history of prolonged or complicated fracture healing. It is used for only two years because of the theoretical risk of bone cancer. After that, it may need to be followed by a bisphosphonate so that treatment effect is not lost. In women with appropriate estrogen levels or males with appropriate testosterone levels after the two-year course, a bisphosphonate may not be needed.

Exercise and Bone Density Loss

Many of my patients over the years have asked me about the role of exercise in their bone health. In some cases, their anorexia nervosa hopes for a medical reason to keep exercising excessively. A very good study out of Canada helped me to answer this question. A group of young women with anorexia nervosa and amenorrhea and a recovered group, who were weight restored and had resumption of their menstrual periods, tracked their exercise. Those who were still ill, who exercised even moderately— and the authors included restlessly walking around in the moderate category—developed worse bone density than ill patients who did not exercise. The good news, though, was that after recovery, even high intensity exercise improved bone density compared with not exercising. It makes sense that when the body is nutritionally stressed and hormonally depleted, requiring it to exercise would further deplete its stores. I address my recommendations about movement during recovery in the Box at the end of this chapter. I specifically discuss athletes in Chapter 16.

Males

When males have hypothalamic hypogonadism, they stop producing sufficient testosterone. It's very important for doctors to ask their male patients
with eating disorders if they've had any change in sexual function. Typically, to receive the diagnosis of hypothalamic hypogonadism, a male must
have two morning blood draws showing a total testosterone level less than
300 ng/dL and manifest at least a few symptoms of low testosterone, such
as decreased sex drive, sexual dysfunction, reduced incidence of spontaneous erections, body hair loss, muscle mass loss, increase in body fat,
decreased energy, low bone density, or depression.

The combination of low testosterone and the stress of malnutrition contribute to early bone density loss. In fact, males with anorexia nervosa
appear to lose bone density faster, at a higher relative body weight, and
fracture more easily, than females.[26] My clinical experience is that doctors
forget to consider bone density in male patients with eating disorders. I've
had male patients who have been malnourished for years, and no one ever
thought to order a DXA. If a male patient of mine has never had a DXA,
even if he is near the beginning of an eating disorder, I'll check a baseline
bone density level. As with females, they should be checked every two years
thereafter until recovered. Annual follow-ups may be preferred during
early diagnosis and treatment, but insurance may not pay.

If my patient has both low bone density and low testosterone levels, the
first-line treatment is with topical testosterone. Testosterone has a similar
effect as bisphosphonates and estrogen, which is to prevent bone resorp-
tion. The goal for treatment is to keep the total testosterone level within
the normal range. Levels can be checked every few months. Of course,
weight restoration remains the overall gold standard of treatment.

There are a few important considerations when it comes to prescribing
testosterone. One is that treatment with testosterone will revive sex drive
and sexual function. If these themes are problematic for my patient, I
recommend he and his therapist work on this before starting hormone
replacement. In addition, National Collegiate Athletic Association (NCAA)
and World Anti-Doping Agency (among others) prohibit therapeutic
testosterone use in athletes, even if medically indicated for an eating disorder. In elite athletes wishing to compete, nutritional management alone
must be pursued.

Testosterone can be stopped once the patient has achieved a healthy
body weight range, as it would be expected that natural testosterone production will resume in the near future. Levels should still be checked to
confirm that this has occurred. Ultimately, no one aims to create
testosterone-fueled monsters, as some patients fear. The idea is to replace
what currently is absent only until the body begins again to produce its
own sex hormones.

In adolescent males (even up through their early 20s) who have low bone density and low testosterone, it is vital to assess whether they have achieved their adult height before proceeding with testosterone therapy. Because starvation temporarily stunts linear growth, young people with anorexia nervosa may stop growing due to their underweight and low sex hormones.[27] A bone age x-ray should be performed on anyone suspected of not having achieved their full height before administering sex hormones, either transdermal estrogen or transdermal testosterone. The x-ray can evaluate whether growth plates have closed. I have taken care of 17 year olds who had the bone age of 13 year olds. If testosterone were administered to that individual, their growth plates would slam shut, and they would stop growing forever. In males who have normal testosterone levels and females past childbearing age, the question is more easily answered; I would readily prescribe bisphosphonates for them.

Linear Growth (a.k.a. The Height Question)

Short stature is a topic relevant to both male and female patients. In malnutrition, patients of both sexes develop growth hormone resistance. This means that they actually have high levels of growth hormone, but the cells do not respond to it. Once again, the cave person brain is working to spare calories for life-saving functions, and growth isn't one of them. Taking growth hormone while still underweight is useless because patients already have high natural levels of growth hormone. It's just that their body can't respond to it. I come back to one of my favorite themes: these patients don't have a hormonal or growth problem, they have a nutrition problem. Thus, there must be a nutritional solution.

Menstrual Periods

Having reviewed brain changes and bone density considerations in anorexia nervosa, let's turn to the topic of menstrual periods. In the past, the diagnosis of anorexia nervosa in a female patient required the absence of menstrual periods, called amenorrhea. However, in 2013 the DSM-5 removed the requirement of amenorrhea from the diagnosis of anorexia in females. That's because it has become clear that menstrual function varies widely from person to person. For instance, in one study, 50 percent of patients resumed their menstrual period once they regained at least a low-normal weight range and 23 percent body fat. However, fully a quarter of patients either maintained or resumed their menstrual period while significantly underweight, with a body fat percentage of only 11 percent. Furthermore, fat percentage measurements have been found to be no better than body mass index (BMI) at predicting menstrual resumption.[28]

Another study showed that 38 percent of patients who were restricting calories lost their period while still at a "normal" BMI. The authors conclude that many adults have symptoms of starvation without clinical underweight.[29] This is entirely congruent with my own experience. Classical teaching holds that 90 percent of women who achieve 90 percent of their expected body weight will resume their menstrual period within six months.[30] Studies have also highlighted the role of stress, regardless of nutritional status and body weight, in the development of menstrual dysfunction.[31]

When a post-adolescent, premenopausal woman has anorexia nervosa, the natural return of the period is often heralded as the "Mother Nature is happy" moment. However, on one hand, I've had many patients whose periods persisted despite eating disorder behaviors, with and without weight loss. They uneasily wonder if they're not yet sick enough, given that their body is "well enough" to menstruate regularly. On the other hand, I've had patients who have been weight restored and in recovery for two years, still waiting in vain for that period to come back. This almost certainly circles back to genetic variability. Even within the same patient, different relapses can induce different menstrual patterns.

In addition to a bone density study, female patients with malnutrition and the absence of a menstrual period need to have a blood estradiol level checked. While normal estradiol levels vary widely through a normal menstrual cycle, consistent levels of less than 30 pg/mL are considered low. When the estradiol is low and weight restoration or work on eating disorder behaviors is ongoing, it is fair to assume that the cave person brain remains quiescent with regards to sex hormones. When the level starts to rise, the weight has been in a reasonable range for 6–12 months, and the period still hasn't returned, we can use another tool in the tool kit: pelvic ultrasound.

Pelvic ultrasound is more often used in Europe than in the United States. Its premise is sound. Low estrogen levels from hypothalamic hypogonadism will actually make a woman's ovaries and uterus shrink back toward pre-pubescent sizes. The pelvic ultrasound can evaluate ovarian maturity and uterine size.[32] If the pelvic ultrasound shows a small uterus and immature ovaries, then the hypothalamus has not yet woken up, due to insufficient weight restoration or insufficient time at the restored weight. A study showed that almost 90 percent of women required weight restoration to a BMI over $20 \, kg/m^2$ for ovarian maturity to occur. Furthermore, at a BMI of $19 \, kg/m^2$, only 40 percent of women had achieved reproductive maturity.[33,34]

In the final analysis, even after eating disorder recovery there are patients who still have menstrual irregularity or who carry the diagnosis of polycystic ovarian syndrome (PCOS). I'm always willing to refer them to an endocrinologist (optimally someone with some eating disorder expertise) when their needs fall beyond my own knowledge base and scope of practice.

The Pill

Oral contraceptive pills neither protect the bones nor "jump start" the period. This has been proven again and again by well-designed studies. Despite this, many gynecologists and general physicians continue to receive the wrong information during medical school and residency on this topic.[35] As a result, many of my patients with amenorrhea due to an eating disorder have been prescribed the Pill for indications that it absolutely does not work for.

It seems that doctors and patients alike are at risk for assuming that if a woman bleeds every month on oral contraception, then she and her bones are getting what they need. This is wrong and dangerous thinking. For one, virtually anyone with a uterus and a vagina, when given oral contraceptive pills, will bleed during the placebo days. This isn't "jump starting" anything. It's giving someone a hormone-induced monthly blood loss.

Two, if patients and their doctors feel relieved and protected while on oral contraception, their level of concern about fixing the underlying problem—the eating disorder—is likely to ebb. It's easy for the eating disorder voice to say, "See, you're getting a period now, so you aren't sick enough anymore to push ahead on your meal plan and see your therapist."

Three, starving patients can ill afford the loss of menstrual blood every month. The whole reason the hypothalamus rolled back to preadolescence was to spare the body this additional drain on resources.

And four, being on the Pill prevents a woman from potentially having that yay-Mother-Nature moment in which she restores weight to the point that her natural menstrual cycle resumes ... assuming, of course, she's not one of those patients who resumes her period at a low weight.

However, I remind patients that "eggs happen." Amenorrhea is not adequate for pregnancy prevention. If the Pill is the only form of consistent birth control a woman is willing or able to take, and she's sexually active with a male partner and doesn't want to get pregnant, she should definitely take the Pill. Otherwise, it shouldn't be used in those with eating disorders and amenorrhea.

Case Resolution: Josh

Josh's new eating disorder physician shares his bone density and testosterone results with him. The diagnosis is osteoporosis, given the Z-score of −2.6 and low testosterone levels. Josh is also given the diagnosis of hypothalamic hypogonadism, and his doctor explains that his testosterone remains low because he never restored enough body weight for his hypothalamus to wake back up. Most likely, his intensive workout regimen after residential treatment, when he wasn't fully weight restored, contributed to rapid bone density loss. He also took no rest days for his body, which contributed to his stress fracture.

The specialist warmly acknowledges the good choice Josh made to intensify his work with his outpatient team when tempted in the face of his injury to restrict calories again. She reminds him that allowing his fracture fully to heal, while nourishing his body and allowing his weight to rise to a better target range, are likeliest to allow him to practice the sports he loves for the rest of his life. By contrast, staying underweight and pushing too hard to cross-train vigorously or jump back in early will result in further injuries and keep him sidelined.

The prescription is further weight restoration, close work with his team, and rest, gradually adding in some mindful movement, including some lifting. Josh decides to take a break from competitive cycling. Because he will not be competing in events that require drug testing, he accepts transdermal testosterone for his osteoporosis. He will use this daily until he achieves his target weight range. At that point, the testosterone will be discontinued for a few weeks, and his own levels will be tested again to see if his hypothalamus has woken back up. A DXA can be checked 1–2 years after he has maintained his higher body weight to determine if he will need further treatment for his bone density. He is informed it will likely never normalize; however, it can improve.

His doctor notes that, at his age, he can expect higher sex drive and sexual function than he currently experiences. The testosterone replacement will help with this but not overdrive it. If normalized sex drive and function are concerning to Josh, this can be addressed in therapy.

Case Resolution: Aniya

Aniya learns that she has hypothalamic hypogonadism. While her worst Z-score of −1.8 was read as "normal" on the report, her doctor emphasizes that this is by no means actually normal for such a young woman who does weight-bearing exercise and, in fact, reflects bone density loss that should be addressed. The pelvic ultrasound that confirmed a small uterus and ovaries helps convince Aniya that the weight she thought was normal was in fact too low. She had been thinking that achieving her 18-year-old, pre-illness body weight and not engaging in any eating disordered behaviors were sufficient. However, she realizes now that her body is telling her—through a quiescent hypothalamus, bone density loss, and preadolescent sized uterus and ovaries—that it "wants" to be at a higher adult weight. She declines the Pill once she learns that it does not help bones, nor does it help "jump start" periods. Only her overall nutritional health can do that.

Aniya is willing to reengage with her former eating disorder therapist and dietitian to do further weight restoration. She admits that gaining weight scares her, and she realizes she was not as solidly in recovery as she had thought. She is offered the estrogen patch and oral cyclic progesterone as a bridge for bone health to the time when she has achieved a weight at which her period naturally restarts. However, she reasonably asks for six months to restore weight and see if her body naturally cycles. Since she has had no fractures or complications, the doctor agrees.

Case Resolution: Aidan

Aidan and his parents learn that growth hormone will not be effective for him because he already has high growth hormone levels in his blood and growth hormone resistance due to his malnutrition. In addition, testosterone use could potentially close his growth plates prematurely and ensure that he will stop growing. A hand x-ray for bone age confirms that, despite being 17 years old, he has the bone age of a 14 year old. It is very appropriate to check Aidan's bone density because it almost certainly will show some degree of bone density loss, perhaps osteoporosis, and the Z-scores should be determined using his bone age of 14 instead of his chronological age of 17 years. His bone density may be a medical finding that is very motivating for recovery. Even if the DXA results are still normal, he has a higher risk for fracture simply due to his anorexia nervosa. Sustained weight restoration is his most appropriate treatment. He has a long road ahead of him given the severity of his eating disorder. Any weight loss at home should swiftly result in escalation to a higher level of care again.

Exercise during Recovery

Compulsive or obsessive exercise can be a feature of any eating disorder. Patients can come to feel that movement is about punishing themselves, burning calories, or weight loss. Healing this particular aspect of patients' relationships with their bodies is a key feature of the recovery process.

For years, when I lectured about hormones and bones, I would cite the study that showed that any exercise while underweight worsens bone density, and I would conclude, "Serious exercise is a privilege of full recovery." This remains true. However, I've now revised my statement to include, "but movement during weight restoration makes recovery sustainable."

Many eating disorder providers and programs insist that patients minimize physical movement during eating disorder recovery. Their logic is that patients should focus all their calories on restoring their bodies and weight. Additionally, they rightly question whether patients in the depths of their mental illness and starved brain can regulate movement and engage mindfully, as opposed to grimly counting calories or pushing themselves to extremes as they perhaps had been doing.

I am convinced now, however, that eating disorder specialists should permit (where medically and psychologically appropriate) and oversee physical movement throughout the recovery process, regardless of level of care. The brilliant physical and occupational therapists in the hospital at my previous job started me on this pathway. Very weak patients would brighten and glow as they saw rest, nutrition, and expert physical therapy (PT) and occupational therapy (OT) result in stronger, more independent bodies. They accepted nutrition and rest more readily because they saw such rapid improvements in their functional status.

In my current outpatient clinic, this has become even clearer. From athletes to artists who rarely put on a pair of sneakers, in patients of all sizes,

I offer to help get them moving as early as possible in the recovery process, to the degree that they wish to participate and are able. Asking patients not to do physical activity during recovery unwittingly reinforces their eating disordered perception that movement is for burning calories. When we tell them not to move or they'll burn too many calories, we are validating the eating disorder logic.

Instead, the treatment team optimally can agree on a slow, stepwise increase in movement, increasing calories as needed. The therapist can process with a patient how it feels to do a wide variety of exercise—yoga one day, a walk the next, and some free weights the third, with rest days each week. Might this contribute to some bone density loss while patients remain low on sex hormones? It might. But I'm convinced that creating a sustainable recovery plan that leads patients to long term health most often involves movement. Their achievement of full eating disorder recovery earlier will certainly be best for their bones in the long run. One caveat is that patients who cannot medically or psychologically engage in movement safely should be encouraged to wait until their recovery is further along.

As a final word, everyone working to recover from an eating disorder should put aside their step-tracking devices, whether on their phones or worn as a watch, and move through the world mindfully. Any focus on "the numbers," from weight to steps to calories burned to miles, risks servicing the eating disorder rather than one's true values and goals.

Notes

1 www.bones.nih.gov/sites/bones/files/bone_mass.pdf. Accessed March 14, 2018.
2 Allaway HC, Southmayd EA, De Souza MJ. The physiology of functional hypothalamic amenorrhea associated with energy deficiency in exercising women and in women with anorexia nervosa. *Horm Mol Biol Clin Investig.* 2016 February; 25(2):91–119. doi: 10.1515/hmbci-2015-0053.
3 Misra M, Golden NH, Katzman DK. State of the art systematic review of bone disease in anorexia nervosa. *Int J Eat Disord.* 2016 March; 49(3):276–292. doi: 10.1002/eat.22451.
4 Faje AT, Fazeli PK, Miller KK, Katzman DK, Ebrahimi S, Lee H, Mendes N, Snelgrove D, Meenaghan E, Misra M, Klibanski A. Fracture risk and areal bone mineral density in adolescent females with anorexia nervosa. *Int J Eat Disord.* 2014 July; 47(5):458–466. doi: 10.1002/eat.22248.
5 Lucas AR, Melton LJ 3rd, Crowson CS, O'Fallon WM. Long-term fracture risk among women with anorexia nervosa: a population-based cohort study. *Mayo Clin Proc.* 1999 October; 74(10):972–977. PubMed PMID: 10918862.
6 Vestergaard P, Emborg C, Støving RK, Hagen C, Mosekilde L, Brixen K. Fractures in patients with anorexia nervosa, bulimia nervosa, and other eating disorders—a nationwide register study. *Int J Eat Disord.* 2002 November; 32(3):301–308. PubMed PMID: 12210644.
7 Crabtree NJ, Arabi A, Bachrach LK, Fewtrell M, El-Hajj Fuleihan G, Kecskemethy HH, Jaworski M, Gordon CM. International Society for Clinical Densitometry. Dual-energy X-ray absorptiometry interpretation and reporting in children and adolescents: the revised 2013 ISCD Pediatric Official Positions.

J Clin Densitom. 2014 April–June; 17(2):225–242. doi: 10.1016/j.jocd.2014. 01.003.

8 Duckham RL, Baxter-Jones AD, Johnston JD, Vatanparast H, Cooper D, Kontulainen S. Does physical activity in adolescence have site-specific and sex-specific benefits on young adult bone size, content, and estimated strength? *J Bone Miner Res.* 2014 February; 29(2):479–486. doi: 10.1002/jbmr.2055.

9 Warden SJ, Mantila Roosa SM, Kersh ME, Hurd AL, Fleisig GS, Pandy MG, Fuchs RK. Physical activity when young provides lifelong benefits to cortical bone size and strength in men. *Proc Natl Acad Sci USA.* 2014 April 8; 111(14):5337–5342. doi: 10.1073/pnas.1321605111.

10 Mountjoy M, Sundgot-Borgen J, Burke L, Carter S, Constantini N, Lebrun C, Meyer N, Sherman R, Steffen K, Budgett R, Ljungqvist A. The IOC consensus statement: beyond the Female Athlete Triad–Relative Energy Deficiency in Sport (RED-S). *Br J Sports Med.* 2014 April; 48(7):491–497. doi: 10.1136/ bjsports-2014-093502.

11 Olmos JM, Valero C, del Barrio AG, Amado JA, Hernández JL, Menéndez-Arango J, González-Macías J. Time course of bone loss in patients with anorexia nervosa. *Int J Eat Disord.* 2010 September; 43(6):537–542. doi: 10.1002/eat. 20731.

12 Gatti D, El Ghoch M, Viapiana O, Ruocco A, Chignola E, Rossini M, Giollo A, Idolazzi L, Adami S, Dalle Grave R. Strong relationship between vitamin D status and bone mineral density in anorexia nervosa. *Bone.* 2015 September; 78:212–215. doi: 10.1016/j.bone.2015.05.014.

13 Golden NH, Lanzkowsky L, Schebendach J, Palestro CJ, Jacobson MS, Shenker IR. The effect of estrogen-progestin treatment on bone mineral density in anorexia nervosa. *J Pediatr Adolesc Gynecol.* 2002 June; 15(3):135–143. PubMed PMID: 12106749.

14 Klibanski A, Biller BM, Schoenfeld DA, Herzog DB, Saxe VC. The effects of estrogen administration on trabecular bone loss in young women with anorexia nervosa. *J Clin Endocrinol Metab.* 1995 March; 80(3):898–904. PubMed PMID: 7883849.

15 Strokosch GR, Friedman AJ, Wu SC, Kamin M. Effects of an oral contraceptive (norgestimate/ethinyl estradiol) on bone mineral density in adolescent females with anorexia nervosa: a double-blind, placebo-controlled study. *J Adolesc Health.* 2006 December; 39(6):819–827. PubMed PMID: 17116511.

16 Sim LA, McGovern L, Elamin MB, Swiglo BA, Erwin PJ, Montori VM. Effect on bone health of estrogen preparations in premenopausal women with anorexia nervosa: a systematic review and meta-analyses. *Int J Eat Disord.* 2010 April; 43(3):218–225. doi: 10.1002/eat.20687.

17 Goodman MP. Are all estrogens created equal? A review of oral vs. transdermal therapy. *J Womens Health (Larchmt).* 2012 February; 21(2):161–169. doi: 10.1089/jwh.2011.2839.

18 Misra M, Katzman D, Miller KK, Mendes N, Snelgrove D, Russell M, Goldstein MA, Ebrahimi S, Clauss L, Weigel T, Mickley D, Schoenfeld DA, Herzog DB, Klibanski A. Physiologic estrogen replacement increases bone density in adolescent girls with anorexia nervosa. *J Bone Miner Res.* 2011 October; 26(10): 2430–2438. doi: 10.1002/jbmr.447.

19 Southmayd EA, Hellmers AC, De Souza MJ. Food versus pharmacy: assessment of nutritional and pharmacological strategies to improve bone health in energy-deficient exercising women. *Curr Osteoporos Rep.* 2017 October; 15(5):459–472. doi: 10.1007/s11914-017-0393-9.

20 Baskaran C, Cunningham B, Plessow F, Singhal V, Woolley R, Ackerman KE, Slattery M, Lee H, Lawson EA, Eddy K, Misra M. Estrogen replacement

improves verbal memory and executive control in oligomenorrheic/amenorrheic athletes in a randomized controlled trial. *J Clin Psychiatry.* 2017 May; 78(5):e490–e497. doi: 10.4088/JCP.15m10544.

21 Miller KK, Meenaghan E, Lawson EA, Misra M, Gleysteen S, Schoenfeld D, Herzog D, Klibanski A. Effects of risedronate and low-dose transdermal testosterone on bone mineral density in women with anorexia nervosa: a randomized, placebo-controlled study. *J Clin Endocrinol Metab.* 2011 July; 96(7): 2081–2088. doi: 10.1210/jc.2011-0380.

22 Stathopoulos IP, Liakou CG, Katsalira A, Trovas G, Lyritis GG, Papaioannou NA, Tournis S. The use of bisphosphonates in women prior to or during pregnancy and lactation. *Hormones (Athens).* 2011 October–December; 10(4):280–291.

23 Vujasinovic-Stupar N, Pejnovic N, Markovic L, Zlatanovic M. Pregnancy-associated spinal osteoporosis treated with bisphosphonates: long-term follow-up of maternal and infants outcome. *Rheumatol Int.* 2012 March; 32(3):819–823. doi: 10.1007/s00296-011-1816-z.

24 Fazeli PK, Wang IS, Miller KK, Herzog DB, Misra M, Lee H, Finkelstein JS, Bouxsein ML, Klibanski A. Teriparatide increases bone formation and bone mineral density in adult women with anorexia nervosa. *J Clin Endocrinol Metab.* 2014 April; 99(4):1322–1329. doi: 10.1210/jc.2013-4105.

25 Andrews EB, Gilsenan A, Midkiff K, Harris D. Challenges in studying very rare cancer outcomes and infrequent exposures: example of teriparatide and osteosarcoma. *Ann Epidemiol.* 2016 November; 26(11):751–753. doi: 10.1016/j.annepidem.2016.08.011.

26 Mehler PS, Sabel AL, Watson T, Andersen AE. High risk of osteoporosis in male patients with eating disorders. *Int J Eat Disord.* 2008 November; 41(7): 666–672. doi: 10.1002/eat.20554.

27 Modan-Moses D, Yaroslavsky A, Kochavi B, Toledano A, Segev S, Balawi F, Mitrany E, Stein D. Linear growth and final height characteristics in adolescent females with anorexia nervosa. *PLoS One.* 2012; 7(9):e45504. doi: 10.1371/journal.pone.0045504.

28 Winkler LA, Frølich JS, Schulpen M, Støving RK. Body composition and menstrual status in adults with a history of anorexia nervosa-at what fat percentage is the menstrual cycle restored? *Int J Eat Disord.* 2017 April; 50(4):370–377. doi: 10.1002/eat.22600.

29 Berner LA, Feig EH, Witt AA, Lowe MR. Menstrual cycle loss and resumption among patients with anorexia nervosa spectrum eating disorders: is relative or absolute weight more influential? *Int J Eat Disord.* 2017 April; 50(4):442–446. doi: 10.1002/eat.22697.

30 Golden NH, Jacobson MS, Schebendach J, Solanto MV, Hertz SM, Shenker IR. Resumption of menses in anorexia nervosa. *Arch Pediatr Adolesc Med.* 1997 January; 151(1):16–21. PubMed PMID: 9006523.

31 Prokai D, Berga SL. Neuroprotection via reduction in stress: altered menstrual patterns as a marker for stress and implications for long-term neurologic health in Women. *Int J Mol Sci.* 2016 December 20; 17(12). pii: E2147. doi: 10.3390/ijms17122147.

32 Mason HD, Key A, Allan R, Lask B. Pelvic ultrasonography in anorexia nervosa: what the clinician should ask the radiologist and how to use the information provided. *Eur Eat Disord Rev.* 2007 January; 15(1):35–41. Review. PubMed PMID: 17676670.

33 Key A, Mason H, Allan R, Lask B. Restoration of ovarian and uterine maturity in adolescents with anorexia nervosa. *Int J Eat Disord.* 2002 November; 32(3):319–325. PubMed PMID: 12210646.

34 Allan R, Sharma R, Sangani B, Hugo P, Frampton I, Mason H, Lask B. Predicting the weight gain required for recovery from anorexia nervosa with pelvic ultrasonography: an evidence-based approach. *Eur Eat Disord Rev.* 2010 January; 18(1):43–48. doi: 10.1002/erv.982.

35 Mahr F, Farahmand P, Bixler EO, Domen RE, Moser EM, Nadeem T, Levine RL, Halmi KA. A national survey of eating disorder training. *Int J Eat Disord.* 2015 May; 48(4):443–445. doi: 10.1002/eat.22335.

Chapter 4

The Empty Tank

Case: Maria

Maria is a 34-year-old cisgender Latina female who has had anorexia nervosa, restricting subtype, since she was 15. She got married three years ago and adopted a child last year after being unable to get pregnant. She had two residential eating disorder stays during her adolescence and teen years, during which she fully restored her weight, but she always slowly sank back to her baseline state of being chronically underweight. In the past year, her eating behaviors and weight began to slip further, much to her dismay. This started shortly after her son's adoption, which made no sense to her because one of her top goals in life was to become a mother. She always takes care of everyone else first and is diligent to the point of rigidity about making sure the house is clean and in perfect order. She is a great mom, attentive and responsible to her son. However, she struggles with being attentive to herself.

As a result of her chronic malnourishment, Maria has always battled the medical complications of a slowed metabolism, and she has a team with whom she meets twice a month: a doctor, a therapist, and a dietitian. As her weight has slowly fallen in the last six months, she has felt exhausted, cold, weak, anxious, constipated, full, and has struggled with insomnia. She also has had moments where she feels sweaty, agitated, and shaky when she wakes up. These episodes tend to pass after she's had some breakfast with her son. Her hair has started to shed in the shower, and her skin has become fragile. Sometimes when she bumps against something lightly, she ends up with a skin tear or a bruise. Her body image is worse than ever. Her whole life, she's struggled with not feeling sick enough to deserve everyone's concern about her eating disorder, in part because her bloodwork has always been normal.

Needless to say, this entire past year, Maria's eating disorder team has been trying to convince her to return to treatment. They and her husband are worried she might die. She has refused because she doesn't want to leave her son. She feels so guilty that she can't turn this around and get back to the safer place she used to be, and yet at the same time, she is more and more determined not to gain weight. Maria does not drink alcohol and is only on medications for her gastroparesis and bone density, so she is surprised when her doctor checks her labs and calls her in to discuss abnormal results. She learns that her blood glucose is quite low, her liver function tests are abnormal, and her complete blood count shows abnormally low levels of both white blood cells and red blood cells.

Background

Patients with eating disorders and disordered eating are running on an empty nutritional tank. Whether they restrict calories, binge and then purge to emptiness, or binge at night and then restrict all the next day, they spend vast portions of each day empty. I respect that the metaphor of the empty tank applies to their emotional state, too. Eating disorders numb people to their emotions, helping them feel safe from painful, messy feelings. The medical complications of an empty tank can occur in patients of all shapes and sizes, although some of them are more common in patients with very low body weights. Rapid weight loss, long term malnutrition without weight loss, and living at a lower body weight than one's usual range can all prove medically dangerous.

Sudden Cardiac Death and Hypoglycemia

Many people think that patients with chronic starvation die due to a "heart attack." It's important to note the difference between a heart attack and cardiac arrest. A heart attack is what happens when the arteries of the heart get blocked, such that blood flow can't get to the heart muscle, and the muscle is deprived of oxygen. In the deadliest of situations, the blockages are so severe that the amount of heart muscle lacking oxygen causes the heart to stop, and the person dies.

Cardiac arrest, by contrast, refers to the heart stopping due to any cause, for instance an abnormal rhythm (called an arrhythmia) or an electrolyte abnormality. Studies have shown that almost no one with malnutrition from an eating disorder dies from a heart attack.[1] Autopsy results show their heart arteries are clean and open.[2] However, cardiac arrest is generally considered to be a major cause of death in eating disorders.

The fact is, though, that cardiac arrest is really the final common pathway in anyone's process of dying. At some point, whether due to a critical infection, malignancy, accident, or other organ failure, the heart stops. The vital question to answer for those with eating disorders is: what makes their heart stop? Is it a problem with the heart itself, perhaps some strange rhythm or abnormal electrical activity that goes terminally awry? Or is it something else?

My long clinical experience taking care of some of the most medically compromised patients with anorexia nervosa in the country (and watching their heart rates 24–7 on monitors) has shown that practically no one's heart simply slows until it stops. Arrhythmias are rare too, except in the case of certain classes of medication or abnormal electrolytes caused by purging. But if the heart itself is okay, why are patients with restrictive anorexia nervosa dying of cardiac arrest?

I am convinced that the heart stops because of low blood sugar, known as hypoglycemia. When the heart runs out of fuel, it will stop. This means much more focus needs to be placed on patients' blood sugar levels than is currently being done in medical clinics or even treatment programs. Hypoglycemia can occur in a wide variety of medical problems, and in this chapter, I will only focus on why it occurs in the context of restrictive anorexia nervosa.

It's worth briefly mentioning how blood sugar management works in a healthy person. When carbohydrate is consumed, our digestive tract breaks that down to glucose, which is then absorbed into our bloodstream and distributed to our cells. When we eat more carbohydrate than our cells need in that moment, the excess is stored as glycogen in our muscles and liver. Glycogen is our main source of energy when the body calls for more energy than our last meal could provide.

In anorexia nervosa, caloric restriction deprives the body of adequate carbohydrates on a daily basis. Very quickly, the body uses up its 2000 calories or so of stored glycogen. However, the brain can only run on glucose. So, when the energy tank is empty, the body has to create glucose from its own tissues. Muscle tissue breaks down into amino acids, which can be converted into glucose, using fat to fuel the process. Ketone formation is a byproduct. (This is actually the intended consequence of very low carbohydrate diets that are called "ketogenic.") At some point, the body has broken down so much muscle and fat, desperately mining for glucose to keep the brain alive, that the emaciated person doesn't have much more muscle mass to give. At that point, the blood glucose starts to drop regularly, especially between meals.

The longest daily fast is typically overnight. As a result, by morning, blood glucose levels can be perilously low. A family member might tragically find their loved one unresponsive in the early morning hours. Ultimately, the cause of death in those cases cannot be known. However, I've borne witness to a few memorable "near misses," when a patient was found "down" and successfully resuscitated, and the resuscitating team found the blood glucose was undetectable. In these cases, emergent provision of intravenous glucose saved the day.

In the moment, when someone has hypoglycemia (defined as a blood glucose of less than 70 mg/dL), they must immediately consume rapidly absorbed glucose. Juice or glucose tablets are all reasonable—anything without protein or fat, which slows absorption. Patients can get hypoglycemic after meals as well. Consumption of carbohydrates can stimulate excessive insulin production, pushing too much glucose into the cells and leaving the blood levels low. In this situation, a few ounces of juice, milk, or liquid supplement works well.

In the bigger picture, pre-meal hypoglycemia is a sign of impending disaster and must be taken very seriously. Patients need to be told that this is a pre-death warning sign and that they could die overnight or end up with irreversible brain damage from lack of fuel. I always advise eating disorder programs that they should meet new patients with a warm handshake and a finger stick blood glucose test, because failing to diagnose hypoglycemia is a serious problem.

Patients don't have to be symptomatic for hypoglycemia to be dangerous. Many people who have been running low blood glucoses lose their ability to sense lows. In fact, that's even more dangerous because a patient's lack of symptoms contributes to their sense that they are fine. When treated with consistent, monitored nutritional rehabilitation and adequate caloric intake, patients quickly become able to meet their daily glucose requirements, stop breaking down their own muscles, refill their glycogen stores, and eventually rebuild muscle and fat.

Bone Marrow Failure of Starvation

The bone marrow is the rich, cellular matrix inside of our bones. It is responsible for creating our blood cells: the white blood cells that fight infection, the red blood cells that carry oxygen and carbon dioxide, and the platelets that help stop bleeding. During significant malnutrition, the bone marrow can stop working. Bone marrow failure of malnutrition is called gelatinous marrow transformation or serous fat atrophy.[3] Normal marrow is replaced by a non-cell producing "goo" which is fatty and quiescent. Essentially, the body is saying, "I'm starving. Why would I produce blood cells?"

The complete blood count (CBC) is the laboratory test that evaluates blood cell levels. Patients with an empty nutritional tank can develop leukopenia (low levels of white blood cells) with or without neutropenia (low levels of a particular type of white blood cell, the neutrophil, that is an active infection fighter). Strangely enough, patients with anorexia nervosa have not been found, despite their weakened immune systems, to develop more infections.[4] However, if they do become infected, it's very serious. I recommend the flu shot in season, because influenza can be deadly. In addition, patients can develop anemia (low red blood cells) and thrombocytopenia (low platelets). Anemia can cause fatigue and shortness of breath, while thrombocytopenia contributes to easy bruising, nosebleeds, and increased bleeding of all types.

It's very important to communicate the implications of bone marrow failure of starvation. Some of my patients hear vague statements from their doctor such as, "Yeah, your white count is low, but I think that's common."

Others get referred to a cancer specialist for an evaluation of blood cancer or are prescribed medicines to stimulate the bone marrow to start producing cells again. In actuality, the patient does not have a bone marrow problem. They have a starvation problem. Thus, we must refer them to a nutritional solution. Bone marrow will return to normal over several weeks with appropriate nutritional rehabilitation. Marrow stimulating agents and oncology evaluations are inappropriate and can distract from focusing on the eating disorder. Most importantly, I remind my patients who think they aren't sick enough, "You have *bone marrow failure* as a result of your anorexia nervosa. Your body is showing us that you aren't fine."

Liver Abnormalities

Liver dysfunction is also common in severe malnutrition. The aspartate aminotransferase (AST) and alanine aminotransferase (ALT) are enzymes whose elevation denotes liver cell injury. High levels of AST and ALT are broadly categorized as being related to "hepatitis" or liver injury.

There are two main reasons why the AST and ALT might be elevated in someone with anorexia nervosa. The first reason is hepatitis of starvation.[5] When the nutritional tank gets empty enough, the liver cells begin to consume themselves, a process called autophagy. A study showed that more than 50 percent of underweight, hospitalized patients were admitted with hepatitis of starvation.[6] This resolves with nutritional rehabilitation, although the AST and ALT may continue to rise a week into refeeding, a process I call the "comet tail effect." That is, the liver appears to respond to its nutritional status from the week prior. A study showed that AST and ALT levels more than three times normal (that is, around levels of 150 U/L or more) predict hypoglycemia, independent of BMI.[7] The bilirubin levels are not affected by malnutrition or refeeding.

The second reason for AST and ALT elevation is hepatitis of refeeding. Around two months into nutritional rehabilitation, patients may develop a mild case of what is called steatohepatitis or fatty liver. This is a response to high calorie, high carbohydrate intake. It can last a few weeks before resolving completely. If it becomes more severe, a slight decrease in the carbohydrate fraction of the meal plan (for instance, to 40 percent) will help. Of course, anyone who has elevations in their liver function tests should have a thoughtful overall assessment. Alcohol intake, viral infection of the liver, and certain medications can also cause liver cell injury; these factors must all be considered.

Albumin is the main protein in blood and is made by the liver. It is commonly used as a marker of malnutrition in adult general medicine patients. However, albumin levels are almost always normal in patients with anorexia nervosa. This is a conundrum that perplexes insurance companies and emergency room physicians who are looking for reasons (besides inadequate nutritional intake and agonizing emotional dysregulation) to authorize a patient to a higher level of care.

It turns out that albumin is low in adults without eating disorders *in response to the inflammatory condition that made the person lose weight*: cancer, infection, or a rheumatologic/autoimmune condition.[8] The weight loss is just a side effect. By contrast, those with malnutrition from an eating disorder have very low levels of inflammation in their bodies, and albumin remains normal. Albumin is *not* a marker of malnutrition in eating disorders; I have had to educate insurance reviewers about this countless times. In fact, when a previously normal albumin does drop in someone with an eating disorder, it should be regarded as a "canary in the coal mine" that something else is brewing, such as a bladder infection or a pneumonia. In the relatively rare cases where someone with anorexia nervosa does develop a low albumin, I generally suspect something else is going on.

Skin, Hair, and Nails

The last important organ system to discuss is what's called the integumentary system: the skin, hair, and nails. Skin is considered the "largest organ," because it covers the entire surface of our body. It forms a vital barrier between the inside of our bodies and the pathogen rich outside world. With malnutrition, the skin becomes malnourished too, dry and fragile.[9,10] Many malnourished patients look much older than their stated age, especially those in their 20s and beyond. Their facial skin develops lines, and the loss of fat in their cheeks makes the skin sag and look hollow. Skin takes on a papery quality that, as malnutrition becomes more severe, can tear with little trauma, develop petechiae (tiny blood vessels that burst right below the surface and cause red dots), or bruise easily. Hands, particularly when patients over-wash them in the service of anxiety or obsessive-compulsive tendencies, can become so dry that the skin cracks and bleeds. Ironically, given that the goal of this obsessive behavior is to reduce bacterial contamination, any cracks in the skin actually increase the odds of infection.

When malnourished, fingernails can stop growing normally, often emerging as brittle and ragged shadows of their former selves. Diffuse hair loss, called telogen effluvium, can cause loss of up to 50 percent of the scalp hair density. Genetic variability accounts for the fact that some patients with sustained malnutrition retain healthy hair, while others shed hair almost immediately upon engaging in disordered eating.

The full recovery of the integumentary system can take a long time. Because hair growth follows a long cycle, often months of recovery work can pass before patients start to notice regrowth of healthier hair. However, the skin starts to improve within a few weeks of nutritional rehabilitation. Furthermore, rich emollient creams should be applied to the skin several times a day in order to combat the extreme dryness that can lead to cracking and infections. When hand and foot skin is highly affected, I recommend nighttime heavy application of a hydrating ointment followed by cotton gloves and socks, so that it can absorb overnight. Patients with eating disorders often look years younger as they recover.

Case Resolution: Maria

Maria and her husband meet with the outpatient treatment team and listen to their grave concerns about her health and their recommendation for her to return to inpatient treatment. Her doctor highlights the ways in which every one of Maria's organ systems are shutting down. She has bone marrow failure, liver failure, skin failure, and now, most concerningly, hypoglycemia. The doctor shares with her that hypoglycemia may be the cause of brain damage and death in anorexia nervosa. While the team cannot predict when she will die from her eating disorder—because people can be astoundingly resilient and survive well past what would be expected—she now faces the risk of death on a daily basis.

Maria protests. She identifies that she has seen vastly thinner patients than she on the internet. She has personally been friends with more underweight peers in past residential care. She is still a top performer at work. The very idea of entering treatment at this weight is embarrassing to her, because she is convinced that she's not sick enough to require their concern or the disruption in her life. In any event, her baby needs her. She is clear in saying that she does not want to die and doesn't believe she will.

The team persists, noting that Maria's body itself is telling the team how ill she is, from her manifestations of slowed metabolism to her organ failure. The team notes that they, too, wanted Maria to remain outpatient, and they have supported her as best they could for a long time while she resisted treatment. But now, between her medical complications and her rigid, starved brain that is incapable of making even small changes consistently, it's clear that outpatient isn't working. The team lets her know she is no longer safe to drive. What if she gets woozy from low blood sugar and runs into someone else or gets into an accident with the baby in the car?

Maria's husband plays a key role. He is loving and gives her space to voice the anguish of her anorexia nervosa but informs her that he cannot continue to watch her waste away. He's become nervous about leaving her alone with the baby because he's afraid she might drop him due to her weakness or pass out from low blood sugar. With immense sadness, he lets her know that he will begin separation proceedings and ask for full custody unless she proceeds to inpatient care and completes a full treatment course.

Initially, Maria is furious and feels backed into a corner, betrayed, and above all, bewildered that everyone is making such a big deal out of her clearly not-that-serious situation. However, the doctor's words about organ failure do help to give her the permission to realize maybe her distortions are worse than she thought. She asks to go over those results a couple times during the meeting, and by the end she has acquiesced to calling a few highly recommended treatment centers. She agrees to drink a certain number of Ensures every day, regardless of her solid food intake, in order to protect her brain and heart from hypoglycemia.

Months later, having struggled through, then tolerated, then thrived in a higher level of care, Maria admits she can barely remember that meeting or the weeks before it. She feels reconnected with her values and committed to recovery work. Being an adult, and in particular a wife and mother, has changed her entire relationship with the recovery process. Compared with her rebellious teen years in treatment, she now feels she has more of an identity outside of her anorexia nervosa and clear reasons to live and stay well.

The Subterranean Aquifer, Checklists, and Reframing Expectations

When I talk with my patients about the "soul cost" of constantly running themselves ragged, of chronically failing to recognize and attend to their physical and emotional needs, I like to use the metaphor of the subterranean aquifer. An aquifer is a reserve of underground water that can be tapped into when water supplies on the surface run low. I liken the aquifer to each patient's intellectual, emotional, and physical energy stores.

Many of my patients tell me they feel uneasy about taking care of themselves. It can, they tell me, feel more appropriate to get schoolwork done just right, to take care of a friend, or to accomplish a work project, than to sit quietly and take care of themselves. This is what I call "depleting the aquifer." They've been tapping into their reserves for so long that their metaphorical personal water level drops and rarely gets replenished. They are nutritionally drained, emotionally drained and numbed, so that on a day-to-day basis they find it a struggle to do things to take care of themselves. My patients' aquifers often start out plentiful. They are so capable and have such impressive capacity to do work that it takes a lot for them to dry up. This can contribute to their thinking, "Hey, there's no consequence. In fact, I'm praised and rewarded for this. I'd better keep going."

But there are serious medical consequences to letting that aquifer run too low. Even if patients aren't consciously aware, their soul knows that they're further depleted every single day. When the aquifer gets too low, the body and soul will find a way to force patients to hold still and recharge. In the case of the eating disorder, as they get sicker and deplete the aquifer even faster, patients become so unwell physically that they are forced to slow down. By contrast, when a person takes care of herself, then the anorexia has less to work with. If the patient gets her needs met through positive, productive recharge, then the anorexia can't say, "I'm all you've got in this chaotic, dangerous world. Just listen to me."

Why wait until the aquifer is dry to make changes? Better to learn how to meet one's needs before discovering that chronic stress has contributed to the development of an illness. While stress doesn't cause disease by itself, it can absolutely trigger the body's stress responses, which can then set off or worsen any number of illnesses for which someone has a genetic predisposition. I encourage my patients to start contemplating what their personal psychological, social, and physical needs are—everyone's are different—and to begin thinking about how they can start to meet them. I invite them to refill the aquifer and not ever let it run dry again.

Another way of thinking about this same issue is the "checkboxes problem." Many of my patients—and many people I know without eating disorders—offer themselves conditional joy or rest. That is, doing something relaxing is dependent upon getting all of life's requirements out of the way first. For instance, "I can't sit and rest on the couch to read or watch TV until the laundry is folded, the kids' lunches are made, and the bills are paid." Now, of course we all have things to do in life. But if we're honest with ourselves, the to-do list is almost infinite. Whether we bring our work home with us in the form of email at night, or our work takes place in the home with no office to leave at the end of the day, or there's a ton of homework to do, there are always tasks on the list. In medical training, doctors learn to put little open checkboxes next to tasks; so, in my mind, the list has a series of checkboxes next to it.

Too many of my patients resist relaxation or rest until all their checkboxes are checked. Guess what? That means they almost never give themselves permission to rest. They might have seen this same behavior in their home as children, where hard working parents never appeared to take time for themselves in order to serve the greater good. These are honorable, well-meaning tendencies. But when blended with a mental illness that already drives patients to misery with its judgmental, cruel voice, this drive becomes harmful.

I encourage my patients to challenge this philosophy. Sure, they still have a bunch of things to do. But if they don't rest and recharge, even for a short time each day, their bodies will take them down. This could mean their eating disorder gets stronger, or they have a flare of a sensitive GI system, migraines, or chronic pain. As a result, they will actually be far less productive. If we're maximizing for productivity—which isn't necessarily always the right thing to do—then regular recharge and rest will prove much more productive than wringing ourselves dry. Would we ever expect a car to drive 100 miles before receiving any fuel? Can anyone sing before they take a breath? Self-care has to take place like breathing, occurring at regular intervals. Thank heavens breathing is automatic, or patients with eating disorders probably wouldn't take a breath until they got into bed at night.

My final example of this important theme is a way that I learned to combat some of these tendencies in my own thinking. The biblical quotation, "From those to whom much is given, much is expected" (Luke 12:48) always posed a challenge for me. I knew I'd been given a lot, whether in terms of my upbringing or in terms of my health and work ethic. The expectation part was tough because I have really high expectations for myself. When you are really hard working, how do you know when to rein that in? How do you show your gratitude for all the positives in your life without giving and giving until you're empty, until your own aquifer has run dry?

Over time and after reflection, I reframed my understanding this adage. I decided that the act of choosing over-work is no virtue and wasn't synonymous with meeting expectations. This involves realizing that one's energies are finite. I now visualize a pie chart that represents the different aspects of my life that I spend energy on. My new expectation for myself is to expend energy in a way that is congruent with my values.

In my own personal values pie chart, my husband and kids tie for first, then my direct work with patients, then everything else I love and think is worthwhile in life: staying healthy, writing this book, nurturing my friendships, enjoying my extended family. So for me, I can't give 80 percent of my energies in a given day to my patients and come home with 20 percent left for the people who tie for first in my values. I must conserve energy. That means I have to say no to things.

Once I realized that this is my version of meeting expectations, I finally found the reason I needed to say no to certain requests. Saying yes to something I care about, but not as much as other priorities, puts me in energy imbalance. It hurts, don't get me wrong. I'd love to be superhuman and please everybody and show my immense gratitude by saying yes to everything. It also doesn't please everyone else in my life when I have to set boundaries or say no. But ultimately, I am the sole guardian of my energy and the sole curator of my values. I have a privilege that many women in the world absolutely do not have: the power to prioritize what is important to me. I will use that precious gift to the best of my ability. I don't want to push myself to the point where it manifests in physical illness in order to slow me down.

Notes

1 Sachs KV, Harnke B, Mehler PS, Krantz MJ. Cardiovascular complications of anorexia nervosa: A systematic review. *Int J Eat Disord.* 2016 March; 49(3): 238–248. doi: 10.1002/eat.22481.

2 Isner JM, Roberts WC, Heymsfield SB, Yager J. Anorexia nervosa and sudden death. *Ann Intern Med.* 1985 January; 102(1):49–52. PubMed PMID: 3966745.

3 Sabel AL, Gaudiani JL, Statland B, Mehler PS. Hematological abnormalities in severe anorexia nervosa. *Ann Hematol.* 2013 May; 92(5):605–613. doi: 10.1007/s00277-013-1672-x.

4 Bowers TK, Eckert E. Leukopenia in anorexia nervosa. Lack of increased risk of infection. *Arch Intern Med.* 1978 October; 138(10):1520–1523. PubMed PMID: 708174.

5 Rosen E, Bakshi N, Watters A, Rosen HR, Mehler PS. Hepatic complications of anorexia nervosa. *Dig Dis Sci.* 2017 November; 62(11):2977–2981. doi: 10.1007/s10620-017-4766-9.

6 Rosen E, Sabel AL, Brinton JT, Catanach B, Gaudiani JL, Mehler PS. Liver dysfunction in patients with severe anorexia nervosa. *Int J Eat Disord.* 2016 February; 49(2):151–158. doi: 10.1002/eat.22436.

7 Gaudiani JL, Sabel AL, Mascolo M, Mehler PS. Severe anorexia nervosa: outcomes from a medical stabilization unit. *Int J Eat Disord.* 2012 January; 45(1):85–92. doi: 10.1002/eat.20889.

8 Narayanan V, Gaudiani JL, Mehler PS. Serum albumin levels may not correlate with weight status in severe anorexia nervosa. *Eat Disord.* 2009 July–September; 17(4):322–326. doi: 10.1080/10640260902991202.
9 Tyler I, Wiseman MC, Crawford RI, Birmingham CL. Cutaneous manifestations of eating disorders. *J Cutan Med Surg.* 2002 July–August; 6(4):345–353. PubMed PMID: 11951131.
10 Strumia R. Eating disorders and the skin. *Clin Dermatol.* 2013 January–February; 31(1):80–85. doi: 10.1016/j.clindermatol.2011.11.011.

Extreme Presentations

Full disclosure before you begin this chapter: in order to cover as many medical complications of eating disorders in this book as possible, in Chapter 5 I review the problems that usually only occur in patients with profound underweight from anorexia nervosa. These patients, who often do not think they are sick enough for intensive treatment, deserve to have their stories told too. However, if you are going to read this chapter and decide *you* aren't sick enough because you don't have one of these extreme and rare medical problems, please skip it. Come back and read it later, if you want to, when you're further in recovery and in a better place. Or omit it permanently. I have no interest in invalidating anyone's struggle.

Case: Jessica

Jessica is a 25-year-old cisgender Caucasian female with a history of restrictive anorexia nervosa dating back to when she was 11 years old. It has been a long road. She has experienced countless admissions to inpatient and residential programs, many of which ended when insurance cut out too early. That meant she would have to return home just weight restored enough to panic, not having stayed long enough to do the psychological work to tolerate her body changes. Each time, she would try to work with her home team, motivated by a desire to make progress academically and not fall further behind her classmates. However, the relapses kept occurring.

After age 18, the struggle became even harder. Jessica regarded herself as an adult and refused treatment for six excruciating months. She then went through multiple short admissions that failed to offer her lasting recovery. At age 24, her parents won a lawsuit against their insurance company, and she was able to stay in treatment for six months. She emerged fully weight restored and acting like the daughter they remembered: smart, funny, caring, engaged, and thoughtful.

Having done a lot of college work online, she enrolled in a community college near home, where she lived with her parents, and was excited about being a "normal" student again. Then two months later, Jessica was sexually assaulted at a party. Barely able to speak about what had happened, she was flooded with fears that it was her fault or that her weight-restored body was somehow responsible. Her eating disorder mind was reactivated. Restriction and exercise became her only companions, and she adamantly refused her parents' and team's increasingly desperate pleas to return to treatment.

Jessica's weight loss was rapid and extreme, leading her up to present day. After a few months at the lowest body weight she's ever experienced, her eating disorder voice is also the loudest. She has started to vomit almost everything she eats despite never having purged, which scares her. She feels painful fullness after a few bites of food, and sometimes the pain becomes sharp, right in the middle of her stomach. Her eyes have become itchy and light sensitive all the time. At times, she feels like she hears her own voice echoing in her ears and has learned that if she puts her head down on her arms she gets temporary relief. Food intake is further curtailed by the fact that she feels food get stuck sometimes as she tries to swallow it. It floods her with a panicky feeling as she tries to gulp to get it down. After drinking fluids, she sometimes has to clear her throat or cough. Her voice has become softer, more high pitched, and nasal sounding. To her surprise, she develops persistent, mild vaginal bleeding despite not having had a period in six years. Feeling too miserable and weak to resist anymore, and finally fearing for her life, she agrees to admit to a medical hospital that specializes in eating disorders.

Background

Patients should start their care in an expert hospital setting when they become sufficiently medically compromised. Having helped run the top such medical program for adults in the country for many years, I have seen this firsthand. Even a terrific, academically renowned university hospital without eating disorder expertise almost invariably fails adults with severe anorexia nervosa. They are just not equipped with the multidisciplinary team needed to help a sensitive, mentally ill, starving patient navigate everything at once: the moment-to-moment panic and desire to leave, the optimization of all the physical impediments to taking in food, the prevention of injury or harm, the art of refeeding, and the delicate support of someone to do the two things they abhor the most: rest and nourish. Children and adolescents, by contrast, often do receive good initial medical care at standard top hospitals, perhaps because pediatricians receive training in childhood malnutrition or because parents can mandate treatment.

For the care of medically compromised adults with eating disorders, all members of the hospital staff should possess true expertise in this patient population: nurses, nursing assistants, doctors, dietitians, psychologists, physical therapists, occupational therapists, social workers, intake professionals, and support staff. It is worth pushing to admit or transfer to an expert program when the patient is severely medically compromised because state of the art, evidence-based care is provided across the board. Centers with expertise have cared for a high enough volume of patients that they have made countless improvements in how care is provided. A patient deemed a "medical mystery" can often be handled smoothly and productively in a place that cares for similarly ill patients all the time.[1]

While every case of anorexia nervosa is severe, in that it carries the highest mortality rate of any mental health diagnosis, for simplicity's sake I will use the term "severe anorexia nervosa" to describe the patients in this chapter.

Dysphagia

Dysphagia (pronounced dis-FAY-juh) is the term that is used to describe difficulty swallowing oral contents into the stomach, and it can be deadly. Oropharyngeal dysphagia specifically refers to dysfunction of the upper part of the swallow, but since that's a mouthful itself, I will just use the term dysphagia. In severe anorexia nervosa, all of the body's muscles have shrunk and become weak. This includes the swallowing muscles, which now cannot coordinate properly to move a bolus of food or fluid from the mouth to the stomach. Gastroesophageal reflux disease (GERD) can also cause or contribute to dysphagia.

Either as part of the denial of disease severity or because dysfunction worsens slowly over time, patients may not mention or even recognize that they are having dysphagia. Asking a number of questions can help:

> Are you finding that foods, especially dry foods, or pills are getting stuck in your throat? Do you have to swallow a number of times to get them down? Are you coughing after drinking liquids? Has your cough become weaker? Have you had pneumonia recently?

A yes to any of these questions in an individual with severe anorexia nervosa should trigger an urgent speech language pathologist (SLP) evaluation. Up to a fifth of patients admitted to a specialty eating disorder program had dysphagia symptoms, and half of those were found, on evaluation, to have significant swallowing problems.[2]

Dysphagia increases the risk of aspiration pneumonia, where oral contents end up in the lungs instead of the stomach and set up a lung infection. A bite of food, a sip of liquid, or even a swallow of bacteria rich saliva can all lead to aspiration pneumonia. Aspiration pneumonia is one of the ways that patients with anorexia nervosa can die because, even with great antibiotics and even life support, their weakened bodies and immune systems may not be able to pull through.

A capable SLP in the right hospital setting can diagnose dysphagia at the bedside, obtain further data with a video swallow test, and can recommend altered food and liquid textures without compromising caloric intake. SLPs also oversee specific exercises to strengthen the swallowing muscles, and superb nursing can help diminish aspiration risk at meals and overnight. In rare cases, someone who cannot yet swallow safely can have a thin feeding tube passed through their nose into their stomach. After a period of nutritional rehabilitation and exercises, the body heals, and the patient can swallow again.

Other less medically compromised patients with eating disorders may also have the sensation of swallowing difficulty. Referring these patients to a SLP for testing is appropriate. Some learn that psychological distress manifests physically in swallowing difficulty. The muscles are strong, but their function is impeded through a mechanism that the patient cannot consciously control. This is no less scary and intrusive for the patient, but the fix is primarily a psychological one rather than a medical one. Excellent psychotherapy can help patients identify emotional distress and work on relaxation techniques that will help them regain full function.

Autophonia and Lagophthalmos

Two medical problems frequently show up alongside dysphagia in severe anorexia nervosa: autophonia and lagophthalmos. Autophonia, also called patulous Eustacian tubes, refers to the sensation of hearing one's own voice echoing in one's head or having muffled hearing. The Eustacian tube is the "inner ear equalizer" that opens when one yawns or swallows as the pressure changes in an elevator or airplane. When a person loses so much weight that the Eustacian tube stays open all the time, their hearing and voice quality change. Many patients learn on their own, because the symptom is so uncomfortable, that if they put their heads down on their arms in front of them, the "whooshing" goes away. That's because gravity can temporarily close the Eustacian tubes. While not dangerous, it is nonetheless a physical sign to pay attention to and use to motivate patients: "You have lost so much weight that you no longer even have the tiny fat pad that your inner ear needs." Rehydration when needed and weight restoration resolve autophonia.

The other finding that often goes along with autophonia and dysphagia is lagophthalmos (lag-uf-THAL-mus). Normally, a fat pad behind our eyeballs keeps the orbit in position so that our eyelids glide over the eye and touch during a blink or at night during sleep. Each time we blink, we draw a layer of moisture over our eyeballs and prevent the corneas from drying out. Patients with severe anorexia nervosa can lose the fat pad behind the eyeballs. The eyes sink back into the person's head such that the eyelids don't fully close during a blink or at night. This is called lagophthalmos. It's diagnosed by asking the person to close their eyes softly (not squeezing the lids closed) and observing that you can still see the white of the eye.

When the corneas are constantly exposed to air, they can become very dry, causing itchy, red eyes that are photophobic (sensitive to light).

The biggest risk of lagophthalmos is corneal scarring from chronic dryness. To prevent permanent complications, patients should use preservative-free eye drops throughout the day and unmedicated lubricating ointment in the eyes at night to moisten the eyes and improve symptoms. Weight restoration restores the proper lid dynamics.[3]

Pancreatitis

Another potentially life-threatening medical complication in severe anorexia nervosa relates to the sudden onset of abdominal pain and vomiting after meals, even when a patient has never deliberately purged in their life. The three likeliest causes are severe gastroparesis, as I discussed in Chapter 2, pancreatitis (an inflammation of the pancreas), and superior mesenteric artery (SMA) syndrome. Virtually all patients with severe anorexia nervosa have gastroparesis. However, in someone this malnourished with these symptoms, I would always evaluate for pancreatitis and SMA syndrome before proceeding with nutritional rehabilitation.

The pancreas is an organ that performs many vital functions in the body. It produces insulin and glucagon, which it releases directly into the bloodstream. In addition, it releases digestive enzymes into the small intestine through a tube called the pancreatic duct. These enzymes digest fats, carbohydrates, and proteins as they emerge from the stomach. When this process goes awry, pancreatic enzymes can back up and begin to digest the pancreas itself, causing a great deal of pain and inflammation. This is called pancreatitis.

There are many causes of pancreatitis. Overall, the commonest causes are alcohol abuse and gallstones. In patients with eating disorders, severe malnutrition and nutritional rehabilitation can both cause it, in particular the use of total parenteral nutrition (TPN, feeding through a deep vein). A simple blood lipase level is sufficient to diagnose pancreatitis. It must be managed in a hospital, as patients cannot eat with this illness, lest they trigger a fresh wave of pancreatic enzyme production. Pancreatitis requires careful electrolyte monitoring, intravenous fluids, and pain medications.

Superior Mesenteric Artery (SMA) Syndrome

The other etiology of abdominal pain and vomiting in anorexia nervosa that must be evaluated urgently is SMA syndrome. The aorta is the largest artery in our body, and it runs right down the middle of our torso after emerging from the heart, a big highway from which other arteries branch off. The superior mesenteric artery is one such branch, and it supplies blood to the intestines and pancreas. The SMA emerges from the aorta at an angle of about 45 degrees. Normal body fat between the two arteries maintains that angle. The small intestine (specifically, the third portion of the duodenum) passes between these two structures like a soft tube passing between the dull blades of an open pair of scissors.

In severe malnutrition, which in this case refers to very low body weight or very rapid weight loss, the fat pad shrinks substantially. As a result, the SMA-aortic angle shrinks to around 10–25 degrees, closing the two arteries like the blades of the pair of scissors coming together. The duodenum gets mechanically pinched between the two arteries. Now compressed from the outside, it cannot let digesting food through normally. That food backs up into the stomach, and pain and vomiting ensue. Liquids are often still able to pass through unless the obstruction has become complete.[4,5]

SMA syndrome can be diagnosed either by a CAT scan, which evaluates the SMA-aortic angle, or by a barium study with small bowel follow through. In the latter study, the patient drinks some barium, and a camera tracks the progress of the barium through the stomach and then into the small intestine. The video will show if the thick fluid gets backed up at the third portion of the duodenum. Most cases of SMA syndrome reflect partial obstruction, not complete. The question of partial or complete obstruction is a vital question to answer on radiographic studies as it makes all the difference in how one proceeds with nutritional rehabilitation.

Treatment of SMA Syndrome

Treatment of SMA syndrome hinges upon nutritional rehabilitation to the point where the fat pad reaccumulates, causing the angle between the two arteries to increase, opening the "scissors." However, it can be a challenge to accomplish weight gain when the patient has a partial obstruction of the intestine with pain and vomiting.

The best and safest way to feed patients is to start with oral liquid supplements alone, without sacrificing calories. Liquids typically can still pass through an impinged intestine. Gastroparesis should still be aggressively treated with metoclopramide as well, unless the duodenal obstruction is complete. It is vital to remove every possible physiologic barrier for the suffering patient. Unfortunately, consuming only high density liquid supplements, ice cream, and full fat yogurt for up to two weeks can trigger eating disordered thoughts and make already anxious patients even more uncomfortable in the hospital. However, it's far safer and more effective than any other treatment options.

Surgical jejunal feeding tubes (also called surgical J-tubes) placed through the abdominal wall into the small intestine beyond the blockage make great sense, theoretically, for SMA syndrome. They provide nourishment beyond the obstruction while the patient takes nothing by mouth. Unfortunately, J-tubes turn out to be painful and complicated in those with severe anorexia nervosa.

Other surgical management, such as a rerouting of the intestines around the blockage, should be avoided at all costs. Despite a study showing positive results,[6] patients should be given the opportunity to restore weight fully before considering surgery. Full weight restoration prior to surgery consideration is imperative as individuals' lives have been ruined by these surgeries. The site where intestine was sewed to intestine can become scarred and obstructed itself, leading to further operations.

Rarely, a patient may present with complete obstruction from SMA syndrome. In this case, or when gastroparesis is also too severe to tolerate sufficient oral caloric liquids, intravenous feeding (TPN) can be used for a week or two for initial weight gain, and then the patient can switch to oral liquids.

Acute Gastric Dilatation

A rare but critical medical complication of both severe gastroparesis and SMA syndrome is called acute gastric dilatation. The stomach organ expands excessively, as stomach contents have built up over time without being released into the small intestine. With such stretching, the risk is rupture.

Untreated gastroparesis as well as severe SMA syndrome can cause this. Patients with bulimia nervosa and binge eating disorder (BED) can also develop gastric dilatation from the amount of binged foods. The over-stretched stomach can get so full that efforts to purge by vomiting are unsuccessful. Acute abdominal pain should immediately trigger a plain x-ray of the abdomen because acute gastric dilatation can be diagnosed swiftly. Treatment involves decompressing the stomach through a large tube that passes through the nose into the stomach, while anticipating and managing gastric bleeding. Immediate surgical consultation should be requested in an effort to avoid gastric rupture. Prevention is key. Early use of metoclopramide on admission to prevent complications of gastroparesis, early diagnosis of SMA syndrome, and use of only liquid calories all help.

Abnormal Vaginal Bleeding

As I discussed in Chapter 3, patients with anorexia nervosa can continue to have regular menstrual periods, or regain their periods, at very low body weights. As you now know, severe malnutrition typically causes reversion of sex hormones to pre-pubertal levels, and in females, the uterus and ovaries shrink. Without estrogen, the uterine lining thins, a state called atrophic endometrium. This thinned lining can bleed a little at times.

If a patient uses tampons for this spotting or bleeding, the tampons can actually form an ulcer in the vaginal wall. Essentially, the amount of bleeding is too low for tampon use, plus the vaginal wall is fragile from lack of estrogen. The ulcer itself can then continue to bleed, leading to persistent tampon use and exacerbating the whole problem. Diagnosis is made by pelvic exam, looking for vaginal ulceration. Treatment, fortunately, is pretty easy. The ulcer will heal when patients discontinue tampon use. An applicator of estrogen cream in the vagina for a week or so can also help heal the vaginal tissue.[7]

I have seen patients prescribed systemic hormones, such as birth control pills, in an effort to control persistent spotting while underweight. Awareness of their unique physiology would have spared the use of systemic hormones (which don't help) and allowed swift diagnosis and treatment.

Physical Weakness and Fall Risk

Patients with severe anorexia nervosa may lack insight into how physically weak they have become. In hospital settings, falls can lead to broken bones, bleeding, or other injuries. It would be easy to assume that a hospitalized patient in her 20s, who has been overexercising and is eager to walk laps around the unit, would be at low fall risk. However, up to 16 percent of patients with severe anorexia nervosa may be at moderate or high fall risk on admission.[8] Many of my patients have described enforced bed rest in other eating disorder programs, where they were instructed to consume calories and hold still all day. This potentially increases the risk of skin pressure sores in addition to being intolerable emotionally. Good physical and occupational therapy is a vital and often-neglected aspect of care for this group of patients.

Case Resolution: Jessica

Jessica is admitted to a hospital that specializes in severe eating disorders. She has a 1:1 nurse's aide around the clock in her room to keep her physically safe, help her, and support her through meals. When she remembers the many hospitals she's been in that just sent food trays up, and how she pushed the meal around but ate very little the whole time, she realizes how important the 1:1 aide is. She sees a dietitian every weekday for meal planning and meets with a psychologist 1:1 most days of the week for support through this immensely difficult time. The doctors know right away how to diagnose and ameliorate her medical problems. While her lipase comes back negative for pancreatitis, she does have SMA syndrome, and she reluctantly agrees to a temporary liquid meal plan.

Jessica engages with a physical and occupational therapist a few times a week. She is amazed by how weak she had become in her last few weeks at home. They work together until she's safe in the shower, can perform activities of daily living without assistance, and can walk smoothly again. Special cushions are put on her chair so that the sore skin over her sit bones doesn't turn into pressure ulcers. With cessation of tampon use, her vaginal bleeding stops.

Feeling her body become stronger and more independent motivates her, and taking in sufficient calories improves her mood and sleep. Her nurses help highlight all the positive biofeedback her body is giving her about getting nourished. Her glucose stabilizes, her heart rates become less extreme, and her blood pressure improves. Within about three weeks, she is able to eat solid foods again.

In her first week of hospitalization, despite starting at 1600 calories a day, her metabolism speeds up so quickly that she gains no weight. By the time she's ready to discharge to an inpatient eating disorder program a few weeks later, she's gained (unbeknownst to her) about three pounds a week after that first week, which is right on target for this setting. She has no edema (water weight), is having regular bowel movements, is eating 3200 calories a day of balanced meals and snacks, has normal laboratory values and much improved vital signs, and remembers again what her values are and why she wants recovery. The days aren't easy, but she uses her near-death experience to remind herself that she never wants to be in that situation again. Jessica is ready to work on the psychological side of her eating disorder from day one in her next program because the medical issues have been fully addressed.

The Parables of the Fortress and the Nuclear Wasteland and the Perfectionist and the Appreciative Achiever

These are two parables I have shared with countless patients over the years. When hope feels dim, the recovery process feels too hard, or when the eating disorder voice is so loud and mean that patients wonder if they have the strength to keep fighting, I often turn to one or both of these stories.

I often tell the first story when my patient sits in a crisis of anxiety about the idea of full weight restoration or when the idea of recovery seems overwhelming. In this story, the castle represents recovery, and the wasteland represents the eating disorder.

I am standing on the wall of a castle, the parapet in front of me. I'm looking out over a nuclear wasteland, dusty, dark, and grim. Behind me, within the castle walls, lies a beautiful garden. The trees are richly green and heavy with fruit. Fragrant and colorful flowers grow abundantly. The light is golden, and pathways wind through the garden. My patient is scrabbling around on the ground in the nuclear wasteland. I stand on the castle wall and call to her, "Come in! Come in to this castle and walk with me in the garden."

She says, desperately, "I'm scared!" I keep talking, inviting her to keep getting closer to the castle. I say, "Come stand next to me. See what the castle is like compared to your wasteland, feel the sunlight on your face in the garden, and then you can make a decision about where you want to be." Many of my patients crawl all the way up to the castle gates, only to cower back into the dust, saying they're just too frightened to come through. I remind them that life isn't perfect within the castle walls, but it's a lot better than out in the wasteland.

The next parable is my version of a story a dear friend of mine tells, and he heard the original from one of his Harvard professors, Tal Ben-Shahar, who went on to write books about bringing happiness to life. I tell this story when my patients feel resistant to the idea of resting, recharging, or going a little easier on themselves. They worry that if they are kinder to themselves, they won't achieve as much or live up to their own expectations.

Two hikers, the Perfectionist and the Appreciative Achiever, set off to climb a mountain. The Perfectionist arrives at the summit and is full of dissatisfaction. He says, "I didn't climb the mountain fast enough, I didn't train hard enough, I didn't take the optimal route, and my equipment didn't work as well as it should have."

The Appreciative Achiever arrives at the very same summit, takes a deep breath, and looks around in wonder. He says, "What a beautiful view. What a joy to have used my strength to accomplish this. How lucky I am to be standing at the top of this mountain." Both hikers summited. They both achieved the very same accomplishment. But the Perfectionist couldn't celebrate and had only criticism for himself and the experience, while the Appreciative Achiever was able to live in the moment and reflect joyfully on what he had done.

Our souls will bend and ultimately break under constant self-criticism. Constant self-judgment is a toxic environment to live in. We have to remember to celebrate all our victories, large and small. This doesn't mean we become complacent or stop working to improve. It means that our souls need to receive acknowledgment when we've done something we worked hard for. That accomplishment doesn't have to be big or important; it just needs to be recognized.

Otherwise, when we give ourselves the consistent message of, "You're inadequate and disappointing," we will despair and run out of energy. Physical illness, chronic pain, or exacerbation of a mental illness will stop us in our tracks and force us to disengage from life because the soul can't thrive under such circumstances. Be an Appreciative Achiever, not a Perfectionist.

Notes

1 ACUTE Center for Eating Disorders at Denver Health. www.denverhealth.org/acute.

2 Holmes SR, Sabel AL, Gaudiani JL, Gudridge T, Brinton JT, Mehler PS. Prevalence and management of oropharyngeal dysphagia in patients with severe anorexia nervosa: A large retrospective review. *Int J Eat Disord*. 2016 February; 49(2):159–166. doi: 10.1002/eat.22441.

3 Gaudiani JL, Braverman JM, Mascolo M, Mehler PS. Lagophthalmos in severe anorexia nervosa: a case series. *Arch Ophthalmol.* 2012 July; 130(7):928–930. doi: 10.1001/archophthalmol.2011.2515.

4 Mascolo M, Dee E, Townsend R, Brinton JT, Mehler PS. Severe gastric dilatation due to superior mesenteric artery syndrome in anorexia nervosa. *Int J Eat Disord*. 2015 July; 48(5):532–534. doi: 10.1002/eat.22385.

5 Neri S, Signorelli SS, Mondati E, Pulvirenti D, Campanile E, Di Pino L, Scuderi M, Giustolisi N, Di Prima P, Mauceri B, Abate G, Cilio D, Misseri M, Scuderi R. Ultrasound imaging in diagnosis of superior mesenteric artery syndrome. *J Intern Med.* 2005 April; 257(4):346–351. PubMed PMID: 15788004.

6 Pottorf BJ, Husain FA, Hollis HW Jr., Lin E. Laparoscopic management of duodenal obstruction resulting from superior mesenteric artery syndrome. *JAMA Surg.* 2014 December; 149(12):1319–1322. doi: 10.1001/jamasurg.2014.1409.

7 Gaudiani JL, Heinrichs G, Narayanan V, Mehler PS. Tampon use in patients with anorexia nervosa can cause persistent vaginal bleeding: a case series. *Int J Eat Disord.* 2011 December; 44(8):752–755. doi: 10.1002/eat.20861.

8 Laging MA, Brinton, JT, Sabel AL, Gaudiani JL, Mehler, PS. Baseline functional mobility in hospitalized persons with anorexia nervosa: a retrospective study of inpatient physical therapy during medical stabilization. *J Acute Care Phys Ther* 2017; 8(1):28–39. doi: 10.1097/JAT.0000000000000045.

Chapter 6

Starting to Eat Again

Case: Taylor

Taylor is a 26-year-old cisgender East Asian American female graduate student with anorexia nervosa, restricting subtype. Her eating disorder started when she was 12, and she went through partial hospitalization care at that time and then had an outpatient team. By high school, she felt confident in her recovery. Throughout college, she maintained a somewhat low weight and grew increasingly rigid about her food intake and exercise habits. Now in graduate school, the academic pressures in addition to a part time job have increased her stress and anxiety, and in response she engages in a lot of judgmental and critical self-talk. Her caloric intake falls slowly over time as food rules regain their power. Her weight remains stable, which is confusing and rather frustrating for her.

As Taylor's concentration and energy decrease, and she isolates more so as not to eat socially, her family becomes concerned. Her parents and best friend compassionately share that they see her struggling with her anorexia nervosa again. Taylor tries to brush them off, noting that her weight is "fine," so she's not sick enough to merit their concern. She is embarrassed and ashamed of attracting their attention when she'd rather just be invisible at this point. Her loved ones aren't deterred, having seen this before. They say it's not about how she looks, it's about how she's managing her emotions through food restriction again. They see the difference when she's restricting because she's withdrawn, snappy, rigid, and unhappy. They ask her to engage an outpatient eating disorder team again and take care of herself.

In her heart, Taylor is ready to work on recovery. She doesn't like the person she becomes when her anorexia nervosa is in charge. Not only does she push her loved ones away, but also studying takes three times longer as her brain lacks concentration and memory. However, she's plagued by the fear that she's permanently ruined her metabolism. She knows that when she was 12 she had to eat over 3000 calories a day to restore weight slowly, but she's more than twice that age now. She worries that if she starts eating more again she'll never be able to stop. She anxiously imagines a dietitian putting her on a meal plan that will raise her body weight quickly and yet still not satisfy her hunger. She's fearful that her body will get better faster than her soul, and that all too quickly, no one will take her emotional needs seriously. Nevertheless, Taylor finds a therapist, dietitian, and doctor who all specialize in eating disorders, and she shares her fears.

Background

Reintroducing nutrition is key to the eating disorder recovery process in malnourished patients of all sizes and shapes. All the therapy in the world will not help unless the patient is also eating enough calories to close the energy deficit. For some patients, this process has nothing to do with weight and everything to do with learning how to eat satisfying, energizing meals at regular intervals throughout the day, free from worries about food group restrictions. For other patients, it involves learning to address their needs holistically so that bingeing on and purging foods does not become a numbing proxy for feeling and managing emotions. And for others, it involves a painstaking process of transforming from a starved, depleted body to a vibrant, stronger body.

A registered dietitian with expertise in eating disorders is a vital asset in the nutritional rehabilitation process. You can identify such a dietitian by the Certified Eating Disorders Registered Dietitian (CEDRD) designation, a credential overseen by the International Association of Eating Disorders Professionals (iaedp), which requires documentation of extensive eating disorder experience, ongoing learning, and contribution to the field. Therapists, nurses, doctors, and other specialists can also qualify for the CEDS designation. In the case of dietitians who have not yet gotten their CEDRD, you can get a sense for their experience in and commitment to the field by looking at their website and interviewing them. Eating disorder dietitians will not advertise weight loss tips, nor espouse pseudoscientific claims like "sugar is evil," nor endorse any fad diet scheme. While staying within scope of practice, they will nonetheless have a compassionate, highly informed awareness of mental illness and be supportive motivators. Eating disorder dietitians are responsive to and not overwhelmed by eating disorder fears and anxieties.

The concepts discussed in this chapter are broadly applicable to malnourished individuals across the weight spectrum, although the risk for refeeding syndrome appears to apply more to those at a lower body weight.

The Hypermetabolism of Nutritional Rehabilitation

By now, you know that restriction of calories does indeed slow the metabolism. The degree to which it slows is dependent upon the degree of restriction and the person's genetic variability. I know patients who lose absolutely no weight despite severe caloric restriction because their metabolism slows to defend their body weight vigorously. I also know patients who don't quite consume their usual 3000-calorie a day maintenance meal plan for a day or two and drop weight practically overnight. This is written in the genetics for the most part.

Currently, the scientific eating disorder community has encouraged people to use the term "nutritional rehabilitation" rather than "refeeding." I think this is reasonable because the former term is both more scientifically specific and also somewhat less paternalistic than the latter term. However, there will be times in this chapter when I use them interchangeably as the word "refeeding" remains commonly used.

What many people do not know is that the act of nutritionally rehabilitating and restoring weight from malnourishment can take a remarkably large number of calories. As the cave person brain switches from hibernation/caloric conservation mode to rebuild-the-body mode, the metabolism speeds up quickly. The same person who was maintaining weight at 800 calories a day after weeks or months of restriction now needs, three weeks into refeeding, to consume 3500 calories a day to restore just two pounds of body weight a week.

We still don't know why or how this happens. The hypermetabolic state that occurs almost universally in patients who begin again to take in energy is one of the last "black boxes" physiologically. Where do the extra calories go? Why do some patients need up to 5000 calories a day for slow, steady weight restoration? The jury is still out.

What we do know is that this hypermetabolic state is a reality for almost all patients, although the degree varies by person. Unless one knows this, recovery at home without a supportive team is impossible. Absolutely no one with anorexia nervosa would believe on their own that they need to eat until painfully full just to start to restore weight slowly ... not with a disease that fears an extra lick of frozen yogurt might cause, to them, calamitous weight gain.

What this means is that the nutritional rehabilitation process early on is almost never intuitive, but rather prescriptive. Because eating disorders are mental illnesses, patients' intuitions about food are already going to be skewed. In addition, refeeding takes place, at least initially, in a body that has been slowed to hibernation levels by starvation. Bellies get full after a few bites. Bloating, constipation, reflux, and body image distortions can make the first weeks and even months of this process a physical and emotional "street fight." Families, thrilled to see their loved ones finally making progress in recovery, will help best if they show consistent compassion for how difficult the process actually is.

Some individuals receive the incorrect recommendation (from online resources, not expert dietitians) to consume extremely high calorie meal plans almost indefinitely for months or years, as the body weight rises well past a prior, individualized set point. They are told that commitment to this strategy will result in future healing and wellness as long as they keep force feeding. This is unscientific and never indicated.

Eating enough food heals the metabolism slowed by caloric restriction. However, if an individual starts to restrict again, their metabolism will once again fall. In my long career in this field, I have seen patients of all different sizes, shapes, ages, genders, races, abilities, and ethnicities become hypermetabolic during refeeding. When I discuss this, my patients' disbelief is moderated by a spark of hope that perhaps, after all, they're not the one human in history whose metabolism is indeed permanently slowed.

The Refeeding Syndrome: Phosphorus and Edema

This leads us to the first critical medical complication of nutritional rehabilitation: the refeeding syndrome. The refeeding syndrome describes the potentially deadly development of low phosphorus and other electrolyte levels in the blood and fluid shifts into body tissues that can occur when a starved person begins to take in nutrition.

In the starved state, a person breaks down muscle and fat to create glucose, as I described in Chapter 4. Despite normal electrolyte levels in the blood, however, overall body stores of electrolytes may be low, as the body has "mined" electrolyte stores from body tissues in order to have access to normal levels in the bloodstream.

Insulin levels start out very low during caloric restriction because insufficient carbohydrates are being consumed. When patients begin to eat more, insulin levels shoot up in order to drive life-saving glucose into hungry cells. Insulin also pushes electrolytes into cells, particularly phosphorus. This makes sense as phosphorus is one of the key electrolytes in cellular respiration, the process by which cells take in nutrients and turn them into energy to fuel the cell's function. With phosphorus moving out of the bloodstream into cells, and also being used as cells become more energetic again, the blood levels of phosphorus can drop. High insulin levels can also cause the kidneys to retain salt and water, rather than excreting those as usual. As a result, fluid retention called edema can develop from the toes all the way up to the lungs.

Low phosphorus levels can cause muscle weakness and breakdown, including weakness in breathing muscles and heart muscle, as well as seizures, breakdown of red blood cells, and many other serious problems. The full blown refeeding syndrome refers to catastrophically low levels of phosphorus and/or dangerous edema that occurs in patients taking in nutrition after having been in a starved state. This is not limited to those with eating disorders and can occur in individuals who are homeless, have alcohol or drug dependency, have been in a serious accident and haven't yet been fed in the hospital, and who have experienced severe burns, among others.

The full blown refeeding syndrome only occurs in patients whose nutritional rehabilitation process has not been properly overseen medically. It is entirely preventable. First, practitioners need to know that the refeeding syndrome exists, and second, they need to monitor blood phosphorus levels and other electrolytes closely during the nutritional rehabilitation process. Phosphorus levels that start to drop can be identified and remedied through phosphorus supplementation. Low phosphorus levels are properly called "refeeding hypophosphatemia."

"Refeeding syndrome" is only diagnosed when phosphorus levels get low enough for long enough to cause physiologic harm. The prevalence of full blown refeeding syndrome in an expert setting is fleetingly low. Even among the most medically compromised patients, refeeding hypophosphatemia only occurs in 30–40 percent.[1] Identified quickly, these patients then can be prescribed appropriate phosphorus supplementation either by mouth or, in extreme cases, through their veins as well. This swift diagnosis and treatment prevents the refeeding syndrome.

Refeeding edema, meaning the retention of salt and water, can range in severity from "triggering," as patients look in shock at swollen feet, ankles, and tummies, to dangerous. Fluid-saturated tissues can make the overlying skin fragile and liable to break down, splitting or forming an ulcer. Once again, it is exceptionally rare in an expert setting for a patient to develop fluid retention in the lungs as a result of refeeding edema. This would constitute full blown refeeding syndrome.

Breathing complications can occur when a very underweight patient has weak breathing muscles, develops heart muscle weakness from underweight or another cause (called congestive heart failure), or fails to receive proper management for hypophosphatemia.

Low albumin levels, a protein synthesized by the liver and discussed in Chapter 4, predict edema formation.[2] When a patient develops a low albumin level, I set expectations with them about the likelihood of their developing refeeding edema. I reassure them about the transient (but scary) body changes that will likely occur and set up a plan to manage and minimize the edema. Refeeding edema is different from rebound edema that occurs due to stopping purging, which I review in Chapter 9.

Edema is never a sign of healing, despite this myth being perpetuated in certain circles. It may, however, be inevitable for a matter of a few weeks (and no more) during the renourishment process. Management includes keeping legs elevated when seated, using compression stockings during the day if tolerated, decreasing the carbohydrate fraction in the meal plan to around 40 percent to reduce insulin levels, and patiently waiting for the edema to resolve. Diuretics should only be used if the skin is at risk from breakdown due to the degree of edema, and then for as short an amount of time as possible.

So, with refeeding hypophosphatemia constituting the most dangerous medical complication of the nutritional rehabilitation process, what can we do to prevent it? Who gets it? We don't know all the answers to these questions, but we do know a lot. Study after study has shown that low body weight is one of the most important independent risk factors for refeeding complications.[3]

Risks for refeeding hypophosphatemia include prolonged periods of undernourishment, rapid and significant weight loss, concurrent medical problems like cancer or infections, and electrolyte levels that are abnormal even before refeeding begins.[4] Studies have shown that certain other lab parameters, such as low prealbumin levels in the blood, can independently predict higher rates of refeeding hypophosphatemia in hospitalized patients.[5] We used to think that starting calories very slowly in starving patients would prevent refeeding complications. As a result, in my early years in the field, we would start patients out on a meal plan of only 800 or 1000 calories a day. It turns out we were wrong. All we were doing was causing the underfeeding syndrome.

The Underfeeding Syndrome

The underfeeding syndrome refers to initiating calories at too low a level in someone who has been starving. Recent studies have clearly shown that when starved patients don't start on high enough calories, their weight continues to drop, their organ systems continue to suffer, and their cognitive abilities remain rigid and anxious.[6] In fact, we now know that the risks of underfeeding syndrome are greater and more common than the refeeding syndrome.

Excellent studies show that starting calories at 1600 a day or higher, even in very underweight, medically compromised patients, is safe from the perspective of phosphorus levels.[7,8,9] This holds true for individuals of all ages, from adults to adolescents. In the latter population, some centers recommend starting calories as high as 2500 a day.[10] This message has been slow to permeate the eating disorder community in both outpatient and residential settings. Providers are still starting calories too low for patients, worried about the refeeding syndrome. In part, this is because patients may not have access to a doctor who will readily check phosphorus levels once or twice a week as directed by their dietitian. However, starting calories much higher than in the past comprises the evidence-based standard of care.

I can hear the chorus of anxious patients telling me, "Dr. G, that is WAY too much food." I assure each and every patient that no matter what they were eating in their disorder, their brilliant cave person brain will rev up its metabolism when exposed to adequate food. I teach them that in the first two weeks of refeeding, their metabolism is likely to outpace even my prescribed calorie increases, and they may actually lose weight. I have watched this process occur countless times in both the inpatient hospital and outpatient settings.

Many patients with anorexia nervosa become convinced at some point during nutritional rehabilitation that they have gained "10 pounds overnight." I respond with compassion, data, and an attempt not to participate in internalized size stigma: "How painful it is that your mental illness is causing such distortions. I know that makes this process hard. However, your body is extraordinary and knows just what to do. Every bite of food is actually healing your body." Amazingly, within weeks to months of adequate caloric intake, even before an underweight individual may have reached their target weight, the body's cells and organs are functioning properly.

Starting to Renourish

Let's turn to the details of nutritional rehabilitation, both in the outpatient and in the inpatient hospital setting. I always work in conjunction with expert dietitians around the country, and I've been lucky enough to learn from some of the best over the years. So, while I may establish the starting caloric level with my patients, I rely on their dietitian to create and oversee the meal plan itself. In the outpatient setting, patients should start calories at a minimum of 1600 a day.

The macronutrient balance should contain approximately 50 percent of calories from carbohydrates, 30 percent from protein, and 20 percent from fat. Calories in the outpatient setting can be increased by around 500 every week. Increasing more quickly is safe but may be hard for a patient who sees their team members only once a week. Calories should be raised until the patient is consistently restoring 1–2 pounds a week of non-edematous weight in the outpatient setting.

In my experience, refeeding edema is less common in the outpatient setting than the inpatient. Typically for outpatients, a phosphorus level should be checked with a basic metabolic panel of bloodwork once a week, and phosphorus supplementation should be started if the phosphorus level drops below 3 mg/dL. Multiple oral preparations exist, most by prescription, and they can be taken three times a day until the next blood draw, at which point the dose can be altered. The side effect of taking phosphorus can be mild nausea or looser stools, so patients should be prepared to ease back on their bowel regimen while on phosphorus.

Food Options to Manage Gastroparesis

Let's talk about the nutritional management of gastroparesis, the slowed stomach emptying introduced in Chapter 2, that can pose such challenges during early nutritional rehabilitation. It turns out that when digestion is slowed due to starvation, high fiber foods worsen fullness and belly distention. Many patients with restrictive eating have lists of "safe" foods that feel acceptable to eat and lists of "fear" foods. Safe and fear foods may vary widely among different individuals, and oftentimes fiber-containing foods rank among many patients' safest foods.

Nonetheless, a low fiber diet is best for the first four to six weeks of nutritional rehabilitation. This may be the only time a doctor urges a patient to eat almost no fruits and vegetables. In addition to their fiber content, vegetables have few calories in them. With limited gastric "real estate," we have to make sure every bite is as dense, nutritious, and caloric as possible. I compassionately remind my patients that these challenges are why I always work as a team with a therapist and dietitian, so that all three of us can give the patients lots of support.

Liquids and semi-solids move through a slowed stomach more easily than solids. For the first few weeks of nutritional rehabilitation, to minimize belly discomfort, I recommend that the patient and their dietitian make a meal plan that's at least 30 percent liquid/semi-solid. That could mean yogurts, chocolate milk (my favorite), ice creams, etc. This recommendation is harder on those who are dairy allergic or intolerant, but there are still ways to accomplish it.

Traditionally, it's known that higher fat content in the diet worsens gastroparesis too. However, I draw the line at following this for those with eating disorders. For one, there's often already such nutritional fat phobia that I'm not going to contribute to that with a recommendation to follow a low fat diet. Second, my clinical experience of working with patients with severe gastroparesis tells me that eating low fiber and more liquid and calorie-dense food is far more important than eating low fat food. And third, fat is a vital nutrient in the nutritional rehabilitation process.

In both the outpatient and inpatient settings, patients can struggle with fullness and abdominal discomfort as their calories get higher. I've had many patients tell me, "Dr. G, I just cannot increase to 3000 calories a day. I'm too full as it is, at 2600 a day." I am sympathetic to the profound discomfort of refeeding. However, when the weight restoration process has plateaued because of a high metabolism, they must keep pushing up on calories.

I pose the following question: Are they choosing to eat relatively "safe" foods to get to 2600 calories a day? That may mean pretty large volume meals that will contribute to painful fullness. While the prescribed caloric increase is non-negotiable, the patient can control how they take in those calories. If they have to eat a meal with a certain number of calories in it, that could be consumed as 16 bowls of very safe foods, or as one dense peanut butter and jelly sandwich and a glass of whole fat chocolate milk. In the first case, the belly will be incredibly uncomfortable, but the eating disorder will feel safer. In the latter, the belly will be more content, but the eating disorder might be uncomfortable. Volume-neutral options to increase calories include adding more peanut butter to a sandwich, drinking juice or milk instead of water or non-caloric beverages, increasing the fat content in yogurts, adding some more fats like cream cheese to bagels, or the use of high calorie liquid supplements.

Generally, because gastroparesis can become dangerous, I urge patients to choose the lower volume, calorie-dense meal plan. It's generally better to eat six smaller meals than three larger ones, when it comes to gastroparesis. The smaller volume the stomach has to empty, the better.

Nasogastric Tubes and Starting Care in a Hospital Setting

Patients who enter medical hospitals that do not specialize in eating disorders often have a very negative experience with nutrition. Trays get delivered to the room with no supervision, bathrooms are unmonitored for purging, and less-than-helpful commentary about body size and shape is shared by well-meaning hospital staff. But let's face it: plenty of patients with eating disorders end up in an inexpert medical setting, and for whatever reason, it's not an option to transfer to a center of excellence. In that case, I make the following recommendations.

Since calories must be non-negotiable, patients should be asked if they wish to consume them orally or by tube feeding. Some patients prefer the latter, because tube feeds "medicalize" the process. Without highly supportive mental health professionals around, tube feeding might be the most patients can commit to until they have reached an eating disorder treatment program. If they choose oral calories, the hospital staff (often with the support of the family) have to provide a 1600 calorie meal plan and inform patients they either need to complete 100 percent or drink a nutritional supplement to get to 100 percent.

Within 24 hours, a patient who choses to eat food, but cannot or does not achieve this, should receive a nasogastric feeding tube. In patients under 18 years old, the parents can make this decision and enforce it. In adults, tube refusal and food refusal should prompt hospitals and family members to increase the pressure to transfer to a center of expertise as quickly as possible. I have seen patients sit in excellent university hospitals for weeks, refusing food, failing to progress, and remaining too sick for a residential program. When transferred to a highly expert hospital setting, these same individuals suddenly make progress nutritionally, heal their organ damage, get stronger, and are rapidly able to proceed in their recovery journey.

When a hospitalized patient does receive a nasogastric feeding tube, low fiber tube feeds should be used. Round the clock caloric provision diminishes the risk of hypoglycemia and reduces the volume per hour that is introduced into the stomach. Hospital staff are often accustomed to starting tube feeds on post-surgical patients at rates that are far too slow for someone with an eating disorder. A typical starting tube feeding rate for nutritional rehabilitation might be around 60 ml/hr over 22 hours a day. That can sound like a lot to nursing staff and doctors. I respectfully remind them that this is only two ounces an hour! An infant can manage more than that when drinking from a bottle or nursing. A medium latte has 512 ml in it, and most people don't sip at one of those over eight hours. If a patient with an eating disorder receives tube feeding at the slow rate of a post-surgical patient, time will be wasted, and organ failure will progress.

In the hospital setting, acuity of illness requires that calories be stepped up faster to avoid the underfeeding syndrome. Calories should be increased by 400 every three days until the patient is gaining two to three pounds a week. Electrolytes should be checked, depending on admission levels, anywhere from daily to once a week, replacing phosphorus when it falls below 3 mg/dL. Ideally, once the brain gets a little nourished, the patient will agree to start eating food again, and tube feeds can be tapered off.

In eating disorder programs, tube feeding can be used productively for overnight calories when the meal plan has become burdensomely high, or to catch up on calories missed during the day. A nasogastric tube can remain in place for up to six weeks with good care. Risks include sinus infection, reflux, aspiration pneumonia, and vocal cord irritation or injury. More permanent feeding tubes also exist, inserted through the abdominal wall and terminating in the stomach or in the small intestine.

Surgical Feeding Tubes

These more permanent tubes are called percutaneous endoscopic gastrostomy (PEG) or percutaneous endoscopic jejunostomy (PEJ) tubes. They can be placed by a surgeon, interventional radiologist, or gastroenterologist. PEG tubes terminate in the stomach, while PEJ tubes terminate in the jejunum, which is part of the small intestine. They are used in many different patient populations, not just in patients with eating disorders. PEG tubes should only be used when there are significant medical impediments to receiving nutrition by *any* other means.

PEG tubes should never be placed just because someone will not take in adequate oral nutrition. The fact is, nearly all patients with eating disorders already have a functional tube to their stomach: it's called their esophagus. If patients will not take in adequate calories by mouth because of their severe mental illness, they will also restrict tube feeds. I understand the magical thinking that patients and families can have in thinking that "just getting a tube in" will permit adequate caloric intake. However, I have witnessed time and time again that patients with a PEG will either underdose their tube feedings, dilute the feeds with water to get in fewer calories, or sabotage the tube itself.

Plus, surgical feeding tubes aren't without risks. Their placement can be quite complicated, with intense pain and nausea that in my clinical experience lasts longer than in those without an eating disorder. Removing a PEG before it is healed, six to eight weeks after placement, can cause catastrophic abdominal infections. Thus, placing a PEG in a patient with a history of impulsive actions is contraindicated. Ultimately, surgical feeding tubes should be reserved for patients who truly cannot take in nourishment by mouth. A history of severe and persistent difficulty swallowing, medical inability to keep food in the stomach due to intractable vomiting, or complete obstruction due to SMA syndrome are all reasonable indications for a percutaneous tube.[11]

Total Parenteral Nutrition

Total parenteral nutrition (TPN) refers to nutrition administered via a deep vein. A central line or peripherally inserted central catheter (PICC line) is placed, and a dietitian or doctor orders a bag of nutrition that can be infused right into the bloodstream. Whenever possible, it is always preferable to use the gut for nutrition, rather than the bloodstream. As long as the intestine works even a little bit, I recommend using food or liquid supplements.

TPN carries several major medical risks. One, the placement of the central catheter can cause a lung to deflate, called pneumothorax. Two, a bag of pure nourishment straight into the blood doesn't only nourish the patient, it also can nourish bacteria. TPN used over time represents a "when," not an "if," when it comes to serious bloodstream infections, which may prove deadly. TPN can be used for a matter of weeks if someone is absolutely unable to take food by mouth due to GI problems that are related to underweight, such as severe gastroparesis or SMA syndrome, and if they cannot for whatever reason tolerate a feeding tube through the nose. Once needed body weight is restored, however, the gut should again be used.

Micronutrients: Thiamine and Zinc

There are a small number of vitamins and minerals that are truly evidence based to give during nutritional supplementation. The most important of these is thiamine, or B1 vitamin. Thiamine helps several enzymes vital to metabolism, and it is most needed during times of high metabolic rate and glucose intake.

Acute thiamine insufficiency, especially during early refeeding, can cause a distinct delirium syndrome characterized by the combination of confusion, staggering gait, and eye problems. This is called Wernicke's encephalopathy. Diagnosed predominantly in individuals with severe alcoholism and malnutrition, it has also been described in patients with anorexia nervosa and is considered a risk during refeeding.[12,13]

While Wernicke's encephalopathy can be reversed with thiamine administration, if left untreated, it can progress to Korsakoff's amnestic syndrome. Korsakoff's syndrome causes irreversible amnesia and confabulation (making things up and believing they are true). The administration of 200 mg of oral thiamine daily for at least ten days is appropriate in the nutritional rehabilitation of all malnourished patients, not just those with anorexia nervosa.

Zinc is a micronutrient whose deficiency in chronic malnutrition has been established by what's called "level B evidence." That means that there's at least one good study, or several studies with limitations, that have reached this conclusion. Zinc is involved in over 300 human enzymes. Its deficiency, ranging from mild to severe, is associated with numerous findings: severe height restriction, skin and hair fragility, poor immune state, low testosterone, anemia, cognitive decline, and others.[14] There is no simple, cheap test either for zinc or thiamine deficiency.

Because zinc is inexpensive and harmless, I tend to recommend a course of it at the beginning of refeeding for all of my outpatients, particularly those with complaints of poor hair and skin quality. I prefer my patients to take zinc as a lozenge that absorbs through the cheek. I recommend 15 mg zinc gluconate lozenges once a day for a month or two. High dose zinc administration chronically can interfere with copper absorption and should thus be avoided.[15]

Target Weight Range

All this talk of nutritional rehabilitation brings me to the topic of the target weight range. This subject has nothing to do with weight loss in those with larger bodies and only refers to those who are underweight. Most patients with anorexia nervosa dread and fear gaining weight. Therefore, the subject of "how much weight is my team going to make me gain?" is of paramount interest and worry. Ultimately, I always make this decision in conjunction with my patients' therapist, dietitian, and optimally with the patients themselves. It's not a topic that should even be discussed until well into the refeeding process. With a starved, paranoid cave person brain and a critical fear of even one pound of weight gain, no one should be tormented early in recovery by the idea of some number range they are supposed to reach, weeks or months hence.

However, at some point, it's reasonable to know what one is aiming for. I remind my patients that I can't "land a helicopter on a dime." That is, they might say, "Okay, Dr. G. I'm okay with weighing x weight, but not an ounce more." I explain to them that everyone's weight varies naturally and that a weight goal is always a range. I urge them never to get on a scale again (really, no one needs to) because this is something that their team can manage for them. The act itself of getting on a scale can be triggering, and depending on the stability of their recovery, a single moment on the scale can undo weeks of productive work. Once weight restoration is complete and the patient has maintained a stable weight for a satisfactory period of time, as far as I'm concerned, they never need to be weighed again.

Ultimately, I keep in mind several factors when estimating an initial goal weight range: the patient's height, childhood growth charts (were they in the 20th percentile or 90th percentile throughout childhood?), pre-eating disorder weight range, and familial body type. I also think it is useful to know the weight where my female patients last had normal menstrual periods or were able to get pregnant unassisted, or my male patients noticed a significant decrease in sex drive and function. Estimating a target weight range for patients forces practitioners to examine their own internalized weight stigma. Some patients' goal weight ranges lie in higher body weights. I never want to ally with their eating disorder or society's fat phobia by rejecting or resisting this fact.

It is impossible to know an individual patient's "body type" when they are emaciated. Individuals who developed their eating disorder in their teens may recollect a pre-eating disordered weight that they hold onto as a target for the future. However, they may not have finished growing yet, and that target may be far too low.

Depending on the patient, their emotional state, medical problems, and duration of illness, I don't always feel the need to restore patients to their target weight in a linear fashion. Some individuals (and all of my adolescents) are best served getting right to their target weight, restoring steadily the whole time and nourishing their brain and bones without delay. Others, who might have experienced many rounds of residential treatment with variable success, and who are fairly medically stable, can be restored to a minimum weight range agreed upon by the team and then held there for a few months. This can let the psychological work catch up with the body, and then further weight restoration can be done when ready.

What is very important is that providers not align with the eating disorder and under-restore patients in the long term. Every patient with anorexia nervosa wants to asymptotically approach their target weight range ("How about 5 pounds less than what you just said?") because they have a mental illness. This serves neither body nor soul well. On the other hand, many patients have experienced true (as opposed to the distortion of the eating disorder or society's view) over-restoration at the hands of well-meaning eating disorder programs. This sets up a failure of trust, further anxiety, and often triggers relapses.

Physicians can be lulled into complacency by so-called "normal weights" because we carry our own internal biases, including size and weight stigma. On the one hand, patients can be dangerously involved in their eating disorders and yet appear to be a "normal weight." This can lead them to be missed by the medical system. On the other hand, individuals in medical settings may be cautioned about a higher body weight when that measurement is not impacting their health in any way, exposing them to the risks of dieting and weight cycling that may well have a negative impact on their health.[16] We must always resist our own learned, sizeist tendencies and continue to see the whole person in assessing their medical status.

Case Resolution: Taylor

Taylor starts seeing her therapist and dietitian once a week and her doctor every two to four weeks. She works with her dietitian to create a meal plan that starts at 1600 calories a day and increases by 500 calories a week for a target meal plan that meets her body's daily needs. They incorporate foods that Taylor accepts as well as a number of foods that she has avoided completely for months. She processes these fears with her therapist and learns from her dietitian about the science of metabolism and food reintroduction.

Her doctor reassures her from their first session that her metabolism is by no means "ruined." The doctor validates how Taylor's "survivor genetics" have protected her from weight loss despite having engaged in such restrictive behaviors, and she identifies that the diagnosis is atypical anorexia nervosa, clarifying that in fact there's nothing "atypical" about it at all. The approach will be a weight-inclusive one; that is, once Taylor is consuming enough calories to meet her body's needs, her weight may fall, stay the same, or rise, and this number will not be a primary focus. In that first session, her doctor also reviews the medical risks of nutritional rehabilitation and how they will optimize the experience for health and comfort. She starts Taylor on over the counter thiamine 200 mg a day for the first ten days of refeeding, as well as recommending zinc gluconate lozenges 15 mg a day for one or two months.

After two weeks, Taylor has started to struggle with fullness as the meal plan increases. Her doctor prescribes metoclopramide for gastroparesis. After a week or two of sleepiness on this medication, Taylor feels much better. She begins taking a dose of polyethylene glycol daily for constipation, which helps too. Taylor uses a mobile application with her dietitian to track what she's eating and how she feels about it. This gives her a sense of accountability to the process, and she is diligent in completing 100 percent of her meal plan even through the fear. She promises to stay off her scale.

Three weeks into the process, Taylor is plagued by fears that she's gained "10 pounds" and is struggling severely with body image. Her doctor uses this opportunity to give her the objective feedback that she has, in fact, maintained her body weight. The team reassures her, because they know she's completing her calories, that this is because her metabolism is now so fast. Taylor learns how much her body image distortions are truly a part of her mental illness and her internalized size stigma and how little they have to do with her actual body.

A few weeks into nutritional rehabilitation, Taylor's team permits her to start engaging again in mindful, joyful movement. Starting with one or two days a week and doing a little more each week (with days for rest), Taylor does yoga and goes hiking, both activities she finds enjoyable and grounding. She starts regarding her body as being strong and able to take her on fun adventures, rather than as being something to tame and dislike. Taylor's relationships with her classmates, family, and friends warm back up. As her brain becomes nourished, she can feel her cognitive function improve. Studying is much faster and easier, she's sleeping better, and she loses the uncomfortable, edgy, anxious feeling she used to experience.

Four months after the intervention by her family and friends, Taylor is in a much better place. She looks forward to the day where she can simply intuit what she needs to eat and when, but she's not quite there emotionally. She still sees her dietitian and therapist weekly. In important ways, her work with her therapist now really takes off because her brain is restored and ready to do the work needed to prevent another relapse in the future. She still has hard days, but she's able to recognize the eating disorder voice without acting on it.

The Balloon Metaphor and "Fear Foods"

When patients begin the nutritional rehabilitation process, they can experience a lot of GI distress. This physical symptom, whether it appears as bloating and distention, fullness, nausea, constipation, diarrhea, or some combination of these, can be easily misinterpreted by the eating disorder. It can hasten to say, "See? I told you this wasn't safe. We have to go back to what we were doing before."

This is particularly true since many people with anorexia nervosa are highly focused on and experience body image distortions around the appearance of their stomach. When patients become underweight or have lost weight very quickly, many have the triggering experience of "seeing" their most recent meal because their stomach sticks out. Their eating disorder brain can interpret this as weight gain and then try to sabotage recovery work. I like to tell the story of the balloon metaphor in this situation.

I tell my patient: Imagine I blow up a balloon and tie it off, and I put it on the table in front of you. If I drape a thin sheet over the balloon, you will see every contour. If I toss a thick horse blanket over it, you might see that something's there, but it would be less evident.

For the first time in a while, you currently have digesting food, stool, and gas at various stages through your digestive system. These are the metaphorical "air" blowing up the "balloon" of your GI tract. Because you have insufficient fat and muscle, your abdominal wall is lying like a thin sheet over that balloon. Your muscles literally aren't strong enough anymore to hold in the contents of your abdomen. Therefore, you can see every meal.

By contrast, I have a nice horse blanket: plenty of fat and muscle. As a result, pretty much no matter what I eat, my belly looks the same. I encourage you to reframe and understand that only people who are malnourished and underweight can "see their meal." As you get stronger and more weight restored, this will resolve. For now, understand that this protuberant stomach is a sign of malnutrition, the opposite of what you are fearing.

Toward the end of nutritional rehabilitation, another belly-related finding is that patients often feel proportionately thicker around the middle than they were before they became ill, even if their weight is within an appropriate range. Everyone is built differently. Some patients who first became ill during adolescence not only need to recover from their anorexia nervosa, but also then need to go through adolescence … even in their 20s or 30s. In particular for females, feminization occurs, with development of curves and an adult body habitus that may or may not be welcome. In addition to the redevelopment of an adult body, patients may yet further gain more weight in their abdomen.

This is completely normal. Mother Nature's nutritional rainy-day fund is stored centrally. After a long famine, the cave person brain will deliberately keep some fat stores there in case the person goes through another famine right away. However, within a year of maintaining an appropriate weight, this will redistribute according to the genetic blueprint of what the person's adult body shape and size was always going to look like.

This brings us to "fear foods." Virtually all patients with eating disorders have a set of foods that are off limits, often called "fear foods." I have had countless patients react in shock when I support the meal plan their dietitian has laid out for them. "But Dr. G, there are processed foods/dairy/wheat/fats/sugars in this meal plan. Everyone knows those are bad for you/cause cancer/trigger inflammation/will make me gain too much weight." First, I let my patients know that I walk the talk. I eat everything and restrict nothing.

Second, I like to ask them, "What if I created a meal plan for you that was virtually guaranteed to cause the following issues: bloating, fullness, nausea, constipation, hair loss, wrinkled skin, fragile bones, a slowed metabolism, anxiety, social isolation, and cardiac damage?" They sense what's coming. I tell them, "That's the meal plan you're following presently, the one that your eating disorder has told you is so safe. Nothing is more dangerous for you than restriction." By contrast, I remind them, everything that their dietitian has recommended is vastly more healthful and scientifically safer.

Notes

1 Brown CA, Sabel AL, Gaudiani JL, Mehler PS. Predictors of hypophosphatemia during refeeding of patients with severe anorexia nervosa. *Int J Eat Disord.* 2015 November; 48(7):898–904. doi: 10.1002/eat.22406.

2 Gaudiani JL, Sabel AL, Mehler PS. Low prealbumin is a significant predictor of medical complications in severe anorexia nervosa. *Int J Eat Disord.* 2014 March; 47(2):148–156. doi: 10.1002/eat.22233.

3 O'Connor G, Nicholls D, Hudson L, Singhal A. Refeeding low weight hospitalized adolescents with anorexia nervosa: a multicenter randomized controlled trial. *Nutr Clin Pract.* 2016 October; 31(5):681–689. doi: 10.1177/08845336156 27267.

4 National Institute for Health and Clinical Excellence (NICE Criteria). *Nutrition support for adults: oral nutrition support, enteral tube feeding and parenteral nutrition, 2nd edition,* NHS Foundation Trust, 2006, revised 2017. www.nice.org.uk/ guidance/cg32. Accessed February 2, 2018.

5 Gaudiani JL, Sabel AL, Mehler PS. Low prealbumin is a significant predictor of medical complications in severe anorexia nervosa. *Int J Eat Disord.* 2014 March; 47(2):148–156. doi: 10.1002/eat.22233.

6 Whitelaw M, Gilbertson H, Lam PY, Sawyer SM. Does aggressive refeeding in hospitalized adolescents with anorexia nervosa result in increased hypophosphatemia? *J Adolesc Health.* 2010 June; 46(6):577–582. doi: 10.1016/j.jadohealth. 2009.11.207.

7 Peebles R, Lesser A, Park CC, Heckert K, Timko CA, Lantzouni E, Liebman R, Weaver L. Outcomes of an inpatient medical nutritional rehabilitation protocol in children and adolescents with eating disorders. *J Eat Disord.* 2017 March 1; 5:7. doi: 10.1186/s40337-017-0134-6.

8 Smith K, Lesser J, Brandenburg B, Lesser A, Cici J, Juenneman R, Beadle A, Eckhardt S, Lantz E, Lock J, Le Grange D. Outcomes of an inpatient refeeding protocol in youth with anorexia nervosa and atypical anorexia nervosa at children's hospitals and clinics of Minnesota. *J Eat Disord.* 2016 December 19; 4:35. doi: 10.1186/s40337-016-0124-0.

9 O'Connor G, Nicholls D, Hudson L, Singhal A. Refeeding low weight hospitalized adolescents with anorexia nervosa: a multicenter randomized controlled trial. *Nutr Clin Pract.* 2016 October; 31(5):681–689. doi: 10.1177/0884533615 627267.

10 Kohn MR, Madden S, Clarke SD. Refeeding in anorexia nervosa: increased safety and efficiency through understanding the pathophysiology of protein calorie malnutrition. *Curr Opin Pediatr.* 2011 August; 23(4):390–394. doi: 10. 1097/MOP.0b013e3283487591.

11 www.verywell.com/supplemental-feeding-to-treat-eating-disorders-4138109. Accessed February 2, 2018.

12 Sharma S, Sumich PM, Francis IC, Kiernan MC, Spira PJ. Wernicke's encephalopathy presenting with upbeating nystagmus. *J Clin Neurosci.* 2002 July; 9(4): 476–478. PubMed PMID: 12217687.

13 Altinyazar V, Kiylioglu N, Salkin G. Anorexia nervosa and Wernicke Korsakoff's syndrome: atypical presentation by acute psychosis. *Int J Eat Disord.* 2010 December; 43(8):766–769. doi: 10.1002/eat.20783.

14 Prasad AS. Discovery of human zinc deficiency: its impact on human health and disease. *Adv Nutr.* 2013 March 1; 4(2):176–190. doi: 10.3945/an.112. 003210.

15 Gropper SS, Smith JL, Carr TP. (2018) *Advanced nutrition and human metabolism,* *7th Ed.* Boston: Cengage Learning. (pp. 500–509).
16 Madigan CD, Pavey T, Daley AJ, Jolly K, Brown WJ. Is weight cycling associated with adverse health outcomes? A cohort study. *Prev Med.* 2018 March; 108: 47–52. doi:10.1016/j.ypmed.2017.12.010.

Part II

Purging

Let's turn from medical problems associated with restriction of calories to medical problems associated with purging. Purging means physically emptying oneself. Vomiting, laxative abuse, and diuretic abuse are the three most common ways to purge, and excessive exercise can also be considered a means of purging. Sometimes bingeing precedes purging.[1] According to the DSM-5, bingeing means eating a large amount of food in a rapid manner, then feeling painfully full and guilty afterwards. Some patients believe they have binged because the amount of food is more than they personally usually consume, even if it would not be objectively considered an inordinate amount of food by others.

By DSM-5 definition, patients with bulimia nervosa binge and purge at least once a week for at least three months and are not typically underweight, although they may be medically malnourished. With anorexia nervosa, purging subtype, patients restrict calories and purge them (with or without bingeing). As per the definition of anorexia nervosa, the patients do become significantly underweight. Atypical bulimia nervosa, under the DSM-5 heading of other specified feeding and eating disorder (OSFED) is the diagnosis given to patients who engage in binge/purge behaviors less often than for a diagnosis of bulimia nervosa.[2]

The prevalence of bulimia nervosa is around 1–1.5 percent when meeting all the DSM-5 criteria, although up to 20 percent meet subthreshold criteria.[3] Females outnumber males by a factor of 3–10:1.[4] Overexercise can be considered a purging mechanism, but it does not result in the type of physiology described in this chapter. Insulin restriction in those with type 1 diabetes mellitus can also be considered a means of purging, and I discuss this in Chapter 13.

Purging carries three main categories of medical risk: physical damage to the body, electrolyte disturbances and dehydration, and the complications of stopping purging. Chapter 7 offers an overview of why purging causes medical problems. Chapter 8 covers in greater detail what happens to the body physically as a result of purging, while Chapter 9 reviews blood electrolyte changes and the medical complications of stopping purging.

Notes

1 "Bingeing" has two accepted spellings, one with and one without the "e." The eating disorder field typically uses the version with the "e."
2 American Psychiatric Association. (2013). *Diagnostic and statistical manual of mental disorders (5th ed.)*. Arlington, VA: American Psychiatric Publishing.
3 Hail L, Le Grange D. Bulimia nervosa in adolescents: prevalence and treatment challenges. *Adolesc Health Med Ther.* 2018 January 4; 9:11–16. doi: 10.2147/AHMT.S135326.
4 www.nationaleatingdisorders.org/statistics-research-eating-disorders. Accessed April 24, 2018.

Chapter 7

30,000-Foot View
What is Purging? Why Does it Cause Medical Issues?

Background

The medical complications of purging arise from the type, frequency, and duration of purging. Cessation of purging, also called "detox," can also be medically dangerous. Patients who purge face a number of serious challenges. First, regardless of body weight or size, purging can make a person dangerously ill very rapidly. As you know from Part I, in pure restriction, the cave person brain is designed to recognize starvation and adapt virtually all body systems to use less energy in a protective manner. Accordingly, physiologic change happens slowly. By contrast, when purging is involved, a person can be fine in the morning and dead by sundown. Purging can abruptly change electrolyte levels—potassium in particular—as well as hydration status; the body simply cannot adapt quickly enough. Death can occur swiftly and without warning.

Another obstacle faced by patients who purge is that the medical system often causes them psychological or physical harm. Size bias causes medical practitioners to blurt out, "You have an eating disorder? You look fine to me. You're not even underweight." Insurance companies may deny a needed higher level of care on the basis of weight bias: their own, or that which is built into the DSM-5. Or insurance reviewers might decide that a patient's electrolytes aren't "abnormal enough" to merit life-saving residential treatment.

These interactions can have a profoundly chilling effect on patients. They reinforce exactly what the eating disorder voice has been telling them: "See, you're not sick enough. You clearly have to be worse off for anyone to take this seriously." Tragically, some patients can also have these same thoughts reinforced by family members, friends, and even strangers. Furthermore, patients who purge have often received inadvertently bad or even dangerous medical care in emergency departments of hospitals, school infirmaries, or elsewhere.

Why Binge and Purge?

The act of bingeing and purging can fulfil certain psychological needs. For instance, purging can play the role of diffusing anger, sadness, loneliness, or frustration. It can help someone feel numb. It can even bring on a sense of euphoria. Purging may not be at all about the calories. It may be about needing to feel empty, which speaks to many patients' fear of fullness, of being in and aware of their physical bodies as well as of their emotional needs and responses. Purging can also be a mode of self-harm, punishing a body that the mental illness insists is unworthy and unacceptable. Recovery cannot be successful unless patients find a way to get these needs met in other ways.

Unless medical practitioners recognize these aspects of the disease, they can make incorrect assumptions about what purging does for the patient, and in so doing cause invalidation, alienation, and harm. These interactions don't just have psychological ramifications. They have medical ones too because they teach patients learn to avoid medical care. This is one of the many reasons I always work closely with therapists and dietitians as part of a patient's treatment team. Recovery is far more complex than "just stop purging."

Vomiting

Studies show a wide range of the prevalence of specific purging behaviors, with vomiting the most commonly used modality, followed by laxative abuse and diuretic abuse. Many people engage in multiple modalities.[1] Vomiting can be triggered manually, where the person's finger or an object like a spoon triggers the gag reflex. In the former case, patients can end up with calluses and abrasions on the back of their hand from grazing the teeth, a physical finding called Russell's Sign. Over time, vomiting can become almost effortless.

Laxative Abuse

Laxative abuse can start insidiously with patients who have become constipated from metabolic slowing. There are two main types of laxatives, osmotic (those which draw water into the intestine in order to help stools pass more easily) and stimulant (which force the intestinal muscles to contract and propel stool). The former class are safe and rarely abused. The latter class includes senna and bisacodyl, and these are the dangerous ones if abused. Don't be fooled by pretty labels on boxes bought from organic grocery stores: herbal teas, for instance, can also contain senna and can contribute to laxative abuse.

No calories are lost with laxative abuse. Rather, individuals develop a compulsive need to have nothing inside them, to be "empty." Patients may use laxatives until they have nausea, cramps, and diarrhea. A progressive obsession can develop with the appearance of the stomach, along with fears of constipation. Patients can lose touch with normal bowel function; they panic, thinking they are constipated if they don't have diarrhea five times a day. They can begin to plan their days not only around food consumption but also around proximity to bathrooms. They may engage in fewer social interactions, since laxative abuse also can involve flatulence as well as incontinence. Studies have shown that individuals that abuse laxatives have higher rates of suicidality, self-harm, feelings of emptiness, and anger.[2]

Diuretic Abuse

The third main type of purging is diuretic abuse, which is facilitated by the purchase of prescription diuretics off the internet. These medicines force the kidneys to excrete salt and water. As with laxatives, no calories are lost through diuretic abuse. Rather, diuretic abuse leads to weight loss through severe dehydration.

The final common denominator of medical harm from purging is that severe dehydration and severe electrolyte abnormalities, especially low potassium, can cause the heart to stop. This can occur at any body weight or size and at any moment. Some patients who purge a great deal maintain relatively normal electrolytes longer than would be expected. As always, this is because of genetic variability. There is no safe amount of purging.

Temperamental Factors

Patients who purge may have different temperaments from those who purely restrict. While this is a generalization that by no means applies to all patients, individuals who purely restrict food intake are often great students, diligent, and responsible. They rarely have to be reminded to finish a task and are classically perfectionistic, socially anxious or shy, sensitive to criticism, earnest, and often modest. On the other hand, those who purge can have some (or all) of these same traits, but they often also tend to have more of a "wild child" side to them.

The best quotation I have heard about those who purge (and I don't know to whom to attribute it) is that people who purge are "attracted to complexity and then overwhelmed by it." Perhaps not surprisingly, as this quote suggests, patients who purge are easily caught up in complicated social relationships. They can be passionate, risk takers, thrill seekers, outgoing, and more sexually precocious. They may seek physical intimacy as a means of connection and validation, don't mind being noticed, and more often have comorbid substance use disorder.[3,4,5] At the same time, they have all the intelligence, anxiety, and sensitivity of patients who purely restrict; they can overextend themselves and then binge and purge as a calming or numbing mechanism.

Only Sick if the Potassium is Low

Many patients who purge believe that they are only sick enough to merit treatment and abstinence from behaviors when their electrolytes are abnormal. This is perpetuated in a multitude of ways. For one, family systems and personal expectations can inadvertently contribute to the establishment of this belief. A young man who develops bulimia in the context of high personal and familial expectations around academics and sports accomplishments might drive himself until he collapses and is taken to the hospital, where tests reveal his potassium to be very low. Given the measurable medical issue, everyone insists that he rest and recuperate. They support and nurture him in a way that he doesn't receive on an everyday basis, or that he typically rejects because he has such high standards for himself and feels he doesn't deserve that compassion and attention. Once that potassium normalizes, though, and he's rested for a few days, life resumes. He may be hypersensitive to any message that he's now "fine," and then the eating disorder takes over again.

Without a question, it's a big problem when patients who purge don't take their illness seriously unless their labs are abnormal. For starters, it's hard to convince them to engage in treatment. In addition, once a patient has entered treatment and stopped behaviors, anywhere from outpatient to inpatient medical care, the electrolytes turn around pretty quickly. That means that a week into treatment, when lab work comes back normal, they may sadly conclude that they are now "fine" and don't need any more help. It means that a doctor cheerfully telling them their bloodwork is normal may send them into an escalation of eating disorder behaviors because the news feels so invalidating.

This is, of course, all part of the mental illness. It can torment concerned family members who increasingly walk on eggshells, lest a stray positive comment be used as reason for a patient to jump back into eating disorder behaviors. Ultimately, providers have to keep giving the message that there is no one measure—not a lab value nor a weight—that correctly and uniquely labels the severity of an eating disorder or its worthiness for treatment.

The Two-Sided Coin

The story of the two-sided coin emerged from countless conversations I've had with patients over the years, as they try to make sense out of what their eating disorder is doing for them. I put my hand out in front of me, palm up, and point to my palm saying, "This is the golden, glowing side of your coin. It includes all your traits and accomplishments that get attention and praise from your parents, coaches, and teachers."

But, and I flip my hand over and point to the back of it, everyone has another side to their coin. I tell the patient that what I see over and over again is that with the golden side can come a darker side. That's not a moral judgment. It refers to the vulnerabilities that such remarkable patients can also possess: sensitivity, anxiety, high recharge need, and rigidity.

An exquisite sensitivity to praise or criticism, for instance, can be painful, especially in childhood when there is so little life experience and so few coping skills to manage it. A deep need, by comparison with their friends, for extra reassurance, support, connection, and self-care, can feel shameful. No one else seems to need to check in with loved ones regularly, asking, "Am I all right? Are you mad at me?" No one else seems to need extra sleep a night. No one else seems to need extra cuddles. In fact, my patients have often heard from loved ones, again with all good intentions, "Why are you letting this bother you so much? Let it roll off you! Save your tears for the important stuff." I have even wondered if the magnitude of my patients' sensitivity and need for support feels *big* to them and ends up contributing to the distortion that their body is too big and needs to be changed.

While my patients get lots of attention for the golden side of their coin, they often don't get much support for their darker side. In part, they've worked hard to look like they don't have a darker side. They never developed the words to say, "I'm lonely. I'm scared. I'm overwhelmed." Or if they did, they felt that these messages weren't taken seriously, and they shrank away from feeling worthy enough to really be allowed to feel anything but fine.

I see in many of my patients the lack of a consistent ability to do the following psychological tasks: "I know how I feel. I'm kind to that feeling. I can soothe myself." Unable to perform these three key tasks, they may turn to eating disorder behaviors of starving, bingeing, purging, or overexercise to numb and distract.

I like to highlight my patients' strengths in order to help them find compassion for their struggles. The two-sided coin story can help remind them that they are allowed to be both sides of their coin and to honor both. This story also helps me be a better physician and to appreciate what my patients have lived through. It reminds me to be patient, to watch my words because those sensitive radars are still up, and to be gentle. It keeps me focused on not invalidating my patients because there's often a strong history of not feeling supported.

In my parenting, it brings me face to face with my own Type A, anxious personality and how that might lead me to respond to my daughters' needs.

In the past, one of my two children might come to me with a tummy ache, and I'd go into "Mom, MD" mode, working on the differential diagnosis. "Are you hungry? Do you need to poop?" Then, and I cringe to remember it, I'd assure her, "You'll be fine, honey."

I know now that my daughter wasn't asking me to solve the mystery of her tummy ache, and she wasn't worried something truly bad was going on that required me to tell her she'd be fine. I was responding to *my* need in these moments. I apparently needed to fix her issue quickly, reassure myself everything was okay, and take myself off the hook for worrying about it anymore. What she really wanted was recognition, sympathy, and comfort. I learned this from listening to my patients' stories.

Now, with nearly all of the problems my girls bring to me, I say some version of, "I'm sorry. That sounds uncomfortable. Would you like a cuddle or would you like to talk about it?" Recognition, sympathy, comfort. My hope is that their beautiful souls will absorb this response, and as they grow older they will have learned to offer themselves the same compassion during challenging times.

Notes

1 Forney KJ, Buchman-Schmitt JM, Keel PK, Frank GK. The medical complications associated with purging. *Int J Eat Disord.* 2016 March; 49(3):249–259. doi: 10.1002/eat.22504.

2 Tozzi F, Thornton LM, Mitchell J, Fichter MM, Klump KL, Lilenfeld LR, Reba L, Strober M, Kaye WH, Bulik CM; Price Foundation Collaborative Group. Features associated with laxative abuse in individuals with eating disorders. *Psychosom Med.* 2006 May–June; 68(3):470–477. PubMed PMID: 16738081.

3 Gat-Lazer S, Geva R, Gur E, Stein D. Reward dependence and harm avoidance among patients with binge-purge type eating disorders. *Eur Eat Disord Rev.* 2017 May; 25(3):205–213. doi: 10.1002/erv.2505.

4 Klump KL, Bulik CM, Pollice C, Halmi KA, Fichter MM, Berrettini WH, Devlin B, Strober M, Kaplan A, Woodside DB, Treasure J, Shabbout M, Lilenfeld LR, Plotnicov KH, Kaye WH. Temperament and character in women with anorexia nervosa. *J Nerv Ment Dis.* 2000 September; 188(9):559–567. PubMed PMID: 11009328.

5 Root TL, Pinheiro AP, Thornton L, Strober M, Fernández-Aranda F, Brandt H, Crawford S, Fichter MM, Halmi KA, Johnson C, Kaplan AS, Klump KL, La Via M, Mitchell J, Woodside DB, Rotondo A, Berrettini WH, Kaye WH, Bulik CM. Substance use disorders in women with anorexia nervosa. *Int J Eat Disord.* 2010 January; 43(1):14–21. doi: 10.1002/eat.20670.

Chapter 8

How Does Purging Physically Affect the Body?

Case: Claire

Claire is a 37-year-old cisgender African American female who has struggled intermittently with bulimia nervosa since she was 16 years old. An outgoing and dedicated professional, she feels like a very high functioning person and wonders why she can't stop her eating disorder behaviors. At least once a week, she will wake up and know it's going to be "one of those days." After work, she will drive, almost on autopilot, to the store. She will buy binge foods, then go home and systematically eat them all. She tunes out during those episodes, barely tasting the food. Once she's full to the point of pain, she'll vomit over and over until she feels empty. Afterwards, a sense of euphoria and relaxation comes over her, mixed with disgust and shame that once again she couldn't resist.

Claire thinks a lot about body image and her weight. Weighing herself daily gives her a sense of safety and makes her feel as if her life isn't out of control. She always wishes she could weigh less and compares her body with the bodies of other women at her gym. She almost never eats junk food outside of a binge. Since heartburn has always been an issue, Claire keeps antacids in her purse. Her teeth have become more sensitive and painful over the years. Usually organized in all realms of her life, Claire has avoided seeing a dentist because she suspects she might have some enamel damage from her stomach acid and doesn't want to answer any questions. One day when she is looking through old photos, she notices that her face has become rounder over the years, particularly at the angle of her jaw.

Claire has never sought treatment because she's not even sure she has an eating disorder and she doesn't feel sick enough to seek help. After all, she's not underweight, she likes food, and she eats pretty normally the rest of the time.

Background

Purging can damage the body physically in many ways. Vomiting can damage the teeth as well as cause bleeding from the upper GI tract due to a variety of different mechanisms. Acid reflux commonly affects those who purge by vomiting. The parotid and salivary glands can swell, sometimes painfully. Laxative abuse results in a host of serious medical, electrolyte, and dehydration-related complications. Thyroid hormone abuse is rare, but it can cause significant harm. This chapter provides details about all of these topics. It also reviews normal thyroid function, autoimmune thyroid dysfunction, and a common medical error that results from misdiagnosis of underactive thyroid in someone with an eating disorder.

Dental Damage

Vomiting exposes the esophagus and mouth to stomach acid that eats away the enamel of the teeth, typically on the inner side of the tooth. It can also cause chemical burns in the mouth.[1,2] As a physician, I've taken care of many patients whose teeth are irreparably damaged by vomiting, such that they require highly expensive dental work. In addition, chronic vomiting can contribute to sores at the corners of the mouth, called angular cheilitis. Vision loss has been reported from purging, where the sudden increase in pressure during vomiting causes delicate blood vessels at the back of the eye to rupture or even leads to retinal detachment.[3] Sudden vision change is an emergency that requires urgent medical attention.

Barrett's Esophagus and GERD

Chronic exposure to stomach acid can cause precancerous cellular changes in the lower part of the esophagus, a condition called Barrett's esophagus.[4] While there is not a high risk of cancerous transformation, every patient with bulimia nervosa who has purged for more than five years should have a screening upper endoscopy to look for Barrett's esophagus. This preventative screening requires an upper endoscopy, in which a gastroenterologist examines the esophagus, stomach, and part of the small intestine with a long, slim, flexible camera. Biopsies are taken to make sure the cells look healthy.

Typically, when patients have purged for a long time, it becomes easier and easier to vomit. Unlike most people, for whom vomiting is a wrenching, miserable experience, the individual who purges chronically comes to be able to vomit easily. This is because the ring of muscle called the lower esophageal sphincter, that typically tightens at the bottom of the esophagus, becomes stretched out and cannot hold stomach contents in.

As a result, patients who purge chronically can develop pronounced heartburn or GERD. GERD is very common in the general population, with 44 percent of the general population experiencing symptoms once a month and 7 percent experiencing symptoms daily.[5] Chronic GERD, too, can lead to Barrett's esophagus.

GERD should be managed medically with a class of medicines called proton pump inhibitors (PPIs) because they have been proven in studies to be substantially more effective than the class of medicines called the H2-blockers.[6] Proton pump inhibitors must be taken 30 minutes before breakfast or before dinner to work effectively. In addition, certain lifestyle changes, such as reduction in caffeine and alcohol intake, cessation of smoking, and avoiding eating large meals before lying down, help reduce GERD.

Rinsing

Some patients engage in a behavior called rinsing, where after bingeing and purging they drink water and purge again, to "rinse" the stomach of any missed food. This can cause severe chills as the core body temperature drops due to repeated exposure to cold water in the stomach. In extreme cases, the patient may become so cold as to qualify for hypothermia, with body temperatures ranging from 32–35 degrees Celsius (89–95 degrees Fahrenheit); this can lead to life-threatening cardiac arrhythmias.

Rumination

In addition to reflux, some individuals who purge develop what is called rumination. Rumination, in this context, does not mean thinking about a topic over and over again. Rather, it refers to the regurgitation of food into the mouth, then chewing it and re-swallowing it. Some people choose their meals based on the ease and taste of ruminating on it afterwards. They can find this soothing or distracting when they are anxious. Shame and a lack of provider awareness about this behavior keeps many patients from admitting to it.[7]

For some, rumination is not a deliberate act. With the loss of lower esophageal sphincter pressure and a stomach that has become used to reverse peristalsis (digestive muscle contractions in the upwards direction that cause vomiting), a patient may feel perfectly fine one moment and then suddenly find their meal rising back into their mouths. In extreme cases, they can suddenly and unintentionally projectile vomit.

In addition to excellent therapy for the emotional aspect of deliberate rumination, there is one evidence-based treatment that physically helps keep food in the stomach: diaphragmatic breathing.[8] I teach patients,

> Place one hand on your chest, and one hand on your stomach. Take a deep, normal breath, and you'll probably see the chest hand rise, while the stomach hand stays fairly still. Now take a deep breath with the chest hand staying still and the stomach hand lifting.

This latter technique is called diaphragmatic breathing. It changes the pressures in the thorax and abdomen such that food essentially cannot flow upwards as easily. Practicing this regularly after meals is the only scientifically proven way of treating rumination.

Upper GI Tract Bleeding

Purging by vomiting can also cause bleeding from the upper GI tract. The lining of the stomach can become irritated by the trauma of distending with a binge and then being forced to vomit. As a result, gastritis, or stomach inflammation, can occur. Ulcers can form as well, and both gastritis and ulcers can either ooze blood or bleed briskly. Infection of the stomach with bacteria called *Helicobacter pylori* ("H. Pylori") can also contribute to stomach ulcers and irritation.

The esophagus can also bleed in the setting of repeated forced vomiting. The most common cause is a partial-thickness tear of the esophagus, called a Mallory-Weiss tear. Mallory-Weiss tears usually bleed more than gastritis. Moreover, a through-and-through tear of the esophagus can be deadly and is called Boerhaave syndrome. Rupture of the stomach itself after a large binge has been reported and, along with Boerhaave syndrome, can cause excruciating pain as blood and gastric contents fill the lung space and abdomen where they don't belong.[9]

Vomited blood will appear bright red when fresh, or as coarse black "coffee grounds" after sitting in the stomach for a while. Regardless, any vomiting of blood requires prompt medical attention. Depending on the presentation, conservative treatment or referral to a gastroenterologist for an upper endoscopy may be recommended. For all but gastric or esophageal rupture, usually cessation of vomiting and a month-long course of a PPI will resolve the problem. Make no mistake, though: upper GI bleeding can be deadly. Any evidence of it should be taken very seriously and understood as a major motivation to pursue recovery from an eating disorder.

Parotid Glands and Face Swelling

The parotid glands are salivary glands located right in front of the ears, at the angle of the jaw. Most people can't see or feel their parotid glands. However, in those who purge chronically and who have a genetic susceptibility, these glands enlarge, a condition called parotid hypertrophy. This gives patients a squared-off jaw appearance that can sometimes look like "chipmunk cheeks." Salivary glands under the jaw can also swell. In some people, the parotid hypertrophy never goes away or may only diminish somewhat, even after recovery.

Those patients who do develop parotid hypertrophy can discover that stopping purging can cause the cheeks to swell even more and become painful. This called acute sialadenosis. Sometimes the swelling is so severe that patients develop a sore throat, ear pain, and a headache. It can be very triggering for patients to stop purging and wake up the next morning with a face that has doubled in size. Anyone with parotid hypertrophy should prepare for this when they are ready to stop or even decrease purging.

To prevent or reduce this phenomenon, lemon drops or other tart candies can be consumed every few hours to keep the saliva flowing from the parotid glands. Warm or cool compresses and ibuprofen, dosed three or four times a day and always given with food and plenty of water, will help as well. The discomfort and appearance of acute sialoadenosis will eventually pass within a week or two. Although surgery is occasionally mentioned as an option, I recommend against it.

Effects of Laxative Abuse

Another mode of purging involves laxative abuse, which also carries significant medical risks. I am confident that patients who abuse laxatives would recommend to someone else: don't start. Laxative abuse might begin in a non-eating disordered way. Constipation, either due to caloric restriction or naturally occurring, can induce a person to buy over the counter stimulant laxatives. Some patients get immensely focused on their bowel habits, and the opportunity to have a bowel movement on demand after taking a medicine can become too tempting to resist. Thereafter, taking more laxatives to induce diarrheal losses can give patients the (mistaken) impression that they are somehow "cleaner and safer" because their digestive system feels emptier. As the eating disorder takes hold, the patient's ability to think rationally about risk and the body's true needs evaporates, whether related to behaviors of restricting, binging, vomiting, exercising, or abusing laxatives. Thus, the use of two stimulant laxatives a day can become the use of ten a day ... or 50.

Human body weight is comprised of around 50 percent water. Laxatives will induce weight loss through dehydration as diarrhea is excreted. However, no calories are lost; the body still absorbs everything as it passes through our long intestinal system. Patients who abuse laxatives are the most dehydrated of all those who purge. This has major implications for cessation of laxative abuse and major weight increases, as I will discuss in Chapter 9.

Abusing laxatives causes severe nausea and cramps. Patients with chronic laxative abuse who receive a colonoscopy can receive the diagnosis "melanosis coli" which means that a brown pigment appears throughout the colon. Melanosis coli refers to accrued pigments called lipofuscins, which are considered a sign of aging in tissues. It remains uncertain whether melanosis coli is a marker for tissue damage or other problems to come, and there's no treatment for it, but it's certainly an abnormal finding.[10] Laxative abuse can also cause pancreatitis and kidney stones.[11,12]

Physicians have hypothesized that long term laxative abuse causes progressive, permanent colon smooth muscle damage, creating a floppy tube that will never wriggle on its own again.[13] The data are actually mixed about this causal association, and more research needs to be done. I have certainly cared for patients with severely damaged, floppy colons (called "atonic"), for whom constipation management will remain a lifelong struggle. However, this might be a chicken and egg problem. Did this individual start out with a floppy, weaker colon (from restriction of calories or genetically weaker tissues), and as a result seek higher and higher doses of stimulant laxatives, or vice versa? We don't yet know. Regardless, there are vastly safer and gentler medicines for constipation than stimulant laxatives, and I recommend stimulants to almost no one.

Effects of Diuretic Abuse

Although diuretic abuse is less common than either vomiting or laxative abuse, in extreme cases, it can cause permanent kidney failure, requiring an individual either to receive dialysis the rest of their life or to get a kidney transplant. The potential for severe dehydration and electrolyte abnormalities due to diuretic abuse is high.

Thyroid Function Overview

I include a discussion of thyroid function and thyroid hormone abuse in this chapter because thyroid hormone abuse is yet another way patients can purge, albeit more rarely. Let's start with understanding how the thyroid normally works. The thyroid gland sits at the bottom of the front of the neck; each of its two lobes is about the size of a clementine segment. The thyroid controls how the body uses energy and responds to other hormones. Thyroid stimulating hormone (TSH) is made in the pituitary of the brain, and it signals the thyroid gland to make T3 and T4, which are the active hormones.

Hypothyroidism

In true hypothyroidism, the gland typically under-functions because of autoimmune damage called Hashimoto's thyroiditis. Lab findings include a low T4 and a high TSH, as the brain makes more TSH to try and signal the damaged thyroid gland to make more active hormone. Symptoms of hypothyroidism include weight gain, low energy, depression, hair loss, and a feeling of being cold. Because this is an autoimmune process resulting from the body attacking itself, the anti-thyroid antibody called anti-thyroperoxidase, or anti-TPO antibody, will be abnormally elevated in 90 percent of cases.[14]

Hyperthyroidism

In hyperthyroidism, on the other hand, the gland overfunctions, often because of Grave's disease, which also an autoimmune problem. Lab tests will show a high T4 and an undetectably low TSH as the brain says, "Whoa, we've clearly got enough thyroid hormone here! No need for more!" Symptoms include weight loss, a very fast heart rate, tremor, anxiety, and the feeling of being hot and sweaty all the time.

Sick Euthyroid Syndrome

During times of intense physiological stress, such as a car accident, critical medical illness, or malnutrition and weight loss, thyroid tests can become abnormal. This is called sick euthyroid syndrome.[15] The thyroid gland itself is healthy, but levels of TSH may be low, normal, or slightly elevated, with a low T3. The T4 may be normal for a while but in more extreme cases can drop.

To understand how a patient with an eating disorder may end up with an incorrect diagnosis of a thyroid disorder, consider a primary care doctor who sees a patient with complaints of being chilly, depressed, and with thinning hair. He might not think to ask about an eating disorder, or the patient might not give the whole story in order to defend her illness. He orders thyroid tests and finds a slightly elevated TSH and a low T4. Looks like hypothyroidism to him. He prescribes thyroid medication, and now this individual with a restrictive eating disorder and weight loss, whose thyroid is absolutely fine, has been prescribed a medicine that can cause significant harm.

When prescribed for patients with true autoimmune hypothyroidism, thyroid medicine, also called levothyroxine, is medically indicated and highly beneficial. However, when given to someone who does not need it medically, especially someone with an eating disorder, it can be dangerous. One, levothyroxine revs up the metabolism to a certain extent. As we know, the cave person brain has protectively decreased the metabolism in the face of caloric restriction. Taking a medicine that undoes that protective function is dangerous in someone with an eating disorder.

Two, excessive thyroid hormone thins the bones. As we saw in Chapter 3, this is also bad news because people with underweight and low levels of sex hormones already may face rapid bone density loss.

Three, levothyroxine in someone without hypothyroidism can cause a rapid heart rate, palpitations, and anxiety. Given that starved hearts are already stressed, taking excessive thyroid hormone can range from uncomfortable to dangerous. And no one with an eating disorder should be on a medication that increases anxiety!

Thyroid Hormone Abuse

When you take all these dangers and then compound them in patients who deliberately abuse thyroid hormone, you realize how much trouble they can get into medically. I've taken care of patients who used the disjointed medical system to their advantage, getting multiple doctors to prescribe levothyroxine (each one thinking they are the only doctor), then filling the prescriptions at multiple different pharmacies. I've also seen patients forge prescriptions or get various types of thyroid hormone off the internet. This is a fairly rare drug of abuse, but it can be deadly.

I recommend checking an anti-TPO antibody level for malnourished, stressed patients diagnosed with hypothyroidism. If that antibody level is negative, the odds are that the person never had hypothyroidism in the first place. They should be taken off levothyroxine, and thyroid levels (TSH and T4) should be rechecked in six weeks. If the antibody is positive, they do have true autoimmune thyroid failure, and levothyroxine can be continued. The rare patient with antibody-negative results may still need levothyroxine, but this decision needs to be made by an endocrinologist who also has eating disorder expertise.

Diet Pill Abuse

I will mention diet pills briefly. I strongly protest their use in absolutely everyone. If there were actually a medication that could healthily regulate a person's relationship with food, allow them to nourish themselves adequately with a wide variety of foods, recognize hunger cues and honor them, compassionately care for themselves, and move their bodies for vitality and joy, that drug would be at the top of the charts. There is no such drug. Diet pills can cause cardiac damage and heighten anxiety; ultimately, they do not work.

Case Resolution: Claire

Claire finds herself falling in love with a kind, compassionate, and fun new partner. Dates and spontaneous outings, however, make her eating disorder nervous. What if they eat at a place without a "safe" option for her? What if she were to be caught in the midst of a binge and purge session? She realizes her new relationship is becoming important enough to her that she's willing to seek help, and so she finds a new primary care doctor to whom she can open up. She describes the behaviors she's been doing all these years, and she learns she meets the diagnosis for bulimia nervosa. Claire is surprised that this doctor doesn't weigh her, an element of the visit that she had been imagining and dreading. The doctor notes that her weight isn't a relevant vital sign, as one cannot gauge by a person's weight whether they are healthy or unhealthy.

Claire's doctor describes all the medical risks of bulimia nervosa. She notes that Claire's rounder face is due to parotid hypertrophy, which might subside after abstaining from vomiting for a period of time. She refers Claire to a good dentist to resume regular checkups. The doctor prescribes Claire a proton pump inhibitor for her GERD, and she refers her to a gastroenterologist for a screening upper endoscopy to rule out Barrett's esophagus.

Claire has her bloodwork checked and gets an EKG in her doctor's office. Fortunately, all these tests come back normal. The doctor kindly assures her that this doesn't mean Claire is "fine." Indeed, just carrying the diagnosis of bulimia nervosa doubles her risk of death, and it will continue to interfere with all the best aspects of Claire's life. The doctor refers Claire to a multidisciplinary team, including a therapist and dietitian with eating disorder expertise. She encourages Claire to see her team regularly and validates that while the recovery process is challenging and can take time, it is well worth it.

Comparing Yourself to Your Sickest Day

My patients can have a tendency to discount their current level of illness by comparing themselves to their sickest day. "But Dr. G, I once weighed x pounds/had a potassium of x. I don't really need to make any changes in what I'm doing. I'm not sick enough." I compassionately name what they are doing when I hear them say this: they are comparing themselves to their sickest day in order to downplay the severity of their current situation.

Instead, I ask them to focus on the gap between their lifestyle within the eating disorder and their vision of a desired life. I invite them to consider their most real self, one formed out of their unique values and traits. That gap, that distance between their current life and their actual ability to live the well version of themselves, is what constitutes being "sick enough" for treatment. Indeed, that distance validates the presence of the illness, defines the work that still needs to be done, and establishes the need for a caring, expert team.

This same mentality holds when it comes to patients who need to step up to a higher level of care. My patient might say, "But Dr. G, I'm not the sickest I've been/as sick as I was the last time I stepped up to a higher level of care." Reasonably enough, they might say that their work, academic plans, family, pets, or other commitments are too important to them to leave for a higher level of treatment. I understand that these aspects of their lives are truly important to my patients. However, rather than implementing recovery work that would allow them to stay in connection with these values, in practice they cannot stop acting on the impulses of their deadly mental illness. By urging my patients to look toward the future, rather than comparing themselves with the past, I try to help them understand they are indeed sick enough to keep making forward progress.

Notes

1 Derchi G, Vano M, Peñarrocha D, Barone A, Covani U. Minimally invasive prosthetic procedures in the rehabilitation of a bulimic patient affected by dental erosion. *J Clin Exp Dent.* 2015 February 1; 7(1):e170–174. doi: 10.4317/jced. 51732.

2 Uhlen MM, Tveit AB, Stenhagen KR, Mulic A. Self-induced vomiting and dental erosion–a clinical study. *BMC Oral Health.* 2014 July 29; 14:92. doi: 10. 1186/1472-6831-14-92.

3 Zhang GS, Mathura JR Jr. Images in clinical medicine. Painless loss of vision after vomiting. *N Engl J Med.* 2005 April 28; 352(17):e16. PubMed PMID: 15858179.

4 Benini L, Todesco T, Frulloni L, Dalle Grave R, Campagnola P, Agugiaro F, Cusumano CD, Gabbrielli A, Vantini I. Esophageal motility and symptoms in restricting and binge-eating/purging anorexia. *Dig Liver Dis.* 2010 November; 42(11):767–772. doi: 10.1016/j.dld.2010.03.018.

5 Locke GR 3rd, Talley NJ, Fett SL, Zinsmeister AR, Melton LJ 3rd. Prevalence and clinical spectrum of gastroesophageal reflux: a population-based study in Olmsted County, Minnesota. *Gastroenterology.* 1997 May; 112(5):1448–1456. PubMed PMID: 9136821.

6 Sakurai K, Nagahara A, Inoue K, Akiyama J, Mabe K, Suzuki J, Habu Y, Araki A, Suzuki T, Satoh K, Nagami H, Harada R, Tano N, Kusaka M, Fujioka Y, Fujimura T, Shigeto N, Oumi T, Miwa J, Miwa H, Fujimoto K, Kinoshita Y, Haruma K. Efficacy of omeprazole, famotidine, mosapride and teprenone in patients with upper gastrointestinal symptoms: an omeprazole-controlled randomized study (J-FOCUS). *BMC Gastroenterol.* 2012 May 1; 12:42. doi: 10.1186/ 1471-230X-12-42.

7 Birmingham CL, Firoz T. Rumination in eating disorders: literature review. *Eat Weight Disord.* 2006 September;11(3):e85–89. PubMed PMID: 17075234.

8 Halland M, Parthasarathy G, Bharucha AE, Katzka DA. Diaphragmatic breathing for rumination syndrome: efficacy and mechanisms of action. *Neurogastroenterol Motil.* 2016 March; 28(3):384–391. doi: 10.1111/nmo.12737.

9 Dewangan M, Khare MK, Mishra S, Marhual JC. Binge eating leading to acute gastric dilatation, ischemic necrosis and rupture – A case report. *J Clin Diagn Res.* 2016 March; 10(3):PD06–7. doi: 10.7860/JCDR/2016/16530.7450.

10 Liu ZH, Foo DCC, Law WL, Chan FSY, Fan JKM, Peng JS. Melanosis coli: harmless pigmentation? A case-control retrospective study of 657 cases. *PLoS One.* 2017 October 31; 12(10):e0186668. doi: 10.1371/journal.pone.0186668.

11 Baker EH, Sandle GI. Complications of laxative abuse. *Annu Rev Med.* 1996; 47:127–134. PubMed PMID: 8712767.

12 Gennari FJ, Weise WJ. Acid-base disturbances in gastrointestinal disease. *Clin J Am Soc Nephrol.* 2008 November; 3(6):1861–1868. doi: 10.2215/CJN.02450508.

13 Mehler PS, Rylander M. Bulimia nervosa – medical complications. *J Eat Disord.* 2015 April 3; 3:12. doi: 10.1186/s40337-015-0044-4.

14 Rotondi M, de Martinis L, Coperchini F, Pignatti P, Pirali B, Ghilotti S, Fonte R, Magri F, Chiovato L. Serum negative autoimmune thyroiditis displays a milder clinical picture compared with classic Hashimoto's thyroiditis. *Eur J Endocrinol.* 2014 July; 171(1):31–36. doi: 10.1530/EJE-14-0147.

15 Lee S, Farwell AP. Euthyroid Sick Syndrome. *Compr Physiol.* 2016 March 15; 6(2):1071–1080. doi: 10.1002/cphy.c150017.

Chapter 9

Electrolytes and Stopping Purging

Case: Manuel

Manuel is a 21-year-old cisgender Latino college student. He has always lived in a larger body, receiving countless comments and looks each day. Having tried many diets throughout his life, only to gain more weight, he resolves to make things change in his senior year. He starts a diet that strictly prohibits multiple food groups and as a result feels ravenous all the time. One night, he binges on all the foods he's been craving, and then, full of shame, he throws up. Almost overnight, that becomes his pattern: restricting calories throughout the day, only to binge and purge every night. As he secretly engages in his eating disorder, and his weight falls a little, people around him (including his doctor) compliment him. Knowing what he's doing can't be good for him, Manuel nonetheless feels all the more determined to keep going. He starts to weigh himself compulsively, several times a day. When the scale shows a slightly lower number, his spirits soar. When that number goes up, he despairs. To try and empty himself further, he begins abusing laxatives. At first, it's one or two a day to overcome the constipation he's developed since starting to lose weight. Then the number of laxatives he takes creeps up. He spends his evenings nauseated, crampy, and having multiple episodes of diarrhea. On a day that the scale goes up a little, he grimly orders a bunch of diuretics online and begins taking those too.

Manuel feels awful, emotionally and physically. His friends have all expressed their concern that their warm, kind friend seems to have disappeared from their lives. His church community, previously an essential part of his social and spiritual life, misses him. Manuel rationalizes that he must be fine, because he's still going to all his college classes and getting reasonably good grades. However, he feels weak all the time. When he stands up, he gets lightheaded and sweaty, and his muscles hurt. His throat and mouth are sore from all the purging, his cheeks have become firm and swollen, and his thoughts feel fuzzy and unfocused.

One weekend, realizing he's spiraling out of control, Manuel throws away all his laxatives and diuretics and swears he's "done" and is going to try to eat normally again. He even stays off the scale. By Monday morning, Manuel wakes with swelling in his hands, feet, and abdomen. Panicking, he pulls out his scale and is horrified to see he's gained ten pounds. Now he's certain he's ruined his metabolism and his body, validated in his belief that his weight will skyrocket if he doesn't follow his eating disorder's commands fully. He rushes to the store to buy more laxatives. On Wednesday after class, his chest feeling heavy, he stands up and passes out. His professor calls 911, and he is transported to the hospital.

In the emergency room, Manuel is found to have a resting pulse of 90 and blood pressure of 100/60. When he stands, his pulse rises to 130, his blood pressure drops to 70/45, and he feels dizzy. Labs show a potassium level of 2.8 mEq/L (normal 3.6–5.1 mEq/L), a sodium level of 125 mEq/L (normal 135–143 mEq/L), a bicarbonate level of 36 mEq/L (normal 22–28 mEq/L), and a magnesium of 1.1 mEq/L (normal 1.5–2.5 mEq/L). His EKG shows a QTc interval of 505 msec (normal 350–450 msec). The doctor who cares for Manuel compassionately sits with him, reviews his results, and tells him he's critically ill and must be admitted to the intensive care unit (ICU) immediately.

Background

Years ago, I admitted a wonderful woman in her early 30s, a schoolteacher with anorexia nervosa, purging subtype, to the hospital. Her lab results on admission were frightening: dangerously low potassium and evidence of severe dehydration. As I sat with her on that admission day and expressed how concerned I was, I assured her we'd be working carefully to bring her back into balance medically without causing significant and dangerous medical complications. She looked at me in puzzlement, tears welling in her eyes.

> "But Dr. G," she said. "I had labs that looked just like this 2 weeks ago, and the nurse practitioner in my primary care office called me and said my labs were a 'little off' and recommended I just eat some potato chips and drink some water. I almost didn't agree to come to the hospital because I figured I wasn't sick enough."

This chapter is not intended as some dry medical text on laboratory findings and their treatment. Rather, patients and their loved ones have to become well read advocates when it comes to electrolytes and the process of stopping purging. The problem is, many medical professionals do not know how to interpret laboratory values in patients who purge, much less treat them appropriately and safely. This places some therapists and dietitians in the awkward position of playing de-facto doctor, as they find themselves out of their comfort zone trying to answer patients' questions about lab findings.

The Emergency Department: Life-Saving but Suboptimal for Those with Eating Disorders

A therapist or dietitian may plead with a patient to seek emergency department care out of a very real fear that the patient's heart might stop that night. While it is always correct to seek help when needed, the experience of the emergency department may pose many challenges for patients who purge. Too often, even when the therapist or dietitian is proactive and brave enough to call ahead and give the doctors a heads-up, they get dismissed by a medical system that remains, unfortunately, hierarchical.

The patient, feeling miserable both from the symptoms of her eating disorder and from her dread of the upcoming experience, arrives at the hospital. First, she may sit through long waits while others who are deemed to be sicker get care first. This is necessary for an emergency room setting that must triage care. However, patients with eating disorders can be down-triaged inappropriately, given their tendency to be polite, patient, and poor at self-advocacy. It can be confusing to have a therapist beg you to seek emergency care because she's so worried you're about to drop dead and then wait six hours in a waiting room before being seen.

By this time, the eating disorder may be about done with waiting and inconvenience. The hustle and chaos of the emergency room are overwhelming. Distress and anxiety rise, tolerance wanes, and all the person wants to do is escape home to soothe by engaging in behaviors. Many patients leave before they've even been seen. If the patient does manage to stay, getting an intravenous (IV) line placed can offer the next challenge. In the context of many prior IVs, veins can become scarred. It's uncomfortable to be stuck eight times only to end up with an IV line in the foot.

In the ensuing hours, patients may hear comments like, "It says here you have an eating disorder. You're not that thin. I wish I had a little bit of an eating disorder. I could stand to lose 10 pounds, you know?" Or, "There are actual sick people here. Go home and eat bananas and drink water." Or, "Yeah, your potassium is a little low, but this one time I saw someone with an eating disorder whose potassium was really low! You're not that bad."

These are well-meaning comments. After all, if a person came in with a broken arm, this kind of comparison would feel reassuring and positive. "Okay good, my fracture's not the worst they've seen!" But for someone with an eating disorder, it feels shameful: "I knew I didn't need to be here. I'm so embarrassed I've spent the money/time and caused my family to worry, not to mention keeping those really sick people out there from getting care in a timelier way."

Finally, the nature of the medical care provided is often suboptimal: too much fluid infused too fast, intravenous potassium that burns the vein, a huge dose of oral potassium that causes nausea. No one means to offer suboptimal care. Doctors simply aren't trained in eating disorder medicine, and a busy emergency department is not a great place for a highly sensitive soul. After all this, the patient is discharged from the emergency department with the warm assurance of, "You're fine now. Just follow up with your doctor in a couple of days." With edema already starting to develop, and exhausted to the core, the patient slinks home knowing how not fine they are in their soul. This encounter might save the patient in the moment from cardiac arrest due to low potassium, but it's a revolving door. They've been triggered and then sent straight back into the arms of their eating disorder.

Potassium

Let's go through all of the electrolytes that purging affects. While every laboratory will have its unique parameters for describing normal values, there's a helpful rule I learned as a first-year doctor, the "2–3–4 rule." Generally speaking, magnesium should be about 2 mg/dL, phosphorus should be about 3 mg/dL, and potassium should be about 4 mEq/L. A low potassium level is called hypokalemia.

Potassium levels drop because this vital electrolyte is lost in vomit, diarrhea, and urine in those who purge via vomiting, laxative abuse, and/or diuretics. Any one of these modalities, much less several used at the same time, can cause hypokalemia. The risk for medical complications particularly rises when the potassium falls below 3 mEq/L. At that point, the patient is at risk for muscle weakness or muscle breakdown, including breathing muscle weakness, intestinal dysfunction (usually constipation and cramps), and the most dangerous: cardiac arrest due to an arrhythmia.

Patients who purge must always consider themselves to be at risk for their heart stopping from low potassium. One cannot predict when it will happen. As I discussed in Chapter 4, this is called cardiac arrest. Unless this event is witnessed and expertly managed by cardiopulmonary resuscitation (CPR) almost immediately, it leads to permanent neurologic damage or death. Low potassium can cause cardiac arrest through various arrhythmias, one of the commonest being a deadly rhythm called torsades de pointes.

The first sign that a patient's heart is at risk for the medical emergency of torsades de pointes is a prolonged QTc interval on an EKG. The QTc is a measurement on the EKG between the start of the Q wave and the end of the T wave, corrected ("c") for heart rate. Critical prolongation (i.e., the length of the QT interval) is generally thought to be over 500 msec, although arrhythmias can occur at lower QTc levels.[1] Anyone with this kind of QTc prolongation should be immediately admitted to a cardiac monitoring floor of a medical hospital.

Low potassium levels and medications (including many psychiatric medications) can also prolong the QTc.[2] In the denial of their mental illness, patients might say, "Sure, that might happen to others, but I'm not sick enough for that to happen to me. I'm fine." Ask the grieving parents, partners, and siblings about their loved ones who also knew they'd be fine. The scientific fact is that low potassium can and does kill.

To be clear, not all patients who purge develop abnormal lab values. They can feel terribly invalidated by this fact. All too often, a well-meaning provider questions whether the patient is actually participating in the degree of purging behaviors they say they are. I can only refer patients back to the concept of genetic variability. Some people must have a more protective electrolyte response to purging than others. In these cases, it's not the level of the potassium that primarily drives the recommendation for the patient to seek help. Instead, I recommend recovery work based on the degree to which the emotional suffering of the mental illness and the behaviors themselves are negatively influencing a person's ability to live their values.

Treatment of Low Potassium

Potassium can be supplemented in two ways: by mouth (tablet or liquid) or by intravenous infusion. Potassium tablets are large and can be hard to swallow for some people. The oral liquid tastes terrible. Both forms of oral potassium can cause burning in the stomach, which may already be raw from purging. I've even had a patient think they were having a heart attack when they took potassium pills on an irritated stomach. For that reason, it's best not to take too much potassium at once and always important to take them with plenty of water and, ideally, food.

For that reason, I try not to prescribe more than two potassium pills at once, especially since it can be given several times a day. Oral potassium comes in milliquivalents (mEq), and it's most often prescribed in 20 mEq pills. A general rule of thumb is that for every 0.1 that the potassium level is less than 4.0 mEq/L, the patient needs 10 mEq. So, if the potassium is 3.2 mEq/L, the patient will need at least 80 mEq to get it back up near 4.0 mEq/L, possibly over a couple days (if no further losses take place). For severely low potassium levels or when there is evidence of prolonged QTc from low potassium levels, intravenous potassium is vital. However, it burns the vein and can cause a previously intact IV access to stop working. Whenever possible, potassium should be replaced by mouth.

Bicarbonate and Chloride

The bicarbonate, or "bicarb," denoted as the "CO2" on some lab reports, is a standard part of the basic metabolic panel, sometimes also called a chemistry panel. The bicarb level is a key measure in determining a patient's blood pH balance. A very low bicarb usually means that someone has acidic blood, which can occur in a variety of situations, such as chronic diarrhea, some medication overdoses, muscle breakdown from starvation or a complication of diabetes, or kidney failure. A very high bicarb, on the other hand, is typically a sign that a patient has more alkaline blood. In those who purge, a high bicarb is a marker of severe dehydration, called "volume depletion" medically. The official term for a patient who has a high bicarb is a "contraction metabolic alkalosis."

Whenever the bicarb is over 30 mEq/L (normal is 22–28 mEq/L), in someone who purges, I know that their body is volume depleted. When the bicarb is over 40 mEq/L, I refer the patient urgently to a hospital because their risk of seizure and of other medical complications is extremely high.

Patients who abuse laxatives typically have significant dehydration, but because of the diarrheal losses, the bicarbonate can look normal. The blood acidity from diarrhea (low bicarb) cancels out the alkalotic state of volume depletion (high bicarb). Unfortunately, providers can miss this and assume values are normal when the patient in fact has two serious acid-base abnormalities going on at the same time. Later in this chapter, when I discuss preventing rebound edema and purging cessation, I'll talk more about the implication of a high bicarbonate level. The electrolyte chloride has little independent clinical significance.

Low Sodium and Low Volume Status (Dehydration)

The serum sodium is a confusing electrolyte because of its name. People assume that if their sodium is low, it means that they have a low level of salt in their blood. However, the blood sodium level is more precisely a measure of the ratio between blood salt and blood water. Low sodium levels can plague those with eating disorders of all varieties, from restrictive anorexia nervosa to bulimia nervosa, and there are many different causes.

It's worthwhile to start with a framework for how to understand sodium, so that it makes more sense in any given clinical situation. When someone has a low blood sodium level, called hyponatremia, the first assessment must be their hydration status. In medicine, we use the term "volume status," which reflects both salt and water levels, rather than "dehydration," which officially refers to low blood water levels only. When someone has a virus with vomiting and diarrhea, an injury with blood loss, or they sweat copiously, they lose both salt and water and become volume depleted.

So, let's say a patient has a low serum sodium. Knowing that they purge chronically, we understand they are volume depleted. The fix will therefore be to replenish both salt and water. Sometimes this can be done by drinking fluids and eating salty foods, and sometimes it requires intravenous fluid.

Low Sodium and Normal Volume Status

When a person purely restricts calories, the serum sodium can become low as well. Again, we start by considering the volume status. In this case, the patient is not volume depleted. However, our kidneys need a certain amount of food every day to be able to package up the water we drink and excrete it as urine. Individuals who are eating an appropriate amount of food each day are able to drink more than 15 liters (almost four gallons) of water without any appreciable change in their serum sodium level. The body is exquisitely tuned to keep the serum sodium stable.

However, caloric restriction can result in a reduced ability to package up and urinate excess water. As a result, patients may overwhelm their ability to get rid of water after even two liters of non-caloric fluid intake a day. The body water level rises while the sodium levels remain the same, and as a result, the lab test shows hyponatremia. The fix here is to avoid excessive water intake and increase calories. Often, drinking no more than two liters of fluid a day is sufficient to let the body get rid of the excess water.

Normally, a hormone called vasopressin is released from the pituitary gland to retain blood water. When vasopressin secretion works properly, it keeps our body water levels in perfect balance. In the syndrome of inappropriate anti-diuretic hormone secretion, or SIADH, overly high levels of vasopressin are released. As a result, the blood water level rises and causes hyponatremia. Psychiatric medications, narcotics, and major physiologic trauma can all cause SIADH.

In addition, patients with a disorder called psychogenic polydipsia can develop severe hyponatremia. Psychogenic polydipsia refers to someone with an insatiable craving to drink water. They might obsessively seek it out and then deny having done so. One of my patients adamantly denied ever overdrinking, despite recurrent admissions for severe hyponatremia. Then her parents found her entire car trunk full of empty water bottles. (When faced with this evidence, she still denied having consumed it.) In both SIADH and psychogenic polydipsia, limiting water intake to 2–3 liters a day will resolve the problem as long as reasonable calories are also being eaten.

Low Sodium and High Volume Status

The third and final volume status, excess fluid in the body, is less common in those with eating disorders, at least before treatment begins. General medicine patients with liver failure, heart failure, or kidney failure often have a high volume status. The body cannot get rid of redundant fluid and salt, and it builds up both in the vasculature and sometimes also in the body tissues as edema. In those cases, the excess water in the blood causes hyponatremia.

Treating Low Sodium

The medical correction of hyponatremia can be dangerous. Overly rapid correction can cause irreversible, catastrophic neurologic damage, called central pontine myelinolysis (CPM). Females and those with alcohol abuse are at even higher risk for CPM from rapid correction of hyponatremia. The current medical guidelines recommend that the serum sodium increase by no more than 4–6 mEq/L every 24 hours.[3] That is, if someone has a sodium of 125 mEq/L upon admission, by the next morning, the goal sodium level is 129–131 mEq/L.

For that reason, and because even for doctors sodium problems can be tricky to manage, severe cases of hyponatremia should generally be managed in an ICU. Patients who live chronically at a low sodium levels usually have no symptoms. However, those whose sodium drops rapidly can become confused, with slurred speech, fatigue, exhaustion, and even seizure.

High Sodium and Diabetes Insipidus

High serum sodium, or hypernatremia, is rarer than hyponatremia in those with eating disorders. Normally, when our serum sodium levels rise, even to around 144 mEq/L, our drive to drink fluids becomes intense; we become extremely thirsty and seek water. There are rare individuals with eating disorders who not only resist their hunger cues, but their thirst cues too. Through water restriction their serum sodium level rises, although I've rarely seen it go above 145 mEq/L. Simply drinking fluids fixes this.

As previously discussed, the hypothalamus and pituitary gland in the brain react to malnutrition and weight loss, for instance in the cessation of sex hormone production. In cases of extreme malnutrition, I have witnessed several patients develop a problem called diabetes insipidus, or DI. Confusingly enough, this has nothing to do with diabetes mellitus (which is what most people simply call "diabetes"). DI can be understood as the opposite of SIADH. DI is caused either by failure of the pituitary gland to make sufficient anti-diuretic hormone or by the kidneys' resistance to it. The former occurs in those with severe malnutrition. Anti-diuretic hormone keeps us from urinating away needed water in the blood.

Patients may be insatiably thirsty and drink over seven liters of fluid a day, but because the brain isn't producing the hormone to hold on to that water, they also pee over seven liters a day. These patients develop a sodium that's high, ranging from 144–147 mEq/L. Sometimes hormonal intervention is needed, under very careful medical monitoring. Most often, I recommend proceeding with nutritional rehabilitation, and eventually the proper center in the brain will turn back on and function.

Magnesium

Patients with eating disorders can have overall depletion of their magnesium levels, but it is not one of the electrolytes I focus on too much because it does not appear to have high clinical significance except in medically hospitalized patients. Back in my hospital days, there were some patients who needed supplementation with magnesium for a few days at the start of refeeding, but potassium and phosphorus are far more important. It is worthwhile to note that oral magnesium supplements are nearly useless for improving serum magnesium levels as they mostly just cause diarrhea. To get magnesium levels to rise, one really needs to use intravenous magnesium sulfate.

Calcium

The blood calcium is exquisitely regulated by various hormones, and much of it is bound to the protein albumin. Whenever the body needs a little more calcium, it has the entire skeletal system to draw from, such that our daily dietary ingestion doesn't impact the blood level of calcium. A low serum albumin, relatively rare in those with even advanced eating disorders, can make the serum calcium look low, but a simple mathematical correction shows that the effective calcium level is normal. Other problems such as parathyroid hormone (PTH) abnormalities and abnormal vitamin D levels can also influence the serum calcium.

Kidney Function: Blood Urea Nitrogen and Creatinine

The final component of the basic metabolic laboratory panel to review is the blood urea nitrogen (BUN) and creatinine (Cr). These are markers of kidney function and protein digestion. Cr is the byproduct of normal muscle breakdown. It is used clinically to help determine how well a person's kidneys are working.

There is a difference between a laboratory's normal range for a test and what is actually expected for a given patient. A normal Cr level for any individual varies depending on their weight, muscularity, sex, and age. In general, a larger, muscular young man can have a higher Cr level that is normal up to a level of 1.2 or 1.3 mg/dL. By contrast, an older woman with low body weight and low muscle mass might have a maximum normal Cr of 0.6 mg/dL.

While the laboratory "normal" range usually covers Cr levels of 0.5–1.2 mg/dL, one can quickly see that this number has to be individualized for interpretation. A basic rule of thumb is that every time a person's Cr doubles, their kidney function falls by 50 percent. A young woman with anorexia nervosa, purging subtype, who is chronically volume depleted, might present with a creatinine Cr of 1.2 mg/dL. The lab report shows this is in the normal range. But clinically, I know that based on her age and low weight, it should be no more than 0.7 mg/dL. Therefore, she's already lost half of her kidney function due to chronic dehydration. This is easily missed by clinicians who are not familiar with eating disorders. In this case, the kidney function is typically not lost permanently. Acute kidney injury of this type can arise from dehydration or low blood pressure, and often it can still normalize with recovery work, even after being abnormal for quite a long time.

The BUN is a measure of protein breakdown and kidney function. Normal values are around 7–20 mg/dL. Most often, if a person is in kidney failure, their BUN rises. However, the BUN can be used for other subtle assessments. For instance, when the BUN:Cr ratio is greater than 20:1, it can signal volume depletion.

High protein intake can raise the BUN in a way that is not pathologic. For instance, when a patient is several weeks into nutritional rehabilitation and eating a lot of calories (and thus a fair amount of protein), their BUN can rise. This simply means the body is breaking down that protein normally. Along similar lines, if someone has an upper GI bleed—say, from their stomach or their small intestine—nutritionally this blood is absorbed and digested like a protein meal, and the BUN may increase.

Stopping Purging

Now we come to one of my favorite topics: the severe rebound edema that patients may experience when they stop purging. This is a problem that utterly plagues my patients who purge, holding them back from recovery work and keeping them sick longer. It triggers them to continue or resume behaviors that can cause serious harm. With relatively simple medical concepts, it is easy to make a big difference medically, but few doctors know about it.

Pseudo-Bartter Syndrome

As we've seen time and again, our brilliant cave person brain is working behind the scenes to keep us alive. When someone purges chronically, their cave person brain only understands that they are chronically volume depleted and interprets this as, "We must be dying of dehydration in the desert." It scans the suffering body and interprets that there is a chronic, severe deficiency of salt and water. It concludes, "If I am so lucky as to come upon an oasis in this desert, with access to salt and water, I had better upregulate any hormone that will prevent me from peeing away those life-saving resources." This is exactly what our body does.

Specifically, the cave person brain upregulates production of the steroid hormone aldosterone in our adrenal glands, which sit like little caps on top of our kidneys. Aldosterone plays a few vital roles in this clinical context, some helpful and some not so helpful. First, high levels of aldosterone make our kidneys hold on to nearly every molecule of salt and water we take in, either by mouth or by IV fluids. Conserving water and salt is the main reason the body overproduces aldosterone. Second, aldosterone happens to make the kidneys dump potassium out of the blood and into the urine for excretion.

This overproduction of hormone is called "secondary hyperaldosteronism." The "secondary" part means that the glands are producing it in response to some other condition, not primarily from a tumor. The other term for secondary hyperaldosteronism is "pseudo-Bartter syndrome." As a result of pseudo-Bartter syndrome, patients can end up with painful, triggering fluid retention when they stop purging and start to hydrate. The adrenal glands take a couple weeks to get the message that their owner is now safe and well hydrated. They will keep overproducing aldosterone the whole time. This is the cause of rebound edema in those who purge.[4]

We know that people who purge can end up with dangerously low potassium levels. Thus, the last thing in the world we want is to waste potassium in the urine, but that's what happens in pseudo-Bartter syndrome. As long as someone is dehydrated from purging, they will continue to urinate away potassium. No matter how much potassium I give a patient, if they remain dehydrated from ongoing purging, I will not be able to normalize it easily.

The diagnosis of pseudo-Bartter syndrome is made clinically. There's no blood test. However, the blood bicarbonate level is a great help. Remember that a high bicarbonate level, also called contraction metabolic alkalosis, is a marker of volume depletion. When a patient who purges has a bicarbonate level of $30\,mEq/L$ or more, I am confident they have pseudo-Bartter syndrome. The one exception is in those who purge via laxative abuse, who as described above may have a normal bicarbonate level due to two concurrent acid-base abnormalities. If they take enough laxatives regularly to cause diarrhea, even without a high bicarb, they too have pseudo-Bartter syndrome.

Treatment of Pseudo-Bartter Syndrome

The good news is that pseudo-Bartter syndrome can be managed medically, perhaps not to the point of entirely preventing edema, but enough to make a huge difference compared with no treatment at all. With this medical management, I have helped countless patients "detox" from purging, and they've resumed having faith in their bodies again.

There are three key aspects to medical management. One, the patient has to stop purging completely—no easy task, I know. But if they really want to detox off purging, they have to stop altogether. Any purging at all continues to fuel the cave person brain's message to the adrenals: keep producing that aldosterone.

Second, the patient needs gentle hydration. We have to turn off the sensor in the brain that clamors, "Dehydrated!" In the hospital setting, this means intravenous fluids no faster than 50–75 ml/hr, and only until the bicarbonate is under 30 and the serum sodium is normalized. In the outpatient setting, this might mean 2–3 liters of oral fluids a day and unrestricted sodium intake. It does *not* mean that patients should start "flushing their systems" with gallons of fluids. I liken this to a bathtub with a clogged drain. You wouldn't turn on both taps as high as they can go when the bathtub's drain is slow, or the bathtub will overflow. Similarly, in pseudo-Bartter syndrome, it's a good idea not to flood the body with fluids for a couple weeks.

Third, and vitally, the aldosterone itself must be blocked. A cheap, highly effective medicine called spironolactone accomplishes this. Spironolactone is a weak diuretic, used in such diverse medical problems as acne, congestive heart failure, and high blood pressure. Spironolactone directly blocks aldosterone. Additionally, it helps boost potassium levels, thus accomplishing the two most necessary tasks.

Some of my patients look concerned when I mention spironolactone and say, "Um, Dr. G, the whole point is that I have a problem with diuretics and purging. Why are you putting me on a diuretic?" I reassure them that spironolactone is too weak a diuretic to be abused. I prescribe anywhere from 25 mg of spironolactone daily to 100 mg daily in cases where patients have had truly severe edema in the past. Even those with low blood pressure can typically tolerate spironolactone just fine, although I ask patients to watch for any dizziness. Usually patients need just two to three weeks of spironolactone if they are following all of the detox from purging rules.

There is an exception to this rule, however, and that is in patients who abuse laxatives. Laxative abuse forces an immense amount of body water out of the cells, out of the blood, and into the lumen of the intestine, where it is excreted as diarrhea. Far more fluid can be lost via the colon than via vomiting or diuretics, simply because the intestinal system has such a large surface area. As a result, patients who abuse laxatives typically present as the most dehydrated of all patients who purge. Whether a patient has anorexia nervosa, purging subtype, or bulimia nervosa, a substantial portion of decreased weight in those who abuse laxatives may come from volume depletion rather than actual body weight loss. That means their pseudo-Bartter syndrome is going to be particularly severe.

Unfortunately, spironolactone doesn't work as well in those who abuse laxatives. Therefore, I have heartfelt conversations with my patients who do so. I talk about how vital it is to stop the abuse, and that I will give them a higher dose of spironolactone for a longer period of time than normal. I ask them to throw away their scale at home because even with best medical management, their weight and size will change rapidly as their desperately dehydrated bodies finally are allowed to hydrate. Often, I will use 50–100 mg of spironolactone a day for six weeks, as long as they have stopped purging, and I will check the patient's blood potassium level once a week initially to be sure it's not going too high. I note that even if they and I do everything "right," they are still likely to end up with some edema. It will go away over a few weeks, but it's going to be hard on the psyche. I additionally promise to follow them medically very closely to manage their bowel regimen. Stimulant laxatives must be stopped altogether and replaced by safer, osmotic laxatives. There is no medical reason to "taper" stimulant laxatives.

Even with great medical care, detox from purging can be a time of immense challenge for patients with eating disorders. Change is already a scary theme, and the body can change very quickly during early recovery work. This is because going from a dehydrated state to a hydrated state, even without edema, changes the weight, size, and shape of the body over the course of a few days. Most of my patients have heard a well-meaning person in their life say, "But it's just fluid weight. It's not real weight." However, fluid weight can be just as frightening for my patients who purge as "real" weight. Where the eating disorder may have become obsessed with emptiness at all costs, simply living life hydrated can pose a painful challenge.

Lots of therapeutic and dietary support will be needed during this time, as well as comfort and kindness from friends and loved ones. Of course, patients who purge less, and some who have different genetic susceptibilities, may never experience fluid shifts or substantially abnormal laboratory values. That doesn't mean they aren't sick enough to seek recovery. It simply means they will have less medical complexity during the recovery process.

Case Resolution: Manuel

In the ICU, the doctors are familiar with eating disorder medicine and make the diagnosis of bulimia nervosa. The team assesses that Manuel has profound volume depletion, and they know about the risks of pseudo-Bartter syndrome. They begin normal saline that has a little potassium in it at 75 ml/hr and give Manuel 50 mg of spironolactone a day, starting that first day, even when he has low blood pressure. Manuel's serum sodium is checked every four hours because they know it should not rise more than 4–6 mEq in 24 hours. The ICU team administers 60 mEq of oral potassium upon arrival, and then prescribes 40 mEq twice a day, knowing that more than that will just make his stomach ache. Intravenous magnesium is started, and this continues until his levels are consistently above 2 mEq/L. Two days later, Manuel has a normal serum sodium, normal potassium, normal bicarbonate, normal magnesium, normal vital signs, and his EKG QTc interval has normalized as well.

Manuel is transferred out of the ICU to the medical ward, and he feels absolutely miserable. His body looks and feels different to him because he is no longer dehydrated, even though he has no edema. Knowing that he has to make meaningful progress toward recovery, he eats the food the hospital brings him and does not purge, but it's a huge struggle, especially without psychological support. The social worker offers to connect him with residential eating disorder programs, and he reluctantly accepts these referrals. His eating disorder tells him to refuse, that he can simply go home and "do this by himself," but in his heart, he knows he needs a higher level of care. He worries that being in a larger body will mean that he's not sick enough to enter residential care, but upon completing intakes, he learns that he does indeed meet the guidelines. He transfers from the hospital to residential programming and completes a full course of treatment. When it's time for him to discharge from the facility, the staff members make sure that he has referrals to a terrific eating disorder therapist, dietitian, and doctor, upon return to school.

The Sponge Metaphor and Finding Self-Compassion

When discussing dehydration, rehydration, and edema, I tell patients the sponge story. There are three types of sponges. On one side of the spectrum, there's the hard, dry sponge that's been sitting on the counter for a week. On the other side of the spectrum, there's the sopping, dripping sponge you get after running the sponge under the water. In between, there's a soft, pliable sponge that doesn't have an extra drop of water in it.

I tell my patients who purge that presently they are like the dry, hard sponge. I want to avoid making them like the sopping sponge. Instead, I want for them to be the middle sponge. To do this, we have to do the equivalent of putting the dry sponge in the sink and dripping water slowly onto it while checking it regularly ... not flooding it with the faucet fully open.

I recommend oral intake of food, 2–3 liters (60–90 ounces) of fluids daily, and IV fluids if a patient has symptoms of dizziness or orthostatic vital signs that don't respond to cessation of purging. Patients with bicarbonate levels above 35 mEq/L and serum sodium levels below 130 mEq/L almost always need IV fluids. Patients with blood work that looks a little better than this, and who don't have symptoms that demand IV fluids, can often improve with good multidisciplinary team support, attention to purging cessation, and improvement in oral intake.

Many individuals with eating disorders find that their eating disorder voice makes them react to their own thoughts, actions, accomplishments, and needs with a meanness they would never express to a loved one. I once saw my friend, the brilliant psychiatrist Dr. Kimberli McCallum, give a lecture on mindfulness. The teaching she offered on self-compassion affected me deeply, and I have passed a version of it along to patients ever since.

I ask my patients to imagine a recent experience in which they judged themselves unkindly. They might have said to themselves, "That was stupid of me," or "I'm so inadequate" or "What a disappointment I am." While everyone can learn from difficult situations and be open to doing better next time, none of these reactions are particularly constructive. They just make us feel small and empty.

We must first recognize when we are being self-critical. Then, we can reframe the situation and say, "That was a painful experience" instead of judging. The moment we relabel what occurred as "painful" instead of reacting with harsh judgment, something shifts. Our inner compassion emerges—fully functioning and able to soothe children, friends, and pets, if not the self—and it actually can offer comfort. We acknowledge that, for whatever reason, the experience was painful to us. We can offer compassion for that fact. Then, rather than continue to ruminate on it, we release it and move on.

Notes

1 Al-Khatib SM, LaPointe NM, Kramer JM, Califf RM. What clinicians should know about the QT interval. *JAMA*. 2003 April 23–30; 289(16):2120–2127. PubMed PMID: 12709470.

2 Arunachalam K, Lakshmanan S, Maan A, Kumar N, Dominic P. Impact of drug induced long QT syndrome: a systematic review. *J Clin Med Res*. 2018 May; 10(5):384–390. doi: 10.14740/jocmr3338w.

3 Verbalis JG, Goldsmith SR, Greenberg A, Korzelius C, Schrier RW, Sterns RH, Thompson CJ. Diagnosis, evaluation, and treatment of hyponatremia: expert panel recommendations. *Am J Med*. 2013 October; 126(10 Suppl. 1):S1–42. doi: 10.1016/j.amjmed.2013.07.006.

4 Bahia A, Mascolo M, Gaudiani JL, Mehler PS. PseudoBartter syndrome in eating disorders. *Int J Eat Disord*. 2012 January; 45(1):150–153. doi: 10.1002/eat.20906.

Part III

Patients in Larger Bodies

We've now discussed in detail the medical complications of caloric restriction and of purging, both of which can occur in individuals with bodies of all shapes and sizes. Part III turns to patients in larger bodies, specifically the medical problems of weight stigma and of binge eating disorder (BED), the commonest, and perhaps least talked about, of all eating disorders. Not everyone with BED is in a larger body, and not every person in a larger body has BED. In fact, most people in larger bodies do not meet criteria for BED.[1] You cannot tell who has an eating disorder or who is healthy or unhealthy just by looking at them.

You might notice that I did not use the words "overweight" or "obese." This was quite deliberate, and outside of this mention, you won't find these words anywhere in this book. A chapter on BED must lay out some vitally important concepts that have to do with weight stigma, shame, diet culture, and social justice. I will also challenge, with medical evidence, some fundamental assumptions that people (including doctors) have about those in larger bodies. In this chapter I will focus predominantly on patients with BED in larger bodies as well as some of the overlapping implications for any individual in a larger body. The reason for this is not to exclude smaller-bodied patients with BED, but to bring needed attention to the social justice issues and medical implications of size stigma.

Emerging from my medical training, I thought I knew a fair bit about higher body weight. My training focused on the role of weight gain in the development of certain medical problems and the role of weight loss in the mitigation of those problems. Unfortunately, my training wasn't only dramatically incomplete, it taught me to cause harm. There was no discussion of weight stigma, social justice, privilege, or size diversity. My goal in this chapter is to make the case for a different language, a different awareness of the data, and a different take entirely on the care of patients in larger bodies. I will draw upon the written and spoken teachings of leaders in the field of BED and of advocacy, recognizing that the field, and my knowledge of it, continues to expand.

BED is characterized in the DSM-5 by recurrent episodes of binge eating, as defined by eating a large amount of food, in a relatively short period of time, associated with a sense of lack of control and distress over the quantity or pace of eating or type of food consumed. The binges are associated with at least three of the following criteria: eating rapidly, eating until uncomfortably full, eating large amounts despite not feeling physically hungry, eating alone due to embarrassment about the nature of the binge, or feeling disgusted, depressed, or guilty after the binge. Bingeing must occur once a week for three months, on average, and no purging or other compensatory behaviors are used.[2] Typically, individuals with BED also restrict calories or specific food groups in the course of their disorder. The deprivation-binge cycle is well known both to those who meet formal criteria for BED and to anyone who has ever dieted before.

BED was only formally added to the DSM-5 in 2013, which means that medical research on BED lags behind that on anorexia nervosa and bulimia nervosa. However, clinicians have been aware of it for years. Prevalence estimates for BED are that 2–4 percent of the population likely meet the criteria for BED at some point in their lives, and people of all genders are affected equally.[3] This means, for instance, that in the United States alone between six and 12 million people likely meet the criteria for BED.

These data may substantially under-represent the actual prevalence. New data show that all eating disorders may be far more common than previously thought in individuals from the lowest socioeconomic strata, who are rarely represented in such studies. Those with food insecurity, for instance, rely on food banks to feed themselves and their families. They experience starvation and food deprivation not primarily because of a fear of weight gain but because of lack of access to food.

Groundbreaking research studied individuals presenting to a food bank who agreed to be interviewed about their eating patterns and answered questions related to eating disorder behaviors. This vitally important studiy showed that the more food insecure people were, the higher their likelihood of eating disorder behaviors.[4] Regardless of the cause of food deprivation, the cave person brain responds. It doesn't know the source of undernourishment. It only knows that it has a drive for food, a need to protect the body weight, and a starved brain that reacts in unexpected ways around food, as did the men of the Minnesota experiment (see Chapter 2). This is a striking example of the fact that eating disorders do not just affect young, thin, wealthy, white girls, and it pointedly reminds us how many people lack access to diagnosis and treatment of their eating disorder.

Let's talk about the terms I will use in this chapter and the ones I will not. Words that pathologize higher body weight are out. You know by now that this isn't because I eschew Western medical traditions and science—quite the opposite. Pathologizing words, though, make doctors miss vital realities about their patients' health, and they shame patients. Instead, I will use the phrase "people in larger bodies" or "higher weight individuals." Activists have reclaimed the word "fat" in order to destigmatize it, to remind us that it is simply a descriptor, rather than a judgment. I ask my patients in larger bodies, "What words would you like me to use to refer to your size, when needed?"

Any higher body weight is viewed by society and much of medicine as not only medically dangerous but morally lax. BMI charts often paper the walls of a medical office. Medical office furniture fails to accommodate patients with larger bodies, either having restrictively narrow arms that prevent comfortable sitting or spindly legs that could potentially give out. The examination gown may be far too small, making an already awkward encounter deeply undignified and further heightening shame. Blood pressure cuffs may not fit, yielding not only poor data but also further proof that this patient is not acceptable in the doctor's office. Patients who (reluctantly) go to the doctor for a sore throat can end up receiving dieting recommendations and warnings about their weight before their chief problem is even addressed.

Notes

1 www.nationaleatingdisorders.org/learn/by-eating-disorder/bed. Accessed August 3, 2018.
2 American Psychiatric Association. *Diagnostic and statistical manual of mental disorders (5th ed.)* Arlington, VA: American Psychiatric Publishing; 2013.
3 www.nationaleatingdisorders.org/statistics-research-eating-disorders. Accessed April 15, 2018.
4 Becker CB, Middlemass K, Taylor B, Johnson C, Gomez F. Food insecurity and eating disorder pathology. *Int J Eat Disord.* 2017 September; 50(9):1031–1040. doi: 10.1002/eat.22735.

Chapter 10

Binge Eating Disorder (BED) and Weight Stigma

Case: Janet

Janet is a 41-year-old cisgender Caucasian female executive who has been in a larger body her whole life. When she was six years old, her older sister and school friends started to tease her about her weight. At age 11, she and her mother did their first commercial diet together. She lost a few pounds over the course of a few months and felt miserable the entire time, highly self-conscious of every bite she ate and with an increasing sense that her body was "wrong." Once off the diet, Janet grew in height and gained weight, a fact that her experienced pediatrician noted was absolutely appropriate during adolescence, but that Janet understood as a failure. In her family, she and her mother were the "big" ones who were always dieting, while her father and sister always had smaller bodies who could "eat anything." Janet keenly felt the messages, both spoken and unspoken, that her father and sister sent her way: "If you could only control your eating, you'd be thin like us."

Over the next several decades, Janet tried virtually every diet imaginable. She would lose weight only to gain it back, plus some. She had always been athletic, and she played two varsity sports in high school and then intramural sports in college. Everywhere she went, she could feel people eyeing and judging her size.

In her 20s, Janet started working full time and quickly climbed the corporate ladder. She developed a pattern a few times a week of eating nothing all day after waking up feeling determined to "turn it all around." By evening, she would be so exhausted and ravenous that she would order lots of food and eat it all almost without tasting it, until she felt uncomfortably full, deeply embarrassed, and very isolated. Other days, especially when she had work events to attend over meals, she would eat more regularly and not end up bingeing at night. Her weight continued to cycle up and down over the years, always ending up a little higher each year.

Janet hadn't gone to a doctor during her 30s, both because she was healthy and because she absolutely dreaded the experiences from her 20s of seeing physicians who only focused on her weight, sternly advising her on her "obesity" and warning her of future medical issues or early death. They would hand out advice like, "Just eat less and move more," as if it had never occurred to her. Society was constantly giving her messages that she was unacceptable because of her higher body weight, as if she hadn't been on diets since she could remember.

Around her 40th birthday, Janet felt ill and weak, mentally foggy, dehydrated, and she started losing weight rapidly. A few months later, after passing out at work, she ended up in the emergency room and was diagnosed with type 2 diabetes. The outpatient diabetes dietitian sternly advised her to lose weight "right away," or warned that she could end up with an amputation, kidney failure, or a heart attack. Janet redoubled her efforts to restrict calories and carbohydrates. Her binges only occurred once a week now, despite constant, fierce hunger, because she was so worried about her health. Having been physically active her whole life, Janet's right knee started to hurt. Her new primary care doctor referred her to an orthopedic surgeon who barely looked at her x-ray or examined her before letting her know that she'd better lose weight because no surgeon would ever consider operating on her in the future unless she lost 10–20 percent of her body weight.

Janet started feeling desperate. She considered bariatric surgery. Then she started following some blogs and podcasts that talked about Health At Every Size®,[1] learned there was an eating disorder that perfectly described what she was experiencing, and discovered a movement that fostered body acceptance. She sought out a dietitian, therapist, and doctor who were eating disorder experts, hoping they could help her find a new way forward.

Background

Weight stigma is a pervasive and serious problem in this country.[2] Doctors are among the worst offenders when it comes to weight bias.[3,4] That means that doctors are quick to conclude that people in larger bodies also have negative attributions like laziness or lack of willpower and may provide worse care as a result. When I discuss this topic with doctors, I have been asked, "Well, isn't this 'epidemic' of higher weight just as pervasive and serious? Shouldn't we professionally be recommending a diet for all our patients with a high BMI?" The full answer is complicated and nuanced, but in a word: no. It's clear that whatever this country is doing—socially, medically, with public service announcements—it is not working. Health has not improved. We need another approach.

Diets do not work. The multibillion-dollar commercial machine that tries to sell people the promise of thinness (for health, for self-esteem, for self-confidence) is a false and often damaging industry. Virtually every study shows that people who engage in a diet (typically meaning restriction of calories below what the body needs on a daily basis, often with nutritional categories off limits) may lose weight temporarily only to gain it all back, plus more.[5] You now know why this makes scientific sense. Our cave people brains don't know if we are consuming insufficient calories because of lack of access to food or because of intentional restricting. They just register "famine" and proceed to drop the metabolism, increase anxiety and food obsessions, and defend the body weight. After prolonged deprivation, feeling ravenous and eating more calories than the body needs for energy is biological, not a lapse of willpower.

Health and Size

It's also vital to challenge the notion that higher body weight necessarily means less healthy.

A study of 29,000 diverse men and women found that reduced exercise capacity was a powerful predictor of mortality while BMI was of limited importance.[6] This study upheld findings by the Veterans Exercise Testing Study which showed that the *lowest* death rates of 12,000 middle-aged veterans were observed in the "obese men with a high exercise capacity."[7]

Evidence continues to grow that healthy people in larger bodies, with cardiovascular fitness, may indeed live longer than those in thinner bodies.[8] Furthermore, the act of engaging in regular aerobic exercise and/or resistance training causes life-prolonging changes in a number of cardiovascular risk factors, independent of any change in body weight.[9] Significant changes in mortality are consistently found only at either extreme of weight.[10] When epidemiological studies evaluating the relationship between body weight and mortality control for fitness, exercise, diet quality, weight cycling, diet drug use, economic status, and family history, higher weight disappears as an independent risk factor for higher mortality.[11]

I cite these robust outcomes studies because the overwhelming (and wrong) belief remains in this country that being thin means being healthy and leads to a longer life. People in a wide spectrum of body sizes and shapes may be healthy, or they may be sick. However, doctors routinely continue to bring their own, often incorrect, biases about weight and health to the bedside.[12]

Poor Medical and Surgical Care

This brings me to a somewhat radical-sounding declaration: the number one medical complication in those with BED and/or larger bodies is the poor overall general medical and surgical care that such patients receive at the hands of doctors. It's not diabetes, high blood pressure, or high cholesterol. It's harm—both psychological and medical—that comes from often well-meaning medical professionals. Individuals in larger bodies have been shown to avoid healthcare settings due to prior experiences of harm and body-related shame. The stress of going to the doctor keeps them from seeking regular medical care.[13]

A great example of weight stigma causing poor healthcare outcomes is when patients are told to lose weight or risk being denied needed surgery in the future. Bias can start in the exam room. A one glance assumption that someone's body weight caused her knee pain generally does not reflect best practices. Additionally, where a thin person with knee pain might be referred to PT, yoga, or massage, the patient in a larger body may receive only a recommendation to diet.

Losing a large amount of weight and keeping it off is very rare. We can imagine, though, a desperate patient with severe knee pain who severely limits caloric intake over a sustained period of time to try and qualify for knee replacement surgery. On the day of her operation, she will show up malnourished as a result, regardless of her weight, which does not bode well for her ability to tolerate and heal from the surgery. In fact, weight loss before knee surgery is not evidence based to improve outcomes.[14]

Doctors cite studies showing that high body weight can be linked to medical complications like diabetes, obstructive sleep apnea, and poorer wound healing. Knowing that these medical conditions can correlate with worse surgical outcomes, they prescribe weight loss. However, one large study examined the effect of a 5 percent decrease in body weight on post-operative infection and hospital readmission in almost 11,000 cases of knee replacement surgery. Only 12 percent of patients even "attained" this weight loss in the year before surgery, and they had identical outcomes with those who did not lose weight.[15]

Another study noted that presenting to surgery malnourished from taking in too few calories and breaking down body tissue (i.e. losing weight) may itself cause poor wound healing and infection—the very complications weight loss is supposed to prevent.[16] In fact, a study of almost 78,000 patients undergoing knee replacements showed that a high BMI was not independently associated with most surgical complications. Rather, a low blood albumin level (a protein in the blood that can correlate with inflammation as well as poor nutrition) was associated with increased death rates and other complications.[17]

So once again, weight bias and a lack of awareness of the medical literature can cause doctors to make recommendations that a) may be impossible for a patient to follow and b) prevents a patient from getting optimal care, such as knee surgery when needed. A surgeon might argue that they won't offer a surgery if there will be significant risks of complications afterwards. But if it is actually impossible to lose that weight safely, keep it off, and show up for surgery adequately nourished, then it's a surgeon's job to do the best they can after fully informing the patient of risks. The patient then decides if the benefits outweigh the risks.

The shame/blame game is in full effect here, even when not intended as such. In systems of stigma, however, one cannot stop with doctors saying, "I didn't mean to cause harm. This is what my training taught me." We have to ask more of physicians and invite them to consider the topic from another angle. Patients cannot be expected to advocate on their own—although some brave souls will—because they are on the other end of the power differential with physicians, and years of accrued micro-aggressions and shame may leave them silenced in the medical office.

Better Practices

What is the right way to care medically for patients with BED, then? The field and my knowledge of it are evolving every day. Currently, the answer starts with: it's not about the weight. Physicians must move toward a non-assumptive approach, asking patients about their relationship with food and movement because otherwise the opportunity to diagnose and treat BED will be missed in patients of all body sizes. My policy is never to check body weight on any of my patients unless I'm monitoring planned weight restoration in the context of nutritional rehabilitation. I tell my patients that their weight isn't a primary outcome and doesn't predict their health.

Once again, genetic susceptibility plays a role in people's health outcomes with relation to environmental exposures. Some will develop serious medical problems—conventionally associated with higher body weight—at a relatively "normal" weight. Others have absolutely no medical problems in the context of much larger bodies. Genetic variability (not willpower) play a powerful role. This leads me to the overarching movement that guides best evidence-based care for all patients, called the Health At Every Size (HAES®) philosophy.

Health At Every Size

HAES is a model that grew out of the anti-diet and fat acceptance communities in the late 1980s and early 1990s. It emerged from conversations among clinicians who were seeing the failure of intentional weight loss and realizing it was an unethical intervention, eating disorder specialists who connected problems across the weight spectrum with weight stigma, and activists who wanted better medical care.[18] The HAES movement encourages people to accept and respect the natural diversity of body sizes and shapes, to eat in a flexible manner that values pleasure and honors internal hunger cues, and to move for joy and to become more physically vital. It advocates for access to respectful healthcare and health policies that acknowledge the importance of social justice themes.[19] It supports attending to emotional health and receiving validation for the micro-aggressions and harm that have been inflicted on individuals and oppressed populations in a size-biased society.

HAES does not mean "everyone at every body size is healthy," as some mistake it to mean. Such a statement would be scientifically untrue. The HAES message is subtler, and at the same time wonderfully inclusive of people across status, gender, size, and other spaces of marginalization.

Working in an attuned way with one's body and eating and moving in a flexible way to the extent one chooses can improve health independent of weight change. The HAES approach is weight-inclusive and may involve accepting weight gain, weight loss, or no weight change at all. Even as HAES princples are incorporated into patients' lives over time, doctors can help optimize patients' medical issues through thoughtful diagnosis and treatment. Patients should not be held hostage to medical providers' weight loss recommendations.

So, let's imagine a person who has been stigmatized for their body size, starting within their childhood home where children most need to feel safe and unconditionally cherished. They've been through countless diets and weight cycling, causing their metabolism to slow and speed up again. The best way to offer optimal medical health is to invite them never to diet again, to eat in ways that honor culture, social engagement, taste buds, and energy needs. There's no such thing as a "bad," "disallowed," or "cheat" food.

This is not an invitation to eat "pure 'junk' food," as some wrongly choose to interpret. In our society, people think the absence of strict (and often unscientific) food rules must mean a free for all. Once again, I come back to my message of moderation. I recommend to my patients (and personally practice) eating fresh, colorful foods with plenty of fruits and vegetables, home-cooked when possible, consumed mindfully, generally not in front of the TV or in the car. The balance of carbohydrates, fats, proteins, and fiber does not need to be mentally counted or too exact. There is no place for fear or guilt when enjoying sweets, processed foods, and whatever counts as "unhealthy food" at a given time, in moderation. In general, "real foods" taste better and are more satisfying. By this I mean, for instance, real ice cream, bread, and cheese, rather than low fat or low calorie versions of these.

Intuitive eating is a powerful, diet-rejecting nutrition philosophy taught by many eating disorder dietitians.[20] For patients who have spent their whole lives dieting and being body- and food-shamed, intuitions about what and how much to eat may initially be out of reach. HAES-informed dietitians can meet patients where they are, initially creating meal and portion suggestions and reminding patients not to postpone eating. Over time, the patient is able to tune into hunger, satisfaction, and a relationship with food that is separate from body shape and size.

Individuals can be encouraged to move in ways that improve their experience in the world, within their level of ability and desire—to play with their children, explore the beauty of hiking trails they feared they would never see again, and complete errands and professional obligations with less exhaustion and pain. Moving for joy covers almost infinite options, ultimately centered around the patient's preference, access, and ability. Some might find it joyful to be able to get around their home more easily. Others experience joy from elite athletic performance. The point is that movement is performed not to compensate for (or permit the consumption of) calories, but to celebrate the body and live one's values.

There are many barriers to operationalizing the HAES model; these aren't problems with HAES itself. One is that only a small fraction of the population has access to HAES-informed specialists, either because of geography or because of financial limitations. Even when someone has the security of good health insurance, it often doesn't cover eating disorder services. Also, it's all well and good to recommend someone move for joy, but their bodies may literally not be safe in spaces where movement is done. There may be a lack of clothing that fits comfortably and appropriately to exercise. Hostility in gym environments, where there is no option for movement to take place outdoors, or where it's not safe to walk on the street alone can pose major impediments. And discrimination based on religious affiliation, sexual orientation, gender presentation, and race can cause bodies literally to be unsafe. These are among the reasons that the BED community has become so tightly linked with social justice movements.

Physicians reading this chapter may have a look of disbelief on their faces. "Are you telling me that when you have a patient with diabetes, fatty liver, and obstructive sleep apnea, you literally don't recommend weight loss, even though studies show that weight loss significantly ameliorates these problems?" Yep, that's what I'm saying. I do not focus on weight as a primary outcome, but rather on behavioral change. I keep in mind my own internalized size stigma as I try to hold space for patients' distress about their body size, while promoting a weight-inclusive approach. While it may be true that a given individual would have better health due to improvement or even resolution of medical problems at a lower body weight, I'm again left with the reality that diets don't work. I cannot in good conscience prescribe one for a patient, when it may cause harm and will not result in the desired outcome.

I also often hear, "But I have a friend who did lose weight and kept it off." In almost every human experience, there are outliers. Policy and medical recommendations cannot be made on the data of outliers. When I speak or blog on this topic, a remarkable number of trolls emerge and scathingly question my credentials and dismiss the science I cite. In my highest self, I try to understand that these people themselves are also victims of a sizeist society. They may be slinging back the same misguided and biased words they were raised on and themselves may have been harmed by.

The fallacy that it's all about willpower or sufficient access to chefs and trainers is just that: a false narrative that sustains shame and doesn't bring about change or health. Society has become brainwashed into thinking that health is a matter of individual grit and worthiness, oppressing entire generations of people in the process and making billions of dollars off their shame. Doctors often occupy what's called "thin privilege," which means that by comparison with the general population, medical professionals have thinner bodies that are more societally acceptable. We may not be aware of how much easier our lives are than those in larger bodies, because we take our privilege for granted and even bristle at the notion that inequality exists. That, and our medical training, make us less compassionate and aware of what our patients' lived experiences are. We often don't even ask.

Bariatric Surgery

What about bariatric surgery, also called gastric bypass surgery? Almost half a million gastric bypass surgeries were performed worldwide in 2013, the last time such a survey was performed.[21] I respect that for some people, surgery has been a positive experience. I by no means am looking to shame individuals who have undergone it, due to their lived experiences in their bodies. In the BED and fat activist community, however, it's called stomach amputation.

Often, the stomach pouch that is left after surgery can contain only an ounce or two of food or fluid, and the intestinal tract is rerouted deliberately to cause malabsorption of nutrients. I have seen multiple patients who underwent gastric bypass surgery end up with a far worse quality of life afterwards. They have constant nausea and abdominal pain, diarrhea, and weight loss to the point of clinical malnutrition. These are patients who still don't meet the formal definition of "underweight" for height; however, they show precisely the same physiologic dysfunction as patients with anorexia nervosa. They can lose the ability to eat socially because meal sizes and food selection have to be so cautiously chosen and are so minimal in volume. Alcohol use disorder skyrockets.[22]

The psychological pre-screening for bariatric surgery has not been validated and is inconsistent. That means that people who aren't simply in larger bodies, but also have the mental illness of BED, are waved through to a surgery that cannot be undone. Postoperatively, the disordered relationships with food and body remain, but the body may be permanently altered. This can be catastrophic for the patient. The often-advertised idea that bariatric surgery simply represents the best, most permanent, and most successful diet you've ever tried is misleading and wrong. It is a potentially irreversible procedure that may cause lifelong suffering, and from my perspective it should be reserved—if ever recommended—only for those who have tried a full HAES approach for a long time, and who have such critical medical problems that the potential benefits are far greater than the risks.

Self-Advocacy

For patients in the medical office, it is always acceptable to decline being weighed. Governmental insurers like Medicare may require the documentation of a weight. This requirement is satisfied if the physician documents "patient refused." One possible reason to be weighed is to dose important medicines, like chemotherapy or anesthesia, correctly. Patients can then ask to be weighed blindly and not be told their weight.

What about children? Public weighing and BMI discussions in schools should stop. Many people have distinct memories (usually tinged with shame or a dawning sense of how society overvalues size) of being weighed in school. I always decline permission for this for my kids. This is between me, my children, and their pediatrician.

It is appropriate to focus public policy efforts on systems of oppression that can contribute to poor health. But we have to get HAES-minded practitioners in the rooms where the public health decisions happen, because it is unhelpful and inappropriate systematically to shame children for body sizes they have little to no say in. These children remain embedded in systems that reduce access to healthcare, fail to provide a variety of cost-effective, fresh foods, destabilize family systems, and interfere with a consistent sense of safety.

I fundamentally believe that when one follows HAES principals the body will take on a size and shape that are genetically determined. A recent paper encouraged

> practitioners (to) locate the problem of fat shame in society as opposed to the individual person's body and provide individuals with tools to identify and resist fat stigma and oppression, rather than provide them with tools to reshape their bodies.[23]

I couldn't agree more.

Resolution of Case: Janet

Janet's new HAES-informed team consists of a dietitian, therapist, and doctor. She sees the doctor first and has anxious reservations about even walking through the clinic door, given her recent experiences. Despite being a successful professional with dear friends, she feels diminished as she enters a doctor's office. However, she notes immediately that the furniture in the office is sturdy, comfortable, and armless, so she sits without discomfort. There are no pictures of thin people on the walls and no infographics about the dangers of higher weight. The nurse warmly assures her that weight will not be checked as it's not a vital sign that the practice follows. The blood pressure cuff fits as does the exam gown.

The doctor takes the time to hear Janet's whole history, asks what her goals and values are for treatment, and spends time discussing the HAES philosophy. She names BED as a mental illness that must be treated as such. The doctor notes that she will never recommend dieting and assures a disbelieving Janet that following HAES precepts without focus on weight has successfully improved other patients' quality of life as well as medical problems. Janet notes that she would like to get back to honoring her athletic past because she's always enjoyed physical activity. After discussing several options for how to get back to this, in light of her painful knee, Janet decides to start with an online trainer whom she can access from home and who has been vetted as size friendly. She enjoys starting to work on strength again and begins taking walks in her neighborhood. When leg cramps and foot pains occur as she starts to get more active, her doctor advises her to buy sneakers that fit properly and recommends massage for tight leg and foot muscles. This resolves the problem.

Janet begins work with her new dietitian and asks for specific recommendations at first because the idea of intuitive eating feels alien and even forbidden to her. She's not even entirely sure what her hunger signals are because she has ignored or suppressed them over the years. The dietitian compassionately supports Janet in the teaching of a new way of interacting with food that's meant to be sustainable over a lifetime. They talk about foods Janet likes, and they create a nutritional strategy meant to meet her needs, satisfy her taste buds, and ensure that she will be eating every few hours so as not to get too hungry. It's hard initially because eating break- fast, lunch, and snacks feels so strange. However, Janet finds she gets to dinnertime satisfied, not ravenous, so her binges dramatically decrease. She has far more energy and better concentration at work.

Janet finds she has much to talk about with her therapist. Together, they name and unpack family dynamics, societal biases, and the ways that Janet can use her voice authentically. They work on body acceptance and self-confidence. They brain- storm together some ways to incorporate the increase in meals and snacks into her already busy schedule and identify things that trigger the desire to binge. Over the following months, Janet finds herself enjoying life in a way she hasn't in years.

In addition, her diabetes improves radically. Her insulin requirements decrease by half, reflecting improved insulin sensitivity. Her stamina increases, and she reconnects with her body as athletic. Her knee pain improves as she becomes stronger. At times, she feels tempted to get on a scale or to eat less to "try and lose some weight." Her team holds space for this desire, set against her background and socie- ty's insistent focus on this, but reminds her that nutritional deprivation will only make her more prone to binges.

Sometimes it feels tiring to have appointments and have to think about these issues so much, especially without the "high" she used to get from crash diets, of seeing her weight change dramatically and having people compliment her. The team validates treatment burnout and continues to urge her to take the long view. This isn't about short term (and soon lost) changes, but about a sustainable, scientifi- cally, and psychologically sound recovery process.

Naming Privilege and Challenging the Narrative

Some colleagues in the BED field recently gave me the gift of their time and teaching. They expressed frustration with the medical profession because of all the harm it has done to patients in larger bodies: pathologizing body size, contributing to constructs of "an epidemic," and promoting the typical doctor advice of "just eat less than you burn." I'm sorry to say that in the past, I too participated in this kind of thinking and patient advice. I never thought about my own thin privilege. It didn't occur to me to consider how my growing up white, cisgender, financially secure, with two loving and educated parents, time and resources for family dinners, generations of Italian ancestors dedicated to the art of delicious and nutritious food served in an emotionally engaged setting, and an able body, might have contributed to my own ease with body and food.

There are at least two major problems with the advice "take in less energy than you burn." One, it's not actually scientifically sound. We saw in earlier chapters that patients with anorexia nervosa who are going through nutritional rehabilitation often have to eat vastly more calories than predicted because of hypermetabolism. Other patients across the eating disorder and body size spectrum have learned that no matter how much they restrict calories, their body weight just doesn't change. Their cave person brains defend their body weight through metabolic slowing just like they were designed to do.

I have fielded questions from doubting physicians who ask me, "Okay, you say diets don't work. If that's so, then why aren't there prisoners of war whose body weight 'resisted' starvation? They're all emaciated." There are a lot of things wrong with this question, but I've been asked some version of it many times.

The answer is that people in society do not live in literal prisons. We are genetically programmed to seek out food when we are starved, and unlike prisoners of war, most people have some degree of access to food. Even if so-called excessive food isn't consumed after deprivation, metabolic slowing will cause the body to need less energy and store any extra. Think about it from the perspective of a person deprived of water. Their thirst drive will rise and rise. If water is available, at some point, they will drink. It's not willpower; it's biology.

Two, the development of society's current size demographics doesn't emerge from a lack of willpower or inadequate dedication to dieting, as physicians can imply in their advice. It emerges from a society-wide construct of racist, sexist, and classist policies and ideologies that are promoted by a highly profitable food industry and a booming dieting and supplement industry.

Highly palatable and less nutritious foods are consistently marketed more to poor communities of color than to upper class white neighborhoods. The food industry sells Black and Latino folks triple-sized donuts at the gas station and triple decker burgers for just $1 more, then puts up billboards for commercial diet programs and magazine inserts for the magical pill that will burn fat while you sleep. It broadcasts commercials of light-skinned, thin women cavorting around looking like they feel worthy and confident.

The industry powerfully draws out people's insecurities in order to sell them the solution. The same companies that make skin whitening creams in India, advertising them through photo-shopped images of lighter-skinned women who look financially secure, sell skin darkening creams in North America, where glowing beach beauties show that pasty skin is for losers. These are the reasons that social justice advocates and BED advocates have paired up so harmoniously to make their voices heard.

One of my colleagues in the BED field spoke of their frustration with needing to educate doctors about all this because doctors are so resistant and have been responsible for so much pain and suffering in patients of size. I said to her, "But not all doctors are like this. A lot are really open and would like to know about this stuff." I was called out, properly, on my self-regarding response.

I realized that what my response had missed was my recognition that even if I personally do not espouse sizeist views, I'm still a physician. I am a representative of a class that has traditionally played an oppressive role, even if unwittingly. There has to be awareness of this, and the privilege that goes with it, for society to change. The better insight is, "It's not about me specifically. It's about the bigger picture." This requires me to name that privilege and recognize the delicacy of the position of power that I hold. It requires me to think about how I can contribute to dismantling the potential for future damage that my profession will cause to patients in larger bodies. All of us with privilege must consider how we can challenge the narrative and change the system.

Notes

1 Health At Every Size and HAES are registered trademarks of the Association for Size Diversity and Health and used with permission.
2 Phelan SM, Burgess DJ, Yeazel MW, Hellerstedt WL, Griffin JM, van Ryn M. Impact of weight bias and stigma on quality of care and outcomes for patients with obesity. *Obes Rev*. 2015 April; 16(4):319–326. doi: 10.1111/obr.12266.
3 Puhl RM, Luedicke J, Grilo CM. Obesity bias in training: attitudes, beliefs, and observations among advanced trainees in professional health disciplines. *Obesity (Silver Spring)*. 2014 April; 22(4):1008–1015. doi: 10.1002/oby.20637.
4 Phelan SM, Dovidio JF, Puhl RM, Burgess DJ, Nelson DB, Yeazel MW, Hardeman R, Perry S, van Ryn M. Implicit and explicit weight bias in a national sample of 4,732 medical students: the medical student CHANGES study. *Obesity (Silver Spring)*. 2014 April; 22(4):1201–1208. doi: 10.1002/oby.20687.
5 Mann T, Tomiyama AJ, Westling E, Lew AM, Samuels B, Chatman J. Medicare's search for effective obesity treatments: diets are not the answer. *Am Psychol*. 2007 April; 62(3):220–233. Review. PubMed PMID: 17469900.
6 McAuley PA, Blaha MJ, Keteyian SJ, Brawner CA, Al Rifai M, Dardari ZA, Ehrman JK, Al-Mallah MH. Fitness, Fatness, and Mortality: the FIT (Henry Ford Exercise Testing) Project. *Am J Med*. 2016 September; 129(9):960–965.e1. doi: 10.1016/j.amjmed.2016.04.007.
7 McAuley PA, Kokkinos PF, Oliveira RB, Emerson BT, Myers JN. Obesity paradox and cardiorespiratory fitness in 12,417 male veterans aged 40 to 70 years. *Mayo Clin Proc*. 2010 February; 85(2):115–121. doi: 10.4065/mcp.2009.0562.

8 Lavie CJ, De Schutter A, Milani RV. Healthy obese versus unhealthy lean: the obesity paradox. *Nat Rev Endocrinol.* 2015 January; 11(1):55–62. doi: 10.1038/nrendo.2014.165.

9 Balducci S, Zanuso S, Cardelli P, Salvi L, Mazzitelli G, Bazuro A, Iacobini C, Nicolucci A, Pugliese G; Italian Diabetes Exercise Study (IDES) Investigators. Changes in physical fitness predict improvements in modifiable cardiovascular risk factors independently of body weight loss in subjects with type 2 diabetes participating in the Italian Diabetes and Exercise Study (IDES). *Diabetes Care.* 2012 June; 35(6):1347–1354. doi: 10.2337/dc11-1859.

10 Durazo-Arvizu RA, McGee DL, Cooper RS, Liao Y, Luke A. Mortality and optimal body mass index in a sample of the US population. *Am J Epidemiol.* 1998 April 15; 147(8):739–749. PubMed PMID: 9554415.

11 Campos P, Saguy A, Ernsberger P, Oliver E, Gaesser G. The epidemiology of overweight and obesity: public health crisis or moral panic? *Int J Epidemiol.* 2006 February; 35(1):55–60. PubMed PMID: 16339599.

12 Bombak AE, McPhail D, Ward P. Reproducing stigma: interpreting "overweight" and "obese" women's experiences of weight-based discrimination in reproductive healthcare. *Soc Sci Med.* 2016 October; 166:94–101. doi: 10.1016/j.socscimed.2016.08.015.

13 Mensinger JL, Tylka TL, Calamari ME. Mechanisms underlying weight status and healthcare avoidance in women: a study of weight stigma, body-related shame and guilt, and healthcare stress. *Body Image.* 2018 March 22; 25:139–147. doi: 10.1016/j.bodyim.2018.03.001.

14 Martin JR, Jennings JM, Dennis DA. Morbid obesity and total knee arthroplasty: a growing problem. *J Am Acad Orthop Surg.* 2017 March; 25(3):188–194. doi: 10.5435/JAAOS-D-15-00684.

15 Inacio MC, Kritz-Silverstein D, Raman R, Macera CA, Nichols JF, Shaffer RA, Fithian DC. The impact of pre-operative weight loss on incidence of surgical site infection and readmission rates after total joint arthroplasty. *J Arthroplasty.* 2014 March; 29(3):458–464.e1. doi: 10.1016/j.arth.2013.07.030.

16 Schricker T, Wykes L, Meterissian S, Hatzakorzian R, Eberhart L, Carvalho G, Meguerditchian A, Nitschmann E, Lattermann R. The anabolic effect of perioperative nutrition depends on the patient's catabolic state before surgery. *Ann Surg.* 2013 January; 257(1):155–159. doi: 10.1097/SLA.0b013e31825ffc1f.

17 Nelson CL, Elkassabany NM, Kamath AF, Liu J. Low albumin levels, more than morbid obesity, are associated with complications after TKA. *Clin Orthop Relat Res.* 2015 October; 473(10):3163–3172. doi: 10.1007/s11999-015-4333-7.

18 With appreciation for conversations and communications over time with Deb Burgard, PhD, Hilary Kinavey, MS, LPC, and Carmen Cool, MA, LPC.

19 www.sizediversityandhealth.org/content.asp?id=152. Accessed August 3, 2018.

20 www.intuitiveeating.org/ Accessed April 15, 2018.

21 Angrisani L, Santonicola A, Iovino P, Formisano G, Buchwald H, Scopinaro N. Bariatric Surgery Worldwide 2013. *Obes Surg.* 2015 October; 25(10):1822–1832. doi: 10.1007/s11695-015-1657-z.

22 Steffen KJ, Engel SG, Wonderlich JA, Pollert GA, Sondag C. Alcohol and other addictive disorders following bariatric surgery: prevalence, risk factors and possible etiologies. *Eur Eat Disord Rev.* 2015 November; 23(6):442–450. doi: 10.1002/erv.2399.

23 Brown-Bowers A, Ward A, Cormier N. Treating the binge or the (fat) body? Representations of fatness in a gold standard psychological treatment manual for binge eating disorder. *Health (London).* 2017 January; 21(1):21–37. doi: 10.1177/1363459316674788.

Part IV

The Unmeasurables

(a.k.a. The Very Real Medical Problems that Modern Medicine Can't Measure)

In my quest to use objective evidence of body suffering in order to break through patients' denial and motivate them to seek eating disorder treatment, I have come upon many medical problems that cannot be measured. For instance, let's consider migraine headaches. Migraines are a particular type of headache that often starts with aura, where the vision or other senses become abnormal, and then progresses to a splitting headache that can last from several hours to days. Severity varies, ranging from a once-a-year annoyance to a life-altering disability. There is no doubt that migraines are real, but there's no way to measure them. I can't biopsy brain cells to find the problem, and I can't perform a CAT scan or MRI during a migraine episode to establish severity or prove it's occurring. There's certainly no blood test. Doctors simply have to take the patient's word and narrative of symptoms as the sum total of data that can be collected and subsequently develop treatment plans from that.

It turns out that many of these unmeasurable illnesses affect patients with eating disorders. They may not specifically result from the disorder, but they appear alongside it and make treatment more complicated, perhaps because patients with eating disorders have such strong mind-body connections. Many of these disorders worsen with stress, by all means including the stress of an eating disorder, and thus to at least some degree they can be considered a physical manifestation of emotional suffering. Part IV will review irritable bowel syndrome (IBS) and associated conditions in Chapter 11 and postural orthostatic tachycardia syndrome (POTS) and associated conditions in Chapter 12.

All of the unmeasurable problems I'll discuss in Part IV directly obstruct the process of nutritional rehabilitation or eating disorder recovery work. Of course, a large number of medical problems can co-occur with a diagnosis of an eating disorder, but those I describe in this section can bring therapy, nutrition work, and life to a grinding halt because the body symptoms can become so intrusive. Suboptimal management of these medical problems risks further prolongation of the eating disorder as well as alienation of patients from Western medicine altogether.

I must note that I have no formal alternative medicine training at all. I'm sure there are great practitioners of it and crummy ones, just as there are in Western medicine. However, I've now seen too many patients with eating disorders who find themselves invisible to Western doctors. As a result, they may turn to alternative providers who put them on highly restrictive "elimination diets," feeding them starvation-level amounts of bone broth for weeks while selling them handfuls of the provider's own personal brand of super-expensive supplements that have not been quality checked. The eating disorder goes nuts, the bank account shrinks ... and the original symptom still doesn't improve.

One important concept that can interweave among all physical body symptoms, whether measurable or unmeasurable, is called somatic symptom disorder. This disorder is defined in the DSM-5 as body (somatic) symptoms lasting for at least six months that have been distressing or resulted in significant disruption of function and intrusively intense thoughts, feelings, and behaviors.[1] This diagnosis can either bring great clarity and relief to patients, or feel frustratingly invalidating, depending on how it is communicated.

Here's how I discuss it with patients: the mind-body connection is real and cannot always be perfectly explained or measured. Our emotional state affects our physical symptoms. When psychological stress is high and cannot be sufficiently ameliorated through therapy and self-care, it can manifest physically. Typically, stress will appear physically through body systems that already have some dysfunction. A former collegiate athlete who used to have back issues may find themselves with excruciating back pain during times of stress. Someone with lifelong digestive issues may find themselves doubled over with abdominal pain and nausea when overwhelmed. Seizures that correlate with no brainwave abnormalities on testing (called non-epileptic seizures) can develop during exhausting or conflict-filled experiences.

None of these symptoms are made up, and to say "they're all in your head" is unhelpful and untrue. Patients may find themselves deeply distressed by physical symptoms, especially ones that apparently have no obvious medical cause. The key is that somatic symptom disorder usually accompanies complicated medical diagnoses, often unmeasurable, and a holistic approach that emphasizes the whole person, not "just" the medical or psychological, is needed.

This leads me to the sobering reality of most of the diagnoses I will be describing. They're persistent and may not go away altogether, even with the best treatment. I try to set patients' expectations about this reality. Almost all of the unmeasureables described in Part IV can incrementally improve over time, with setbacks, but they may not fully resolve. Some of my most humbling moments in my outpatient clinic have emerged from my inability to make meaningful inroads on some of these issues, after the patient and I have both earnestly done everything we could think of to help.

Note

1 American Psychiatric Association. (2013). *Diagnostic and statistical manual of mental disorders* (5th ed.). Arlington, VA: American Psychiatric Publishing.

Chapter 11

Irritable Bowel Syndrome (IBS) and Associated Conditions

Case: Emily

Emily is a 24-year-old cisgender Caucasian female who has been recovered from her eating disorder for two years. One of the first major triggers of her eating disorder was a very sensitive stomach. Starting in adolescence, she would experience multiple episodes of diarrhea a week and a distended, uncomfortable belly that was worse after eating. During particularly stressful times at school this would be accompanied by nausea and occasional vomiting, and the diarrhea would get worse.

Emily went to her pediatrician, who ran some blood tests and sent her to a gastroenterologist. The gastroenterologist was friendly but spent only ten minutes with her. He said at the end, "Good news. It's irritable bowel syndrome. You just need to work on your anxiety." She felt like she'd been told she was making it up or it was all in her head. With symptoms still prominent, she and her parents saw a naturopath when she was 15, who recommended she eliminate gluten and dairy from her diet.

Emily tried to do this, and her tummy felt a little bit better. She now had the idea in her head that her stomach symptoms were caused by food, so she started reading online blogs. That reading was enough to make her cut many different carbohydrates out of her diet as well as fats and sugars. She decided to try being vegetarian and then vegan. Her parents watched with relatively little concern because their daughter had always been sensible, and after all, the naturopath's suggestion of eliminating gluten and dairy had made an important difference. They knew her tummy had been bothering her for years and figured she was trying to eat more healthily.

Emily's increasingly restrictive food choices made her lose some weight, garnering positive feedback from friends and even teachers. She was startled by this because she had never had any negative body image and now wondered if everyone had noticed some problem she had not. As her weight fell, her diarrhea lessened, although her stomach still hurt after eating. Her mood turned dark, and she withdrew from friends. She slept poorly and felt anxious and exhausted all the time. Her schoolwork remained excellent, so her family attributed her various symptoms to being a "typical teenager."

Emily felt constantly deprived without many of her favorite foods. One night after everyone had gone to bed, she went into the kitchen, and almost without knowing what she was doing, began devouring leftovers. Stomach aching, she went to bed and actually slept well for the first time in months. This unspooled over the subsequent years into a cycle of restricting food groups, losing weight, then bingeing as if she could never satisfy herself, as her weight rose again. A realization that she could vomit after a binge, at age 20, made her eating patterns even more chaotic, and after two years she realized that she had an eating disorder. Prior to that, she had always just thought she was reacting to her sensitive belly, and the fact that her weight wasn't abnormal made her think she didn't "qualify" for an eating disorder.

Emily opened up to her parents, who were supportive supportive although somewhat skeptical about eating disorders in general. She established a team of a therapist and a dietitian, and over the course of two years felt like she had put her eating disorder behind her. However, her belly symptoms persisted. While she tried to manage difficult days without acting on eating disorder impulses, she nonetheless still had painful abdominal distention multiple times a day after eating and periods of diarrhea interspersed with new symptoms of painful constipation. Emily found it was hard to push a stool out even though when it came out it was often soft. She felt she wasn't fully empty after going to the bathroom and spent long hours on the toilet. Several times, after having no bowel movements for days, she actually had to put a finger in her rectum to manually remove hard stool, and would have some bleeding after that. These symptoms, preceding her eating disorder and persistent after eating disorder recovery, finally prompted her to seek a doctor again.

Background

Historically, there have been two major categories of gastrointestinal problems: organic and functional. This use of "organic" doesn't refer to produce raised without pesticides. Rather, it means a type of problem that is structural and visible. Organic problems cause cells and organs to become abnormal physically. You can see abnormalities on a biopsy or an x-ray. Functional problems, by contrast, refer to issues where the cells and structures are perfectly normal, but the ways they function are abnormal. Thus, on a biopsy, a blood test, or a radiographic film, they do not show up. This doesn't mean they are less severe, only that they are harder to diagnose and potentially harder to study in order to find treatments. Recently, the literature has shifted and now refers to functional gastrointestinal problems as "disorders of gut-brain interaction."[1] This is a much better and more scientifically accurate organizing construct.

The Rome Foundation establishes diagnostic criteria to diagnose disorders of gut-brain interaction. Each new set of criteria takes a Roman numeral; the latest set of criteria, released in 2016, are called the Rome IV criteria.[2] Irritable bowel syndrome (IBS) is diagnosed when an individual has recurrent abdominal pain associated with defecation or a change in bowel habits averaging at least one day a week over the preceding month.

IBS comes in three subtypes: constipation, diarrheal, or mixed. My experience treating those with IBS is that these patients have a strong mind-body connection. That is, when they are stressed or anxious, their abdominal symptoms worsen. However, this doesn't mean that patients "imagine" their IBS into being nor that can simply wish the symptoms away. Take again the example of a migraine headache, for which we know that stress can be a trigger. Once it's started, the person cannot say, "Whoops, I'll put my feet up and rest. No need for this migraine." Once started, it's game on. The same is true with IBS.

IBS is not a benign problem. It's not "just IBS." IBS can be extraordinarily severe and debilitating, leading to profound malnutrition when someone has ceaseless nausea, vomiting, and diarrhea, for instance. IBS has been found to cause eight to 22 days of missed workdays a year.[3] Alternatively, it can be a relatively mild annoyance. However, because it's hard to make symptoms go away completely, regardless of severity, patients can be left frustrated and symptomatic. Rather than responding with compassion, doctors (anxious and perfectionistic themselves) may feel the need to minimize the symptoms as being "not life threatening," allowing them to manage their own feelings of inadequacy and frustration that they cannot erase the discomfort for their patient.

Treatment of IBS

The treatment of IBS has many layers to it. The most important overarching theme is holistic care, meaning care of the whole person. I can prescribe all the "right" medications for someone's IBS, but unless they are concurrently working on getting good, consistent nutrition and rest, wielding stress management techniques, seeking regular self-care, and having their emotional needs met, the medicine won't work optimally. It would be like trying to put out a campfire while simultaneously squirting lighter fluid on it. Taking care of someone with IBS gives me the opportunity to remind them of the importance of their multidisciplinary team, validate the time and energy they are putting into their recovery work, and encourage them to take care of themselves and not just everyone else.

A few medications are available for IBS-constipation subtype (IBS-C). My experience is that every patient responds differently to each one, and I may have to try various medications until the best fit is found. Lubiprostone 8 or 24 mcg by mouth twice a day with meals, linaclotide 145 or 290 mcg a day more than 30 minutes before the first meal, or plecanitide 3 mg anywhere from daily to weekly, dosed any time of day, all are approved medications. The goal with each is to improve stool frequency.

IBS-diarrheal type (IBS-D) may be worsened by excessive bile acids produced in the liver and stored in the gallbladder. These bile acids may pull fluid into the intestinal lumen, much like a laxative such as polyethylene glycol will cause, and worsen diarrhea. The first-line treatment for IBS-D, therefore, is a bile-acid binder called colestipol, which comes in pill form. Since it is more palatable than a similar medication only available in a powder called cholestyramine, I typically start patients on colestipol 1 gram daily or twice daily, 30 minutes before a meal. Because colestipol is also a potent binder of medications, it must be dosed several hours from any other pills

Dicyclomine, given as 10 or 20 mg by mouth four times a day, is an anti-spasm medicine that can help with the pain of IBS-D. Taking a medicine four times a day, of course, is also a pain, figuratively. Hyoscyamine 0.125–0.25 mg by mouth three to four times a day as needed is also an anti-spasm medicine. I have seen patients on this latter medicine develop psychiatric symptoms due to an anti-cholinergic effect, while others find this their medicine of choice. There are currently no medicines for IBS-mixed subtype.

I can't count how many times I've seen a patient with IBS on the wrong class of medications. All the IBS-C medicines can cause diarrhea, while all the IBS-D medicines can cause constipation. None of these medicines are proven in the context of concurrent malnutrition.

Many patients ask me if they should follow a meal plan low in dietary fermentable carbohydrates, including fermentable oligo-, di-, mono-saccharides, and polyols (FODMAP) for their IBS. The data seem to indicate that a low FODMAP diet can help reduce symptoms in individuals with IBS, particularly diarrheal subtype.[4] Strictly following a low FODMAP diet, however, means avoiding many fruits, vegetables, dairy-containing foods, and legumes. The list is long and complicated. Designed to be used as a brief elimination period followed by a slow reintroduction phase to see what foods the body does and doesn't tolerate, the low FODMAP diet can nonetheless represent a distractingly restrictive set of food rules. I just cannot recommend it for patients with eating disorders.

Small Intestinal Bacterial Overgrowth

Many patients who have IBS still have some symptoms of distention and discomfort even when they are taking good care of themselves and are on a good prescription medication. They find themselves wondering where to turn next. In such cases, my next consideration is usually small intestinal bacterial overgrowth (SIBO). It turns out that the human body may have as many as 100 trillion bacteria living on or in us, necessary for our good health and perfectly symbiotic with their human host. A healthy small intestine has relatively few bacteria, however. When bacteria grow in the small intestine, they can cause significant GI upset.

SIBO occurs in more than half of patients with IBS. Its manifestations range from mild symptoms that overlap with IBS (bloating, distention, pain) to a severe enteropathy (meaning dysfunction of the intestine) that causes malabsorption, simulating celiac disease. In extreme cases of SIBO, patients may also develop a relative pancreatic insufficiency. The problem is that when there are too many bacteria in the small intestine, they begin to ferment digesting food, releasing either methane or hydrogen gas in the process. While the science continues to evolve on SIBO, it appears that the disorder can disrupt epithelial tight junctions—where two intestinal cells meet—increasing small intestinal permeability to endotoxins. Endotoxins are molecules found on bacteria that are harmless inside the intestine, but if they cross into the bloodstream they can elicit a strong immune/inflammatory response.[5]

In terms of diagnosing SIBO, breath testing is the most common test, although both false positives and false negatives can occur. The idea is that gases produced by bacteria in the small intestine will cross the intestinal wall and enter the bloodstream, go to the lungs, and be exhaled. A fairly strict set of guidelines exists to make these tests more accurate, and consensus guidelines have been developed on how to perform and interpret these tests for optimal clinical interpretation.[6] Because testing requires dietary alterations and fasting, it is not appropriate to subject patients fragile in their eating disorder recovery work to this process. In the right clinical context, I will skip the test and simply offer a course of SIBO treatment to see if patients feel better.

SIBO Treatment

So, what are SIBO treatments? First, it's important to note that SIBO is not easily eradicated, and it can recur easily. Historically, a course of a non-absorbed antibiotic called rifaximin 550 mg three times a day for 14 days is prescribed. While this is perfectly reasonable as a treatment, I try to use antibiotics as sparingly as possible so as not to (a) kill off "good" bacteria and (b) contribute to bacterial antibiotic resistance.

As a Western medicine doctor, here's a place where I've had to step out of my comfort zone. I was never trained in the use of herbal supplements, in part because they aren't regulated, and thus I have no assurance either that what's in the bottle is what's supposed to be in the bottle (without any hidden additives) or that the recommended dosing is consistent with desired outcomes. However, I firmly believe there is a role for supplements in SIBO treatment.

Specifically, a well-done randomized controlled trial showed that two different herbal remedies were non-inferior to rifaximin, which means they have worked at least as well for SIBO eradication.[7] The advantage is that they may disrupt the normal gut microflora less than rifaximin.

One regimen tested, FC Cidal and Dysbiocide from Biotics, can be ordered online. If patients do not respond to the Biotics regimen, I try the other regimen from the study, Metagenics' Candibactin-AR and Candibactin-BR, which is also available online. For both regimens, the dosing is two capsules of each, twice a day, for four weeks.

I often add in a third supplement that specifically targets methane-producing bacteria, called Atrantil. While no randomized controlled trial exists, a very small case study by the doctor who invented it showed good efficacy of Atrantil in improving IBS symptoms.[8] When I cannot rely on the medical literature for validation of a treatment, I turn to trusted clinicians. To that end, the best gastroenterologist I know regularly uses these supplements in her practice, so I feel secure in doing so with my patients. Atrantil is taken as two capsules two to three times a day with food for two weeks, and then two capsules a day maintenance. Patients may find bloating worsens transiently around the two-week mark, as bacteria die off; this resolves.

Pelvic Floor Dysfunction

If IBS medications and SIBO eradication don't sufficiently resolve symptoms, I consider dysfunction of the pelvic floor muscles. These are a network of small muscles that hold up the uterus (in females), bladder, and bowel. The function and sensation of the rectum, vagina, and urethra have everything to do with the pelvic floor.

Cycles of dieting that cause muscle mass loss may also leave the pelvic floor weak and functioning improperly. Big muscles like our biceps will rehab themselves naturally after malnutrition because we use them normally all the time. By contrast, those who have lost muscle mass in the delicate muscles of their pelvic floor may not regain normal, balanced strength. This is especially true if a patient is always trying to push out hard stool, or always trying to hold in diarrhea, or exercising excessively and putting high pressure on the abdominal muscles. In addition, chronic stress, high anxiety, and the drive to hold a stomach in to create a "flat stomach" can lead to overall high muscle tone and tension.

There are several ways the pelvic floor can function improperly. In high tone pelvic floor dysfunction, for example, the muscles are all constantly contracted. Neither stool nor gas can pass through the rectum and anus easily. Pain with penetrative intercourse, pelvic exams, or tampon use can also occur.

On the other side of the spectrum, pelvic floor weakness might cause a person to have trouble with urine and stool incontinence. The nerve endings in the rectum, which are responsible for the sensation of needing to move one's bowels and of retained stool, can also malfunction.[9,10]

Finally, one muscle might try to move rectal contents forward while another muscle spasms and halts progress. This is called pelvic floor dyssynergia. The Rome IV criteria diagnose pelvic floor dyssynergia (meaning disturbance of muscular coordination) when someone has to strain to pass a stool, feels unable to empty the rectum, or has difficulty relaxing to evacuate stool.[3]

Pelvic floor dysfunction can be diagnosed by a test called anorectal manometry, in which the technician inserts a soft pressure-monitoring balloon into the rectum, and the patient is asked to push, contract, or describe the sensation they experience. A skilled pelvic floor physical therapist, alternatively, can also do a detailed exam, both internal and external, and establish which, if any, muscles are malfunctioning. The physical therapist designs a plan for the patient to follow, ultimately resulting in relief from a wide variety of symptoms.

Pelvic Floor Dysfunction and IBS

How do the pelvic floor and IBS intersect when it comes to symptoms of bloating and distention? Bloating means the sensation the patient has of uncomfortable abdominal fullness, unrelated to the stomach being full after a meal. Distention, on the other hand, refers to actual physical expansion of the abdomen. A study found that patients with constipation (but not IBS) have double the bloating and distention of the general population. However, remarkably, those with IBS-C have a 14 times higher incidence of bloating and distention.[11] While theories vary for what causes the distention, one reasonable theory is that impaired gas transit may be responsible.[12]

It turns out that pelvic floor dysfunction may contribute to impaired gas transit. In a study, patients with abdominal distention received anorectal manometry. They exhibited high resting and with-effort anal sphincter pressures and a prolonged balloon expulsion time.[13] The good news is that expert PT and biofeedback are highly effective in treating pelvic floor dysfunction. These treatments reduce pelvic pain, tailbone pain, pain with penetrative intercourse, urinary incontinence, constipation, and stool incontinence. Given that the therapy is quite intimate, patients with a history of sexual trauma, those with heightened modesty, or those with intense anxiety when unclothed have to consider the benefits and risks of engaging in PT. If they choose to proceed, they should plan to communicate clearly with their physical therapist, go very slowly in the work, and plan to process emotions that emerge with their therapist.

The Gut Microbiota

A lot of my patients ask me whether taking probiotics is useful. The answer is: maybe. To really review probiotics, though, we have to step back and take a brief look at the microbe-gut-brain connection, especially as it relates to eating disorders. This line of scientific inquiry is fascinating and potentially groundbreaking.

To define a few terms, "microbiome" refers to bacterial DNA, while "microbiota" refers to the bacteria themselves. The microbe-gut-brain connection begins when bacteria in the colon consume food and release byproducts that then cross into the human bloodstream, influencing the hypothalamic-pituitary-adrenal axis.[14] Increasingly, it's looking like our psychological well being is substantially influenced by the bacteria that live in our gut.[15] Amazingly enough, in terms of the sheer quantity of DNA contained in a single person, 99 percent of what's in us is microbial. For every human cell, there are ten bacteria. Scientists are coming to understand that our microbiome may have a direct, causal influence on a wide variety of health outcomes.

Let me offer a few astounding examples. When identical twins, one of whom has multiple sclerosis, provide stool samples, and these are introduced into the intestinal systems of mice, the mice that get bacteria from the twin with MS have a higher incidence of autoimmune diseases.[16] Identical twins have far more similar microbiota than siblings or unrelated individuals, even if they live far away from each other and have different environmental exposures, showing that there is a heritable aspect to the bacteria that eventually live in and on us.[17] Health problems like the metabolic syndrome (high cholesterol levels, high blood pressure, and high blood sugar) have been associated with having specific populations of bacteria in the gut, where one twin has the syndrome and another doesn't, suggesting that some bacteria may play a causal role in developing the syndrome.[18]

As a final example, Malawian twin toddlers were studied over time. In some cases, one twin developed a particular kind of malnutrition called "kwashiorkor," where the belly becomes very protuberant. The exact cause of kwashiorkor malnutrition remains unknown, although it appears to be related to protein calorie malnutrition and other environmental insults, resulting in abdominal fluid retention and an enlarged liver. Stool samples from the twin with kwashiorkor and the twin without showed significant differences in their microbiomes. When stool samples from a kwashiorkor and a healthy twin were separately introduced into mice, and the mice were fed the standard Malawian diet, the mice who received kwashiorkor bacteria became significantly more malnourished.[19]

How does this translate to those with eating disorders? Associations have now clearly been proven among appetite, metabolism, weight, and the gut microbiome.[20] Studies have now conclusively determined that those with anorexia nervosa have a far less diverse gut microbiome than controls, and they have a particular deficit in certain bacterial types.[21] Interesting associations have been made between this observation and psychiatric symptoms. For instance, those with anorexia nervosa lack normal quantities of bacteria that produce butyrate, and low butyrate levels correlate with higher anxiety.[22]

Studies have also found that the gut microbiome directly impacts intestinal motility.[23] Alteration of the gut microbiome may be one way in which the body slows its metabolism during starvation. We still don't know exactly why patients with anorexia nervosa can need such high calorie meal plans to gain weight during recovery, but preliminary research suggests this may have something to do with the microbiome too.

Probiotics

So, all we have to do to cure disease is run out and buy a couple bottles of probiotics, right? Not so fast. People do not have tracts of unpopulated colon just waiting for the right probiotic. We're all fully colonized at all times. That means probably the probiotics we take pass right through us without meaningfully changing the composition of our intestinal microbiota. Actual studies continually fail to prove that taking probiotics works. For instance, in a common issue such as yeast infections in women, the hypothesis is that normal vaginal microbiota is disrupted such that yeast overgrows. Probiotics should really help, but the data aren't convincing.[24]

Let's take another problem such as *Clostridium Difficile* colitis (known as "C. Diff"). C. Diff occurs when antibiotic use diminishes good bacteria, resulting in the overgrowth of one particularly bad bacterium. This is a dreadful, mostly hospital-transmitted infectious diarrhea that is very hard to treat and can be deadly. You'd think that probiotics during antibiotic administration, or after a bout of C. Diff, would help prevent disease or recurrence. However, the data are still mixed.[25] Interestingly, a proven treatment for recurrent C. Diff is to infuse "healthy" stool from a stool donor via colonoscopy or enema. While oral probiotics don't clearly work, actually getting a full bacterial load from healthy stool does help the colon recolonize and resist disease.

A top group of microbiome researchers once told me that they themselves don't take probiotics. They said that the science just isn't there yet. They likened being offered a probiotic to a doctor saying to a patient, "Here, would you like this medicine?" "Well, what is the medicine?" "Oh, it's just a medicine, we're not sure what it does." "Well, what are we treating?" "We're not sure. But would you like the medicine?"

True confession: I do recommend probiotics for my patients with IBS and SIBO. After one month of supplement eradication of SIBO, I encourage patients to start on a daily probiotic. My current top two are VSL#3 (which can be prescribed through a pharmacy, improving the odds that it stays cold enough to remain active, as it has to be refrigerated) or Florastor. There are some data to support this.[26] A review article noted that probiotics cannot prevent SIBO, but they can help eradicate it and improve symptoms of pain and bloating, although not stool frequency.[27] Ultimately, everyone's experience of these is different. Some patients absolutely swear by probiotics, and others have never found them helpful (or get more bloated with them). That probably emerges from a combination of genetic variability causing differing responses, as well as placebo effect.

Case Resolution: Emily

Emily's new doctor refers her to a gastroenterologist for a diagnostic colonoscopy just to be sure that no measurable medical problem is presenting atypically. The colonoscopy is normal. Emily knows not to be invalidated by that result because she and her doctor talked in advance about the complicated relationship between the gut and the brain, and she understood the low probability that colonoscopy would reveal anything abnormal. That rule-out complete, Emily's doctor makes the diagnosis of IBS-mixed subtype. Emily is then offered SIBO testing as well as a referral to a pelvic floor physical therapist.

Emily's breath testing comes back positive, so she starts taking FC Cidal, Dysbiocide, and Atrantil for a month. There are an annoying number of capsules to take, but she manages. After about three weeks, her distention is noticeably better, and her stools are a little more regular.

The pelvic floor physical therapist diagnoses her with pelvic floor dyssynergia, and they begin meeting weekly. At first, Emily isn't sure that therapy is helping. However, about eight weeks later, while taking a lower dose of maintenance Atrantil and on a VSL#3 probiotic, she realizes she hasn't had distracting abdominal symptoms for an entire week. Yes, she is still somewhat bloated at times, but she is spending much less time in the bathroom. Yes, when stressed her symptoms worsen. But there are more good days, and her worst day now is better than her best day before.

The Dog in the Street

I recall one of my former patients who was once overlooking a busy street from her hospital window. She saw a dog wander into the road. Fortunately, all the cars slowed and stopped so as not to hit it, but no one got out of their vehicle. It was a standoff, with the dog looking scared and frozen in place, and the cars waiting for it to move. My patient said that's how she felt sometimes in her recovery, as if she were the dog: everyone stopping and staring, but no one getting out to help.

I told her I loved this metaphor and took it further with her. I reminded her that the poor dog was so terrified that he had no idea which way to turn in that moment. Similarly, patients who feel helpless and stuck in moving forward in recovery may not be able to be self-directed and know what to do next. They're likely exhausted, malnourished, anxious, depressed, and frozen in place, like the dog.

I can't expect patients currently engaging in eating disorder behaviors to think to themselves, as if they were the dog in the street, "Ah, I see. I know just what I need to do here. I need to turn around, walk back to the grassy, safe side of the street, and ignore these huge cars bearing down on me."

They don't have to know what to do next. I tell them, "Here's what you can do. You can let your team carry you out of the street without scratching or biting us. You don't have to proactively seek and accept a solution, but you can choose not to resist." By compassionately seeing themselves as the dog in the street, they can let the team help and guide them until they are out of the scariest moments and can start connecting insight with action themselves. Individuals with an eating disorder may not be able to joyfully accept recommended treatment, but they can choose not to resist.

Notes

1 Drossman DA, Hasler WL. Rome IV-functional GI disorders: disorders of gut-brain interaction. *Gastroenterology.* 2016; 150(6):1257–1261. doi: 10.1053/j.gastro.2016.03.035.
2 Simren M, Palsson OS, Whitehead WE. Update on Rome IV Criteria for Color-ectal Disorders: implications for clinical practice. *Current Gastroenterology Reports.* 2017; 19(4):15. doi:10.1007/s11894-017-0554-0.
3 Maxion-Bergemann S, Thielecke F, Abel F, Bergemann R. Costs of irritable bowel syndrome in the UK and US. *Pharmacoeconomics.* 2006; 24(1):21–37. PubMed PMID: 16445300.
4 Pourmand H, Esmaillzadeh A. Consumption of a low fermentable oligo-, di-, oono-saccharides, and polyols diet and irritable bowel syndrome: a systematic review. *Int J Prev Med.* 2017 December 13; 8:104. doi: 10.4103/ijpvm.IJPVM_175_17.
5 Lin HC. Small intestinal bacterial overgrowth: a framework for understanding irritable bowel syndrome. *JAMA.* 2004 August 18; 292(7):852–858. Review. PubMed PMID: 15316000.
6 Rezaie A, Buresi M, Lembo A, Lin H, McCallum R, Rao S, Schmulson M, Valdovinos M, Zakko S, Pimentel M. Hydrogen and methane-based breath testing in gastrointestinal disorders: the North American consensus. *Am J Gastroenterol.* 2017 May; 112(5):775–784. doi: 10.1038/ajg.2017.46.
7 Chedid V, Dhalla S, Clarke JO, Roland BC, Dunbar KB, Koh J, Justino E, Tomakin E, Mullin GE. Herbal therapy is equivalent to rifaximin for the treatment of small intestinal bacterial overgrowth. *Glob Adv Health Med.* 2014 May; 3(3):16–24. doi: 10.7453/gahmj.2014.019.
8 Brown K, Scott-Hoy B, Jennings LW. Response of irritable bowel syndrome with constipation patients administered a combined quebracho/conker tree/M. balsamea Willd extract. *World J Gastrointest Pharmacol Ther.* 2016 August 6; 7(3):463–468. doi: 10.4292/wjgpt.v7.i3.463.
9 Abraham S, Luscombe GM, Kellow JE. Pelvic floor dysfunction predicts abdominal bloating and distension in eating disorder patients. *Scand J Gastroenterol.* 2012 June; 47(6):625–631. doi: 10.3109/00365521.2012.661762.
10 Abraham S, Kellow JE. Do the digestive tract symptoms in eating disorder patients represent functional gastrointestinal disorders? *BMC Gastroenterol.* 2013 February 28; 13:38. doi: 10.1186/1471-230X-13-38.

11 Jiang X, Locke GR 3rd, Choung RS, Zinsmeister AR, Schleck CD, Talley NJ. Prevalence and risk factors for abdominal bloating and visible distention: a population-based study. *Gut.* 2008 June; 57(6):756–763. doi: 10.1136/gut.2007. 142810.

12 Serra J, Azpiroz F, Malagelada JR. Impaired transit and tolerance of intestinal gas in the irritable bowel syndrome. *Gut.* 2001 January; 48(1):14–19. PubMed PMID: 11115817.

13 Shim L, Prott G, Hansen RD, Simmons LE, Kellow JE, Malcolm A. Prolonged balloon expulsion is predictive of abdominal distension in bloating. *Am J Gastroenterol.* 2010 April; 105(4):883–887. doi: 10.1038/ajg.2010.54.

14 Carr J, Kleiman SC, Bulik CM, Bulik-Sullivan EC, Carroll IM. Can attention to the intestinal microbiota improve understanding and treatment of anorexia nervosa? *Expert Rev Gastroenterol Hepatol.* 2016; 10(5):565–569. doi: 10.1586/174 74124.2016.1166953.

15 Mason BL. Feeding systems and the gut microbiome: gut-brain interactions with relevance to psychiatric conditions. *Psychosomatics.* 2017 November–December; 58(6):574–580. doi: 10.1016/j.psym.2017.06.002.

16 Berer K, Gerdes LA, Cekanaviciute E, Jia X, Xiao L, Xia Z, Liu C, Klotz L, Stauffer U, Baranzini SE, Kümpfel T, Hohlfeld R, Krishnamoorthy G, Wekerle H. Gut microbiota from multiple sclerosis patients enables spontaneous autoimmune encephalomyelitis in mice. *Proc Natl Acad Sci USA.* 2017 October 3; 114(40):10719–10724. doi: 10.1073/pnas.1711233114.

17 Demmitt BA, Corley RP, Huibregtse BM, Keller MC, Hewitt JK, McQueen MB, Knight R, McDermott I, Krauter KS. Genetic influences on the human oral microbiome. *BMC Genomics.* 2017 August 24; 18(1):659. doi: 10.1186/s12864-017-4008-8.

18 Lim MY, You HJ, Yoon HS, Kwon B, Lee JY, Lee S, Song YM, Lee K, Sung J, Ko G. The effect of heritability and host genetics on the gut microbiota and metabolic syndrome. *Gut.* 2017 June; 66(6):1031–1038. doi: 10.1136/gutjnl-2015-311326.

19 Smith MI, Yatsunenko T, Manary MJ, Trehan I, Mkakosya R, Cheng J, Kau AL, Rich SS, Concannon P, Mychaleckyj JC, Liu J, Houpt E, Li JV, Holmes E, Nicholson J, Knights D, Ursell LK, Knight R, Gordon JI. Gut microbiomes of Malawian twin pairs discordant for kwashiorkor. *Science.* 2013 February 1; 339(6119):548–554. doi: 10.1126/science.1229000.

20 van de Wouw M, Schellekens H, Dinan TG, Cryan JF. Microbiota-gut-brain axis: modulator of host metabolism and appetite. *J Nutr.* 2017 May; 147(5):727–745. doi: 10.3945/jn.116.240481.

21 Kleiman SC, Watson HJ, Bulik-Sullivan EC, Huh EY, Tarantino LM, Bulik CM, Carroll IM. The intestinal microbiota in acute anorexia nervosa and during renourishment: relationship to depression, anxiety, and eating disorder psychopathology. *Psychosom Med.* 2015 November–December; 77(9):969–981. doi: 10.1097/PSY.0000000000000247.

22 Borgo F, Riva A, Benetti A, Casiraghi MC, Bertelli S, Garbossa S, Anselmetti S, Scarone S, Pontiroli AE, Morace G, Borghi E. Microbiota in anorexia nervosa: the triangle between bacterial species, metabolites and psychological tests. *PLoS One.* 2017 June 21; 12(6):e0179739. doi: 10.1371/journal.pone.0179739.

23 Dey N, Wagner VE, Blanton LV, Cheng J, Fontana L, Haque R, Ahmed T, Gordon JI. Regulators of gut motility revealed by a gnotobiotic model of diet-microbiome interactions related to travel. *Cell.* 2015 September 24; 163(1): 95–107. doi: 10.1016/j.cell.2015.08.059.

24 Xie HY, Feng D, Wei DM, Mei L, Chen H, Wang X, Fang F. Probiotics for vulvovaginal candidiasis in non-pregnant women. *Cochrane Database Syst Rev.* 2017 November 23; 11:CD010496. doi: 10.1002/14651858.

25 Mills JP, Rao K, Young VB. Probiotics for prevention of Clostridium difficile infection. *Curr Opin Gastroenterol.* 2018 January; 34(1):3–10. doi: 10.1097/ MOG.0000000000000410.
26 Guandalini S, Magazzù G, Chiaro A, La Balestra V, Di Nardo G, Gopalan S, Sibal A, Romano C, Canani RB, Lionetti P, Setty M. VSL#3 improves symptoms in children with irritable bowel syndrome: a multicenter, randomized, placebo-controlled, double-blind, crossover study. *J Pediatr Gastroenterol Nutr.* 2010 July; 51(1):24–30. doi: 10.1097/MPG.0b013e3181ca4d95.
27 Zhong C, Qu C, Wang B, Liang S, Zeng B. Probiotics for preventing and treating small intestinal bacterial overgrowth: a meta-analysis and systematic review of current evidence. *J Clin Gastroenterol.* 2017 April; 51(4):300–311. doi: 10. 1097/MCG.0000000000000814.

Postural Orthostatic Tachycardia Syndrome (POTS) and Associated Conditions

Case: Bella

Bella is a 24-year-old cisgender Latina female with atypical anorexia nervosa. She has been restricting calories since she was 16 years old, with brief periods of better nutrition. Despite her restriction and thoughts constantly consumed by calorie counting and body size, to her dismay she has never dropped to a weight that feels acceptably low. From a close-knit Mexican family, Bella has felt isolated for years because she has gotten the message from her peers that Latina girls aren't "supposed" to have eating disorders.

For the last six months, Bella has worried that she's done something to her heart. It constantly feels like it's beating out of her chest, and it gets much worse when she stands up or moves around. Bella used to overexercise in the service of her eating disorder, but for the last few months she has had neither the energy nor the ability to do so. She has experienced waves of flushing and sweating, and she's noticed itchy rashes on her skin, which look like mosquito bites that then fade away after an hour or so. Additionally, she's developed headaches that center over her forehead and cheekbones.

Two months ago while at work, Bella passed out and was taken to the emergency department. Her lab work was all normal, her EKG showed a fast heart rate, and she was referred to a cardiologist. The cardiologist thought that she might have developed the postural orthostatic tachycardia syndrome, or POTS, and sent her for a tilt table test, which proved inconclusive. However, for the last month, she's had two other episodes of passing out, has felt short of breath and exhausted all the time, and has struggled to continue working.

Her doctor arranges for her to have a longer term cardiac recording device implanted. The data reveal that so far, her passing out episodes are always related to a high heart rate but not to any arrhythmia. She is started on a beta blocker, propranolol, which helps her feel a little better at first, but then she starts feeling short of breath again. The eating disorder, in the meantime, is escalating because that voice in her head can't bear that she's not getting to the gym or able to do any activity at all. Realizing she needs more help, and worried that her eating disorder has caused her heart issues, she finds a local therapist who refers her to a dietitian as well.

Background

Postural orthostatic tachycardia syndrome (POTS) is diagnosed when a person has experienced at least six months of rapid heart rate and other symptoms, like dizziness, shortness of breath, palpitations, nausea, sweating, tremulousness, headaches, anxiety, or rage upon standing. It should not be diagnosed when a patient is malnourished, as cardiac findings during malnourishment can mimic POTS. First described in 1893 in a case series on Civil War soldiers, 100 years later this syndrome was formally defined as POTS.[1] The cause is thought to be an excessive sympathetic response to the pooling of blood when a person stands. The sympathetic nervous system is part of the autonomic nervous system—the system by which our cave person keeps us stable, functioning, and responsive to the world on a daily basis. While our parasympathetic system slows us down as the "rest and digest" system, our sympathetic system fuels what's commonly known as our "fight or flight" response.

POTS is therefore a form of dysautonomia, referring to when the autonomic nervous system doesn't work. When patients pass out from POTS—syncope in medical terms—it is not from a drop in blood pressure. In fact, patients' postural blood pressure does not typically change that much from sitting to standing in POTS. Nor are the changes in heart rate from POTS primarily associated with the hibernating heart changes we see in malnutrition, where patients have a slow resting pulse to conserve calories, but a fast pulse upon walking across the room due to weakened muscles.

POTS is generally diagnosed when the heart rate increases more than 30 beats per minute when going from lying down to standing. Alternatively, it is diagnosed when the heart rate goes faster than 120 beats per minute after ten minutes on a tilt table at 60–70 degrees.[2] It more often affects females than males. Some studies have noted that the onset of POTS can follow an infection, leading some to wonder if it represents an autoimmune problem.[3] That is, the body develops antibodies to a disease, which accidentally also attack the autonomic nervous system and thus damage it.

In my experience, people who develop POTS tend to have strong mind-body connections. They often have a higher incidence of migraines, IBS, fibromyalgia, and other problems worsened by stress. Sleep issues are common with POTS and thought to be related to body fatigue, chronic pain, and other somatic symptoms.[4] As a result of the unmeasurable comorbid problems someone with POTS might experience, patients can find themselves having their symptoms minimized or doubted by medical professionals.

Even though we don't have nearly enough information about exactly how POTS starts, or (unfortunately) how optimally to treat the variety of types of POTS, without a doubt it is a real and potentially devastating disease. Patients as young as their 30s can end up permanently in nursing homes due to POTS's debilitating effects, particularly when it presents with chronic fatigue.

Three Types of POTS

POTS comes in three different types: hyperadrenergic (called "hyper-POTS"), neuropathic, and hypovolemic. However, the types can overlap. Hyper-POTS occurs when excessive serum levels of norepinephrine, epinephrine, and dopamine are released when patients stand up from a seated position. The cause of this malfunction remains unclear. One theory is that this could be due to a mutation in the norepinephrine reuptake transporter gene. That is, once norepinephrine is released, it doesn't get "slurped" back into the cell soon enough, and it wreaks havoc while it's active. Patients may experience bouts of intense flushing, rage, and sudden onset diarrhea that occur primarily when they stand up for too long. High angiotensin II levels have been noted, worse with low body mass, as has impairment of nitric oxide-mediated vasodilation. It is common to see elevated heart rates at all times, even when lying down, in patients with hyper-POTS, along with elevated blood pressure, pale coloring, exaggerated tremors, anxiety, and cold, sweaty extremities.

Neuropathic POTS is associated with partial sympathetic denervation of the lower body, causing impaired vasoconstriction in the lower extremities at the level of the arteriole, not the vein. Typically, when someone stands up, gravity makes their blood pool toward their ankles, giving less blood to the heart. Normally, the autonomic nervous system senses this and tightens up the veins and arterioles in the legs, resisting the pooling of blood so that it remains normally distributed throughout the body. When this tightening takes a little more time, such as when you get out of a hot bath that has expanded all your veins, you get lightheaded and feel your heart pounding for a few moments. The heart speeds up to keep pumping that lower blood volume around. Those with neuropathic-predominant POTS, however, have trouble tightening up their arterioles when they stand. This subtype impacts more than half of patients with POTS. It is associated with lower resting heart rates, less anxiety and depression, and more acrocyanosis, the cool, blueish hands and feet described in Chapter 2.

Hypovolemic POTS refers to patients who appear chronically volume depleted, or in common terms, dehydrated. Usually, dehydration or anemia triggers an increase in our renin-angiotensin-aldosterone system, which keeps us from urinating away needed fluids to maintain our blood pressure. However, patients with hypovolemic POTS have inappropriately low levels of plasma renin and aldosterone activity and elevated levels of angiotensin II. They don't respond appropriately to normal hydration and dehydration states, and as a result their pulse rises to compensate.[5]

Introducing Mast Cell Activation

Before I turn to the treatment of POTS, I'll discuss a few associated conditions. I have learned to ask patients about symptoms of these conditions because this information can make all the difference with regards to the treatment strategy I propose. A remarkable number of my patients—both with and without POTS—have symptoms of a problem called mast cell activation (MCA), also interchangeably called mast cell dysfunction (MCD).

The mast cells are a population of white blood cells that contain histamine granules. Histamine is the chemical released in an allergic reaction, causing anything from skin hives to full blown anaphylaxis. Normally, the mast cells hold on to those histamine granules except when triggered by an allergen. However, in MCA, the cells are more likely to degranulate or inappropriately release histamine.

Patients with MCA describe a range of symptoms, usually including at least several of the following: fleeting rashes that come on suddenly and can disappear as suddenly, hives (juicy, soft areas of red swelling on the skin), sinus problems including pressure and pain, joint pains that come and go, sometimes seemingly in response to specific food groups, abdominal pain after eating, fevers intermittently throughout the day, flushing sensations that are sometimes accompanied by sweating, and escalating reactiveness or even allergies to foods or medications. In severe cases, for reasons that are not well understood, exposure to sunlight and heat can trigger severe mast cell reactions, including formation of edema and a "foggy brain." MCA may drive POTS in some cases and can be one of the main causes for the rapid heart rate. Therefore, treating MCA, where present, should form a foundation of POTS treatment.

Treatment of MCA

There are no definitive tests for MCA at present, although some centers use clinical criteria that involve testing the urine or blood after a flushing or rash episode. When patients possess a number of the above symptoms, I tend to treat empirically and see if they feel better on a mast cell stabilizer. If they do, that makes the diagnosis from my perspective.

A number of tools in the medical toolbox can be used for treatment. First, one can begin with simple anti-histamine medications like ranitidine or famotidine (used for reflux) or classic antihistamines like diphenhydramine, loratadine, or cetirizine. If these are ineffective by themselves, I add oral mast cell stabilizers. Oral cromolyn is a liquid solution that must be taken four times a day to be effective because it is so short acting. The common starting dose is 10 mg, or two individual vials, four times a day, and typically it is covered by insurance. The other possible medication is ketotifen 1 mg twice a day. Ketotifen is available in prescription eye drops for seasonal allergies, but for some reason, no drug company has picked up its oral formulation. Therefore, it must be prepared in a compounding pharmacy, where they can make it into a capsule. Neither of these commonly has any serious side effects, although ketotifen can initially cause some fatigue. While it is not covered by insurance, ketotifen is easier for patients to take as a capsule twice a day, so I usually start with it instead of oral cromolyn. If patients don't feel markedly better within two weeks of starting ketotifen, I discontinue it.

If all of these medications fail to adequately control symptoms, I might add the injectable mast cell and basophil stabilizer omalizumab. Omalizumab is an anti-immunoglobulin-E (IgE) monoclonal antibody used for a condition called chronic idiopathic urticaria, which also relates to unexplained persistent hives.[6] Felt to be highly effective in this population,[7] as well as seemingly safe during pregnancy,[8] omalizumab is nonetheless not presently evidence based for MCA. However, exciting research is emerging that IgE may play a key role in autoimmunity, asthma, and perhaps in difficult-to-treat mast cell and basophil disorders.[9] An injected dose of 300 mg is given monthly. The main side effect is the potential for a serious allergic reaction.

Despite MCA causing excess histamine release, I cannot in good conscience recommend a "low histamine diet" for my patients. It turns out that practically every food can increase histamine release, and the restriction of such a diet is not worth whatever very modest benefit might accrue. Such diets are not evidence based and have the potential to be triggering for someone with an eating disorder.

Ehlers Danlos Syndrome

The other condition associated with POTS and MCA is Ehlers Danlos Syndrome (EDS). EDS is an inherited collagen disorder with various subtypes. Patients can have issues with their skin, joints, and vasculature. They are hyper-flexible and suffer from frequent joint dislocations, headaches, taste and smell dysregulation, and other issues. Genetic testing is available although it is not commonly done as patients may find several-year waiting lists to see a geneticist who specializes in EDS.

Patients can be perceived as "too somatic" or "too difficult" when they have EDS because there are so many physical effects from this condition. Once again, this is a case of Western medicine dismissing patients who suffer physically without clear testing to show why they suffer. Future research will likely bring more answers.[10]

EDS has been associated with MCA[11] and eating disorders.[12,13,14] The theory is that abnormalities in the GI system and in taste and smell, as well as perhaps the anxiety produced by constant pain or joint dislocations, may set a patient up for abnormal eating and psychological stress. It is clear that as we learn more about the physical effects of complicated syndromes like EDS, MCA, and POTS, we will serve patients far better.

Essential Treatment for All Types of POTS

Because we still simply don't know enough about the subtle, difficult-to-measure physiology taking place, treatment of POTS at present can be difficult. However, there are some important treatment considerations that can usually improve POTS symptoms, even if they do not "cure" it altogether. I often start by setting expectations with newly diagnosed patients that this may be a chronic, relapsing and remitting problem. It can take years to get POTS under control, and there will invariably be flares.

Fortunately, some patients have a relatively mild version of POTS and respond well to treatments, while others have an exceptionally severe version and seem to have far more side effects than they do benefits from standard care protocols. Once again, there is no way to predict this at the time of clinical diagnosis. Studies of adolescents with POTS show good outcomes overall by 2–10 years from diagnosis.[15] Patience, open communication, compassion, and a willingness to keep trying different treatment modalities are all vital for POTS treatment.

POTS treatment always starts with volume expansion, which means consistent hydration. Good salt and fluid intake throughout the day are vital in all types of POTS. As a marker of adequate hydration, the urine should be almost clear after the first morning void. Intravenous hydration should be avoided—including home infusions via a port—except in the context of serious intercurrent illness (like a diarrheal virus that causes significant dehydration) or chronic debilitating symptoms that are clearly helped by IV fluids.

Additionally, good sleep is vital, although accomplishing recharging rest may prove difficult. Exercise may help those with POTS, such as a recumbent bike and other exercise that does not provoke postural symptoms. However, patients with POTS may also have chronic fatigue, which makes the POTS both more severe and more treatment refractory.[16] This is once again a clinical diagnosis. In those with POTS and chronic fatigue, exercise will typically worsen all symptoms.

Medications to Treat POTS

After these standard interventions, we turn to the medications used for POTS.[17] Patients can have very different responses to medications (both positive and negative), so it's important to set expectations that various month-long trials may be indicated. For patients with hyper-POTS who have any symptoms at all of MCA, I always try to optimize MCA treatment first.

Then, for the POTS itself, I usually start methyldopa 250 mg twice a day. Methyldopa is an old blood pressure medicine in the alpha-2 agonist class. If this is insufficient after a month but has helped a little, I will add another medicine with alpha-2 agonist activity, a clonidine patch of 0.1 mg weekly. Clonidine, a medicine that also relaxes blood vessels, can help the heart beat more slowly. Side effects for both include low blood pressure symptoms, so patients should take it easy when moving from lying down to standing up. If patients develop shortness of breath or actual low blood oxygen levels while on clonidine, I stop the medication.

For those with neurogenic POTS and hypovolemic POTS, I might start propranolol or labetalol, both beta blockers. These specifically slow down the heart rate and can also reduce blood pressure. Low dose propranolol (20 mg a day) has been found to improve symptoms and have few negative effects in adults with POTS.[18] Labetalol can be started at a low dose and slowly increased until patients feel better but don't have side effects of low blood pressure. Beta blockers should not be used in those with hyper-POTS; my clinical experience is that it causes worsened shortness of breath and even low blood oxygen levels. My theory is that it may exacerbate imbalances in the oxygenation/blood flow to the lungs (called "V/Q mismatch"). I've seen patients enter my practice already on a beta blocker and home oxygen at night and be able to stop the home oxygen when they stop the beta blocker.

Midodrine is an alpha-1-agonist used for those with low blood pressure. It can be effective in individuals with neurogenic POTS, but it can cause high blood pressure, and I haven't had as much success with it in my patients. Similarly, I generally recommend against an oral steroid called fludrocortisone. Although used to help boost hydration levels, it often causes water retention, can cause cataracts when used long term, and just isn't well tolerated by patients.

Chronic Fatigue and POTS

My heart goes out to patients who have the combination of POTS and chronic fatigue. A once highly active, organized multitasker can be halted in her tracks, barely able to get out of bed to play with her kids for an hour or two a day. Just taking a shower can require hours of rest afterwards. For these patients, modafinil is a weak dopamine reuptake inhibitor that is used to improve wakefulness. Effective for the highly fatiguing effects of cancer,[19] HIV,[20] shift work sleep disorder, and depression,[21] it is administered as 100 mg by mouth daily. My experience is that this can be a game changer for those with POTS and chronic fatigue.

Managing Syncope (Fainting/Passing Out)

I'll end the section on POTS with a brief note about managing syncope, which is also known as fainting or passing out. Syncope occurs when the brain doesn't get enough blood for whatever reason. Passing out is Mother Nature's brilliant way of getting blood to our brain ... essentially forcing us to get down on the ground and get our brain even with our heart. Patients may have a set of symptoms, referred to as a prodrome, that signal they are about to pass out. Tunnel vision, seeing spots, nausea, sweatiness, ringing in the ears, shortness of breath, and shakiness are all common.

When a patient gets these prodromal symptoms, they should listen to them. The brain wants more blood. Patients should immediately get their brains even with or below their hearts. The best posture is to lie down flat with the legs up. This dumps blood from the legs back into the central vasculature, back to the heart and then up to the brain. Short of that, sitting down and putting the head between the knees works well too. Patients should stay in that position until they feel all the way better. Sitting up and going back about life too quickly can cause patients to pass out, which risks hitting their head or harming some other part of the body. "Drop attacks," or new-onset syncope episodes without any warning, may result from something different and more dangerous and always merit immediate medical workup.

Case Resolution: Bella

Bella's therapist and dietitian are a good match for her. They focus not only on her eating disorder work but also on the challenges of being a Latina woman with an eating disorder. Bella feels seen and heard and makes progress. Bella's doctor learns about her worsening shortness of breath and recommends she buy an oxygen monitor. This shows that her blood oxygen level is falling below normal at intervals throughout the day. She stops Bella's propranolol and, after doing some more reading about POTS, recognizes that Bella may have hyper-POTS as well as MCA causing the itchy rash, sinus pressure, and flushing episodes.

Bella starts on ketotifen and methyldopa, and within a month, she feels some improvements. She no longer feels totally depleted of energy, and her mast cell symptoms are gone. She and her doctor talk about overall good self-care being vital for her POTS, and this helps motivate her in her eating disorder recovery work, too. She knows that good nutrition and rest won't guarantee freedom from POTS symptoms, but engaging in her eating disorder will guarantee worse fatigue, higher risk for passing out, and overall body pain.

Bearing Witness

Sometimes in caring for patients who have unmeasurable medical problems, I come to the point where they are still suffering, and I don't have a next solution to offer. In this case, the ancient role of the physician once again proves relevant: I can bear witness. I can hold space for my patient's suffering without getting impatient, distressed, or overwhelmed. Family and friends may struggle to stay compassionate while seeing their loved one in pain, exhausted, or failing to improve despite countless doctors and tests. The doctor, however, occupies the sacred space of both caring about the patient and yet possessing the neutrality of a non-family member to sit with and welcome further discussion of symptoms.

I promise my patients in these moments that I will continue to walk with them on this journey of finding answers and relief of symptoms. I will continue to read the literature and talk with experts to learn about new treatment modalities. I will welcome their own research without ego and will read anything they send me carefully and with a scientist's eye because no one is more motivated than they to find solutions.

In a modern medical world where practically miraculous diagnostic and therapeutic solutions abound, it can be excruciating to tell a patient that I'm not sure what to do next. However, I can name my instinct to jump in and try multiple treatments at once, hoping to make them feel better. I can name that this instinct poses a risk of causing harm. I can set expectations both with my patient and with myself that we will make thoughtful, evidence-based decisions together, keeping the treatment momentum up while not rushing. And I can bear witness.

Notes

1 Wells R, Tonkin A. Clinical approach to autonomic dysfunction. *Intern Med J.* 2016 October; 46(10):1134–1139. doi: 10.1111/imj.13216.
2 Sidhu B, Obiechina N, Rattu N, Mitra S. Postural orthostatic tachycardia syndrome (POTS). *BMJ Case Rep.* 2013. pii: bcr2013201244. doi: 10.1136/bcr-2013-201244.
3 Garland EM, Celedonio JE, Raj SR. Postural tachycardia syndrome: beyond orthostatic intolerance. *Curr Neurol Neurosci Rep.* 2015 September; 15(9):60. doi: 10.1007/s11910-015-0583-8.
4 Miglis MG, Muppidi S, Feakins C, Fong L, Prieto T, Jaradeh S. Sleep disorders in patients with postural tachycardia syndrome. *Clin Auton Res.* 2016 February; 26(1):67–73. doi: 10.1007/s10286-015-0331-9.
5 Heyer GL. Postural tachycardia syndrome: Diagnosis and management in adolescents and young adults. *Pediatr Ann.* 2017 April 1; 46(4):e145–e154. doi: 10.3928/19382359-20170322-01.
6 Eghrari-Sabet J, Sher E, Kavati A, Pilon D, Zhdanava M, Balp MM, Lefebvre P, Ortiz B, Bernstein JA. Real-world use of omalizumab in patients with chronic idiopathic/spontaneous urticaria in the United States. *Allergy Asthma Proc.* 2018 February 19. doi: 10.2500/aap. 2018.39.4132. [Epub ahead of print].

7 Bernstein JA, Kavati A, Tharp MD, Ortiz B, MacDonald K, Denhaerynck K, Abraham I. Effectiveness of omalizumab in adolescent and adult patients with chronic idiopathic/spontaneous urticaria: a systematic review of "real-world" evidence. *Expert Opin Biol Ther.* 2018 April;18(4):425–448. doi: 10.1080/147125 98.2018.1438406.

8 Namazy J, Cabana MD, Scheuerle AE, Thorp JM Jr., Chen H, Carrigan G, Wang Y, Veith J, Andrews EB. The Xolair Pregnancy Registry (EXPECT): the safety of omalizumab use during pregnancy. *J Allergy Clin Immunol.* 2015 February; 135(2):407–412. doi: 10.1016/j.jaci.2014.08.025.

9 Sanjuan MA, Sagar D, Kolbeck R. Role of IgE in autoimmunity. *J Allergy Clin Immunol.* 2016 June; 137(6):1651–1661. doi: 10.1016/j.jaci.2016.04.007.

10 Lyons JJ, Yu X, Hughes JD, Le QT, Jamil A, Bai Y, Ho N, Zhao M, Liu Y, O'Connell MP, Trivedi NN, Nelson C, DiMaggio T, Jones N, Matthews H, Lewis KL, Oler AJ, Carlson RJ, Arkwright PD, Hong C, Agama S, Wilson TM, Tucker S, Zhang Y, McElwee JJ, Pao M, Glover SC, Rothenberg ME, Hohman RJ, Stone KD, Caughey GH, Heller T, Metcalfe DD, Biesecker LG, Schwartz LB, Milner JD. Elevated basal serum tryptase identifies a multisystem disorder associated with increased TPSAB1 copy number. *Nat Genet.* 2016 December; 48(12): 1564–1569. doi: 10.1038/ng.3696.

11 Seneviratne SL, Maitland A, Afrin L. Mast cell disorders in Ehlers-Danlos syndrome. *Am J Med Genet C Semin Med Genet.* 2017 March; 175(1):226–236. doi: 10.1002/ajmg.c.31555.

12 Lee M, Strand M. Ehlers-Danlos syndrome in a young woman with anorexia nervosa and complex somatic symptoms. *Int J Eat Disord.* 2018 March; 51(3): 281–284. doi: 10.1002/eat.22815.

13 Baeza-Velasco C, Van den Bossche T, Grossin D, Hamonet C. Difficulty eating and significant weight loss in joint hypermobility syndrome/Ehlers-Danlos syndrome, hypermobility type. *Eat Weight Disord.* 2016 June; 21(2):175–183. doi: 10.1007/s40519-015-0232-x.

14 Baeza-Velasco C, Pailhez G, Bulbena A, Baghdadli A. Joint hypermobility and the heritable disorders of connective tissue: clinical and empirical evidence of links with psychiatry. *Gen Hosp Psychiatry.* 2015 January–February; 37(1):24–30. doi: 10.1016/j.genhosppsych.2014.10.002.

15 Bhatia R, Kizilbash SJ, Ahrens SP, Killian JM, Kimmes SA, Knoebel EE, Muppa P, Weaver AL, Fischer PR. Outcomes of adolescent-onset postural orthostatic tachycardia syndrome. *J Pediatr.* 2016 June; 173:149–153. doi: 10.1016/j.jpeds. 2016.02.035.

16 Roerink ME, Lenders JW, Schmits IC, Pistorius AM, Smit JW, Knoop H, van der Meer JW. Postural orthostatic tachycardia is not a useful diagnostic marker for chronic fatigue syndrome. *J Intern Med.* 2017 February; 281(2):179–188. doi: 10. 1111/joim.12564.

17 Shibao C, Arzubiaga C, Roberts LJ 2nd, Raj S, Black B, Harris P, Biaggioni I. Hyperadrenergic postural tachycardia syndrome in mast cell activation disorders. *Hypertension.* 2005 March; 45(3):385–390. PubMed PMID: 15710782.

18 Raj SR, Black BK, Biaggioni I, Paranjape SY, Ramirez M, Dupont WD, Robertson D. Propranolol decreases tachycardia and improves symptoms in the postural tachycardia syndrome: less is more. *Circulation.* 2009 September 1; 120(9):725–734. doi: 10.1161/CIRCULATIONAHA.108.846501.

19 Gerber LH. Cancer-related fatigue: persistent, pervasive, and problematic. *Phys Med Rehabil Clin N Am.* 2017 February; 28(1):65–88. doi: 10.1016/j.pmr.2016. 08.004.

20 Rabkin JG, McElhiney MC, Rabkin R. Modafinil and armodafinil treatment for fatigue for HIV-positive patients with and without chronic hepatitis C. *Int J STD AIDS*. 2011 February; 22(2):95–101. doi: 10.1258/ijsa.2010.010326.
21 Murillo-Rodríguez E, Barciela Veras A, Barbosa Rocha N, Budde H, Machado S. An Overview of the Clinical Uses, Pharmacology, and Safety of Modafinil. *ACS Chem Neurosci.* 2018 February 21; 9(2):151–158. doi: 10.1021/acschemneuro. 7b00374.

Part V

Specific Populations

Many important and unique populations of patients may develop an eating disorder, and Part V offers a series of shorter chapters with a case and a discussion of particular groups of patients. Specifically, Part V covers type 1 diabetes mellitus, avoidant restrictive food intake disorder (ARFID), orthorexia, elite athletes, male patients, gender and sexual minorities, women's sexual and reproductive health, older patients, comorbid substance abuse, and caring for patients who decline treatment.

Keep in mind that detailed psychological and sociological considerations for these and many other populations, while out of this medical book's scope, have been covered in superb texts. Invariably, some people will read this section and feel missed because they cannot find information here about the important combination of medical issues with their eating disorder. I'm constantly learning from my wonderful patients and colleagues and adding topics for future writing endeavors. I always welcome hearing about unique presentations and challenges.

Chapter 13

Type 1 Diabetes Mellitus and Concurrent Eating Disorders (ED-DMT1)

Case: Anthony

Anthony is a 13-year-old cisgender African American male who was diagnosed with type 1 diabetes mellitus (DMT1) when he was nine years old. He had been losing weight rapidly and was ravenous and thirsty for three months prior to his diagnosis. Ever since the day he went to the hospital and was admitted to the pediatric ICU with critically high blood sugars and diabetic ketoacidosis, multiple medical professionals have warned him about the medical consequences of poor diabetic control. They've talked about the risks of early death, heart attack, blindness, kidney failure, and amputation, threats terrifying to a young boy. In addition, diabetic educators and dietitians over the years have earnestly discussed the dangers of being "overweight" and the importance of strict dietary control, carbohydrate counting, and intensive tracking of blood glucose.

Anthony comes from a family of people with larger bodies, and he has many relatives with type 2 diabetes. He and his mom made a number of changes to their nutrition as a result of his diabetes diagnosis and team recommendations, none of which changed their bodies' size or shape. Anthony worries a lot about what might happen to him with his diabetes. He also gets teased by peers and feels shamed by doctors for his larger body. The doctors in particular have often asked him, "Don't you know what can happen to you if you don't take care of yourself?" This is confusing because Anthony does feel he takes care of himself.

At diabetes camp last summer, some of Anthony's friends told him that they'd learned a trick. If they skipped an insulin shot or decreased the amount of insulin given by their insulin pump, they lost weight. It was like magic. They also taught him ways to fake out his medical team, so it looked like he was taking his proper insulin dose. Anthony began to lose weight, and when he returned from camp, family and medical team alike praised him and commented that camp was just what he needed.

At this point, though, Anthony doesn't feel too great physically, as he's constantly thirsty, has trouble concentrating, is tired, and feels guilty for deceiving people. However, he does like the positive attention about his weight. The longer he restricts insulin, the more focused he becomes on losing more weight. He feels he's stuck because one weekend when he tried to get back on an appropriate amount of insulin, he became so puffy and swollen that his hands hurt.

Anthony's hemoglobin A1c level rises, and he has two hospitalizations for diabetic ketoacidosis (DKA) in the course of a month. A hospital dietitian with eating disorder experience sees him during his second DKA admission. She takes the time to sit and ask him compassionately and non-judgmentally about whether he might be deliberately omitting insulin to lose weight. She tells him that this is common and is actually a form of an eating disorder. She notes that help is possible and says she's here to listen. No one has ever asked Anthony whether he might have an eating disorder. He opens up to the dietitian and is referred to an eating disorder team in the community.

Background

Let's start with a quick reminder of what diabetes means. Some people believe that "eating sugar will cause diabetes," which is incorrect. The pancreas is an organ in the abdomen that has both exocrine (meaning producing digestive juices released through a duct into the intestine) and endocrine (meaning producing hormones released directly into the blood) functions. When a person eats carbohydrates, the pancreas produces insulin.

Each body cell derives its energy from the fuel of glucose. Imagine that every cell has a locked door in it; the key to that door is insulin. Without insulin the door stays locked, and glucose remains in the bloodstream. With insulin the door unlocks, the glucose enters the cell, and the cell is nourished.

Two Types of Diabetes

In DMT1, often known as childhood diabetes, the pancreas attacks itself due to an autoimmune process and stops making insulin altogether. Therefore, the only way that glucose can move from the bloodstream to the cells is by injection of insulin. Approximately 1.25 million Americans have DMT1.[1] In type 2 diabetes, known to many as adult-onset diabetes, the pancreas still produces plenty of insulin. However, each cell "door" becomes "double bolted." That means that more insulin is needed to open the door, which is referred to medically as insulin resistance. At some point, the pancreas cannot produce enough insulin to unlock all the double bolts, blood glucose levels rise, and the person is diagnosed with diabetes. Over 29 million Americans have type 2 diabetes.[2]

Why High Blood Sugar Matters

With either type of diabetes the digested and absorbed carbohydrate, now in the form of glucose, remains in the bloodstream rather than entering the cells to energize them. This is medically problematic for a number of reasons. One, the person functionally starves. Even after eating, glucose calories cannot be used by body tissues because glucose remains in the bloodstream. Rapid weight loss is common, and patients can get sick quite quickly.

Two, high blood sugar acts like sandpaper on the most delicate blood vessels in the body, known as the microvasculature. These include blood vessels in the brain, heart, healing tissue, kidneys, nerves, and eyes. Over time, constant "sanding" results in damage, which explains why patients with chronically uncontrolled diabetes are at risk for strokes, heart attacks, foot ulcers that don't heal and may contribute to the need for amputation, kidney failure, nerve pain, autonomic dysfunction including gastroparesis, and blindness.

Defining Some Important Concepts

A few medical terms deserve definitions. Normal blood glucose in someone who is fasting ranges from 70–100 mg/dL, up to 125 mg/dL in someone who is not fasting. Hypoglycemia means low blood sugar and usually refers to a glucose level less than 70 mg/dL, although in patients with diabetes who have been running higher blood sugars normally, a much higher glucose can feel low. Hyperglycemia refers to blood sugars greater than 180 mg/dL.

DKA occurs when the body's cells have had no access to glucose for energy because it all stays in the bloodstream. In response to this starved state, the body breaks down fat and muscle tissue to synthesize glucose, and the byproduct of this breakdown is ketones. Ketone buildup leads to extremely acidic blood, which can cause seizure, coma, or even death if untreated. DKA requires medical hospitalization, often in an ICU.

Finally, the hemoglobin A1c (or "A1c") estimates the average blood glucose level over the past three months, weighted toward the most recent few weeks. It is a predictor of morbidity and mortality outcomes. A normal A1c is less than 5.7 percent, and A1c levels between 5.7 percent and 6.4 percent may indicate pre-diabetes in those at risk for type 2 diabetes. It isn't uncommon for patients to have an A1c of 13 percent or higher at the time of diagnosis.

The Development of Eating Disorders in Patients with DMT1

Why does skipping or underdosing insulin result in weight loss? There are three major mechanisms. One, when a person with DMT1 skips an insulin dose, they trap all the glucose in the bloodstream rather than allowing it into the cells. Then through normal blood filtration in the kidneys, glucose is lost into the urine. Patients thus urinate away glucose calories. Two, a high blood sugar draws water from the body tissues into the blood, where it's then filtered and urinated away. This is called an "osmotic diuresis." Functionally, it's the same as abusing diuretics 24 hours a day, and the ensuing dehydration causes weight loss. Finally, even while the person is eating, the cells are starving because all the blood glucose remains in the bloodstream. The body therefore breaks down its own tissues in search of glucose, and further weight loss occurs.

The DSM-5 mentions insulin omission in its diagnostic criteria for both anorexia nervosa and bulimia nervosa, but the phenomenon of an eating disorder co-occurring with DMT1 and deliberate insulin restriction does not receive its own specific designation.[3,4] Thus, the formal eating disorder diagnosis ends up relating to other findings like body weight and eating disorder behaviors. Someone with a very low body weight and DMT1 would likely receive the diagnosis of anorexia nervosa, while someone with a "normal" or higher body weight and DMT1 would likely be diagnosed with bulimia nervosa, regardless of other purging mechanisms. The overlap between concurrent eating disorders and DMT1, called ED-DMT1 or "diabulimia," becomes clear when one realizes that patients have access, at all times, to a failsafe mechanism to lose weight.[5]

In a society obsessed with weight loss, and a patient population often diagnosed between childhood and adolescence, the opportunity to skip insulin can be dangerously irresistible. Dr. Ann Goebel-Fabbri is a health psychologist who specializes in diabetes. For a fantastic book about patients with ED-DMT1, I recommend her *Prevention and recovery from eating disorders in type 1 diabetes*. She writes, "Teaching a person how to be a 'perfect diabetic' is akin to teaching them how to have an eating disorder."[6]

From childhood, patients with DMT1 are taught to pay attention to meal planning, portion size, carbohydrate counting, and label reading. They receive constant commentary on exercise and weight. Patients may feel chronically deprived by having to follow dietary restraint all the time. They experience a relentless focus on numbers and are judged by doctors and peers based on those numbers. For patients with DMT1 who have inherited temperamental traits of perfectionism, intensity, and anxiety, having the life-threatening consequences of "poor diabetic control" constantly looming can be overwhelming.

In reality, this is a disease in which it's medically impossible to be a "perfect diabetic." Even "optimal" management will result in low and high blood glucoses. The body is complicated, and sometimes the glucose is just going to be different than what one expected. The pressure and burnout from constant vigilance and difference from peers can drive patients to think, "If I can't be perfect, I might as well be truly imperfect and at least lose weight."

Prevalence and Consequences of ED-DMT1

How does this translate in terms of the prevalence of ED-DMT1? The statistics are sobering. Women with DMT1 are 2.4 times more likely to develop an eating disorder than their non-diabetic peers.[7] In one study that monitored patients over four years, 29 percent of young women with DMT1 manifested disordered eating behavior, which persisted in 70 percent.[8] In a study of preteen girls aged 9–13, a full-syndrome or subthreshold eating disorder was identified in 8 percent of patients with DMT1, compared with only 1 percent of their non-diabetic peers.[9] Another study showed that one out of three female and one out of six male patients with DMT1 reported disordered eating and/or frequent insulin restriction.[10] In fact, it is generally agreed that disordered eating or eating disorders, including restriction of insulin, occur in fully 30 percent of all people with DMT1.[11] Compare this with a general population prevalence of anorexia nervosa of 0.1–0.5 percent, bulimia nervosa of 2 percent, and BED of 4 percent.

It turns out this higher prevalence matters a lot. Death rates from DMT1 alone are estimated at 2 percent, and death rates from anorexia nervosa alone are around 6.5 percent. Death rates from the combination of anorexia nervosa and DMT1 are a devastating 35 percent.[12] Another study showed that patients with ED-DMT1 were 3.2 times more likely to die over an 11-year study period. They also died an average of 13 years younger than patients with DMT1 who didn't restrict insulin.[13] Clearly, the co-occurrence of these problems is both prevalent and deadly.

Where does this excess mortality come from? Studies have clearly shown that patients with the most tightly controlled diabetes, typically with A1c levels less than 7 percent, have the same mortality and medical complications as individuals without diabetes. This kind of tight control is very hard to achieve, requires intense work, and causes more episodes of hypoglycemia and more weight gain. By contrast, patients with less tightly controlled, more typical diabetic control have a 30 percent increased mortality compared with the general population, predominantly from heart attack and stroke.[14] Needless to say, a patient with DMT1 who skips insulin in order to run deliberately high blood sugars for weight loss will have a very high A1c and thus a very high risk of all the associated medical complications.

Patients with ED-DMT1 have higher rates of ketoacidosis and more and longer hospitalizations.[15] They also have 2.5–5 times more microvascular complications than those with DMT1 alone. Microvascular damage accounts for the majority of diabetes complications. In one study, 25 percent of patients with DMT1 alone developed retinopathy. By contrast, fully 86 percent of patients with DMT1 and "highly disordered eating behavior" developed this serious diabetic complication that can lead to blindness.[8]

Managing Edema

Treatment of ED-DMT1 is complicated, but it is feasible and vitally worthwhile. It often requires starting in a higher level of care. A number of medical issues must be attended to properly, both for the patient's health and for their trust in the recovery process. One of the biggest barriers to recovery is edema, or fluid retention. This can be intense, uncomfortable, triggering, and persistent.

As we have seen, patients with ED-DMT1 who run very high blood sugar levels have a persistent osmotic diuresis, as if they were abusing diuretics all the time. Even if the individual has never deliberately purged, their body reacts to the chronic dehydration in exactly the same way as in someone who does purge by vomiting, laxative abuse, or diuretic abuse: they develop pseudo-Bartter syndrome, as I've detailed in Chapter 9.

As you may remember, this refers to overproduction of the adrenal hormone aldosterone, high levels of which make the body retain salt and water. Thus, when patients resume insulin and the excessive urination stops, their body will tend to develop severe edema. Patients may try to get back on track with diabetes care only to gain ten pounds in two days and have none of their rings or clothing fit. It perfectly fulfils the eating disorder's fear that "everything will fall apart if we stop using behaviors."

Good management of pseudo-Bartter syndrome in someone with ED-DMT1 calls for use of the aldosterone-blocker spironolactone, usually at a dose of 25 mg a day. After a few weeks, the adrenal glands get the message that the body isn't chronically dehydrated anymore, and they down-regulate production of aldosterone. Potassium levels need to be monitored weekly in this scenario. Spironolactone may not completely prevent the edema, but it will help reduce it. After all, patients resuming appropriate doses of insulin don't only experience edema from pseudo-Bartter syndrome. Insulin itself, as discussed in Chapter 6, causes increased reabsorption of salt and water in the kidneys. Spironolactone won't have an effect on this mechanism. This contribution to edema will go away on its own with time, but patients may need reminders to keep their legs up when seated and a great deal of support and reassurance.

Correction of Hyperglycemia

The overly fast correction of hyperglycemia in someone with a high A1c can lead to debilitating, years-long nerve pain (called neuropathy) and worsened eyesight (retinopathy).[16] This is not broadly known by most non-specialist doctors who, from hospital to outpatient settings, believe the best way to serve the patient is to get their blood glucose and A1c levels down quickly, in order to reduce morbidity and mortality. In reality, physicians should help patients reduce their A1c fewer than two points for every three-month interval. In the hospital, "permissive hyperglycemia," or allowance of higher blood sugars, should be the standard of care.[17]

Choosing a Level of Care

To remain outpatient for treatment, at a minimum the patient must be willing and consistently able to take at least their basal (long acting) insulin and stay out of DKA. If they cannot consistently do this, they must start at a higher level of care. Medical nutrition therapy should emphasize flexible and non-depriving approaches to eating for patients and their families.[18]

Most importantly, the treatment team must be aligned and communicative. The endocrinologist should optimally support the patient in becoming a "good enough diabetic" rather than encouraging them to be a "perfect diabetic," which can set off the overwhelm, perfectionism, and all-or-nothing thinking.

The dietitian should primarily have an eating disorder background. Many patients have told me that their diabetes dietitians were too rigid and numbers oriented. The eating disorder dietitian might feel out of scope of practice working with someone who has DMT1, but families can remind them that the doctor will manage the diabetes. What's needed from the eating disorder dietitian is the teaching that there are no off-limits foods and that moderation is safe.

Excellent literature details the optimal treatment that patients with ED-DMT1 should receive in higher levels of care.[19] It is vital that patients and families go beyond a program's "website assurances" of an expertise in diabetes. Asking to speak with the medical director or the head of nursing in advance of admission is imperative. Patients and families can interview them about how their program manages complicated scenarios, and they can ask how many patients with ED-DMT1 are presently under the program's care. Additionally, a chronic illness therapy group can be very productive, as it allows fellowship and validation of the significant challenges of comorbid chronic illnesses with an eating disorder.

One of the greatest burdens of ED-DMT1 is that once the Herculean effort of recovery from the eating disorder is successfully completed, the diabetes will always be there. In her book, Dr. Goebel-Fabbri identifies the key markers of recovery from ED-DMT1: consistently taking one's appropriate insulin doses, not engaging in rigid dieting, overexercise, or intentionally keeping the blood glucose high, eating in a flexible and healthy way most of the time, and not acting on eating disorder thoughts and feelings.

Case Resolution: Anthony

Anthony is ready to feel better. He knows high school is coming up, and he wants to be able to enjoy it. He also feels worried about his health. He meets with his new eating disorder dietitian and therapist, as well as his endocrinologist, within the first week of his hospital discharge. Anthony's endocrinologist apologizes for having missed the signs of ED-DMT1. He acknowledges to Anthony and his mother that Anthony's race, sex, and body size played into internal biases, preventing him from identifying the eating disorder and focusing instead on weight and numbers, and he promises to work on these biases. He puts Anthony on spironolactone 25 mg a day to reduce some of the edema that has already started to form; the doctor also acknowledges how difficult that edema can be but that it won't last forever.

Anthony works hard over the course of the next year. He makes slow progress on his A1c while benefiting from therapy and from the eating disorder dietitian's refreshing perspectives on food. He no longer feels as deprived. It's exhausting to deal with his diabetes constantly, and at times he feels burned out and rebellious. However, he doesn't take it out on his body anymore.

Notes

1 www.diabetes.org/diabetes-basics/statistics/?referrer=www.google.com. Accessed March 2, 2018.
2 www.cdc.gov/chronicdisease/resources/publications/aag/diabetes.htm. Accessed March 2, 2018.
3 Allan J, Nash J. Diabetes and eating disorders: insulin omission and the DSM-5. *Journal of Diabetes Nursing.* 2014; 18(9):386–387. www.thejournalofdiabetes nursing.co.uk/media/content/_master/3913/files/pdf/jdn18-9-386-7.pdf Accessed March 13, 2018.
4 American Psychiatric Association. (2013). *Diagnostic and statistical manual of mental disorders (5th ed.).* Arlington, VA: American Psychiatric Publishing.
5 With appreciation for the teachings of Erin M. Akers and Dawn Lee-Akers of www.diabulimiahelpline.org.
6 Goebel-Fabbri, A. (2017) *Prevention and recovery from eating disorders in type 1 diabetes.* New York, NY: Routledge.
7 Colton P, Rodin G, Bergenstal R, Parkin C. Eating disorders and diabetes: introduction and overview. *Diabetes Spectrum* 2009; 22(3):138–142. doi: 10.2337/diaspect.22.3.138.
8 Rydall AC, Rodin GM, Olmsted MP, Devenyi RG, Daneman D. Disordered eating behavior and microvascular complications in young women with insulin-dependent diabetes mellitus. *N Engl J Med.* 1997 June 26; 336(26):1849–1854. PubMed PMID: 9197212.

9 Colton P, Olmsted M, Daneman D, Rydall A, Rodin G. Disturbed eating behavior and eating disorders in preteen and early teenage girls with type 1 diabetes: a case-controlled study. *Diabetes Care.* 2004 July; 27(7):1654–1659. PubMed PMID: 15220242.

10 Bächle C, Stahl-Pehe A, Rosenbauer J. Disordered eating and insulin restriction in youths receiving intensified insulin treatment: results from a nationwide population-based study. *Int J Eat Disord.* 2016 February; 49(2):191–196. doi: 10.1002/eat.22463.

11 Jones JM, Lawson ML, Daneman D, Olmsted MP, Rodin G. Eating disorders in adolescent females with and without type 1 diabetes: cross sectional study. *BMJ.* 2000 June 10; 320(7249):1563–1566. PubMed PMID: 10845962.

12 Nielsen S, Emborg C, Mølbak AG. Mortality in concurrent type 1 diabetes and anorexia nervosa. *Diabetes Care.* 2002 February; 25(2):309–312. PubMed PMID: 11815501.

13 Goebel-Fabbri AE, Fikkan J, Franko DL, Pearson K, Anderson BJ, Weinger K. Insulin restriction and associated morbidity and mortality in women with type 1 diabetes. *Diabetes Care.* 2008 March; 31(3):415–419. PubMed PMID: 18070998.

14 Diabetes Control and Complications Trial (DCCT)/Epidemiology of Diabetes Interventions and Complications (EDIC) Study Research Group. Mortality in type 1 diabetes in the DCCT/EDIC versus the general population. *Diabetes Care.* 2016 August; 39(8):1378–1383. doi: 10.2337/dc15-2399.

15 Scheuing N, Bartus B, Berger G, Haberland H, Icks A, Knauth B, Nellen-Hellmuth N, Rosenbauer J, Teufel M, Holl RW; DPV Initiative; German BMBF Competence Network Diabetes Mellitus. Clinical characteristics and outcome of 467 patients with a clinically recognized eating disorder identified among 52,215 patients with type 1 diabetes: a multicenter German/Austrian study. *Diabetes Care.* 2014 June; 37(6):1581–1589. doi: 10.2337/dc13-2156.

16 Gibbons CH, Freeman R. Treatment-induced neuropathy of diabetes: an acute, iatrogenic complication of diabetes. *Brain.* 2015 January; 138(Pt 1):43–52. doi: 10.1093/brain/awu307.

17 Brown C, Mehler PS. Anorexia nervosa complicated by diabetes mellitus: the case for permissive hyperglycemia. *Int J Eat Disord.* 2014 September; 47(6): 671–674. doi: 10.1002/eat.22282.

18 Goebel-Fabbri AE, Uplinger N, Gerken S, Mangham D, Criego A, Parkin C. Outpatient management of eating disorders in type 1 diabetes. *Diabetes Spectrum* 2009; 22(3): 147–152. doi: 10.2337/diaspect.22.3.147.

19 Bermudez O, Gallivan H, Jahraus J, Lesser J, Meier M, Parkin C. Inpatient management of eating disorders in type 1 diabetes. *Diabetes Spectrum* 2009; 22(3): 153–158 doi: 10.2337/diaspect.22.3.153.

Chapter 14

Avoidant Restrictive Food Intake Disorder (ARFID)

Case: Jackson

Jackson is an 11-year-old cisgender Caucasian male whose parents are concerned that his picky eating has turned into an eating disorder. He has had severe reflux and trouble gaining weight since he was an infant. During his toddler years, Jackson would eat only about five foods. However, he never outgrew his toddler pickiness. Food textures, smells, and colors continue to bother him intensely. At the same time, his anxieties around food have grown. He fears birthday parties because he doesn't like pizza or cake and doesn't want to be teased for not eating. After an episode of a GI virus several months ago, he's become increasingly worried that something he eats will make him vomit. This has led to even more restrictive eating patterns.

Jackson's weight has always been around the 10th percentile on the growth chart. At his most recent well-child visit, however, the pediatrician noted that Jackson has fallen off the growth curve and is now below the percentile lines altogether on weight. He has not gained weight or height since he was ten years old. He has more digestive symptoms now, saying he gets full quickly, is constipated, and feels nauseated after big meals, all of which make him feel anxious.

Jackson doesn't think he's fat and wishes he could eat normally. He's a good student and has always enjoyed soccer. With a range of symptoms and concerns, he and his parents present to the pediatrician's office for a follow-up weight check and strategy session.

Background

Avoidant Restrictive Food Intake Disorder, or ARFID, is an eating disorder formally added to the DSM-5 in 2013. It applies to patients whose lack of interest in food, avoidance of sensory aspects of food, or concern about what might happen if they eat (particularly vomiting or choking) makes them unable to meet their energy intake needs consistently. In addition, patients with this diagnosis must experience at least one of the following four criteria: weight loss (or arrested growth in children), nutritional deficiency, dependence on feeding tubes or oral supplements, and significant interference with psychosocial functioning.[1] It tends to occur in younger patients, although it can be diagnosed across the age spectrum, and it has a slight male predominance.

Patients with ARFID do not have the distorted body image or drive for thinness seen in other eating disorders. However, weight loss and underweight are potential triggers for anorexia nervosa, and ARFID can morph into anorexia nervosa if untreated.

Medical Consequences of ARFID

ARFID can lead to severe malnutrition, with all of the same medical complications.[2] Fortunately prompt, expert, multidisciplinary attention can help prevent persistent malnutrition, risk for conversion to anorexia nervosa, and other poor health outcomes. Children in particular may need a higher level of care for a period of time to get the structure, consistent nutrition, and momentum that 24-hour care can provide. A reasonable rule of thumb is that within a few months of diagnosis and the establishment of a team, if there are still considerable malnutrition concerns, weight restoration or resumption of growth has stalled, and the parents or caregivers are burned out from the degree of emotion and resistance to more or different foods, residential care should be investigated.

I have also cared for patients whose severe IBS, other digestive challenges, or other medical issues have led to ARFID. These are adults for whom intense nausea, vomiting, diarrhea, constipation, or bloating ultimately lead to worsening food restriction. There is no drive for thinness or desire to change the body.

These patients benefit from a team willing to communicate frequently to stay on the same page. A doctor who supports a holistic approach and recognizes the emotional triggers for IBS flares can keep the patient from becoming "over-medicalized." That is, such a doctor will refrain from sending the patient for food allergy testing or a series of invasive diagnostic procedures. They will perform a thoughtful workup of abdominal symptoms and then refer the individual to a therapist and dietitian.

Case Resolution: Jackson

Jackson's follow-up weight check shows that, despite best efforts, he has lost an additional half pound of weight. The family talks with the doctor about their options. In choosing between starting with an outpatient team while Jackson continues to go to school, or first beginning with expert residential care, they balance a number of considerations. Ultimately, they choose to start in a residential setting because of the duration of Jackson's symptoms, his increasing physical complaints of abdominal distress and nausea, and their sense that he would be overwhelmed by adding in weekly therapist, dietitian, and doctor visits to his school schedule.

Jackson spends ten weeks in a child and adolescent eating disorder program that has an ARFID track. It's a struggle for him. He experiences homesickness and resistance to the meal plan as well as the nasogastric feeding tube he eventually needs. However, as he restores nutritionally and engages in therapy to work on diffusing and distracting anxiety, he starts to bloom. His parents are closely involved and supportive and do family therapy to learn how best to support him and his recovery. Prior to discharge, the program helps connect the family with an excellent therapist and dietitian in the community who both have ARFID experience.

At the time of discharge home, Jackson is in the 25th percentile for weight, more nearly matching his parents' body types, although still short for his age. He is able to consume all of his necessary calories without belly pain, although he still uses dietary supplements if meals start to drag on too long. His brain has become far less rigid and anxious, and he is expressive about how he can meet his own needs. The outpatient part of his recovery will focus more on sensory work so that he can more comfortably eat a wider variety of foods.

Notes

1 American Psychiatric Association. (2013). *Diagnostic and statistical manual of mental disorders (5th ed.)*. Arlington, VA: American Psychiatric Publishing.
2 Bennett SL, Dunn TM, Lashen GT, Grant JV, Gaudiani JL, Mehler PS. When avoidant/restrictive food intake disorder becomes life-threatening: a case report of an adult male patient. *Colorado Journal of Psychiatry & Psychology* 2017; 2(2): 18–23. www.ucdenver.edu/academics/colleges/medicalschool/departments/psychiatry/COJournal/Documents/Journal%20Issues/COJournalPsychiatryPsychologyV2N2.pdf Accessed March 4, 2018.

Chapter 15

Orthorexia and Food Intolerances

Case: Whitney

Whitney is a 23-year-old East Asian American cisgender female graduate student. She's an anxious perfectionist and an introvert, whose favorite activity is long walks with her dog. Whitney decides at New Year's to become healthier. She's never had a medical problem in her life, besides a somewhat sensitive stomach. She goes online and researches "clean eating," which she's heard about on social media. Deciding to start with a "cleanse," she cuts out multiple food groups for a month.

Whitney feels great. She decides to leave out dairy after her cleanse is over and to move toward veganism. She also starts running daily. When her weight drops a little, she receives compliments. Whitney has never been particularly focused on body image. For her, this new way of eating is more about feeding herself very high quality foods that meet her strict definition of healthful. She connects online with others making the same health commitments, and she feels like she's part of a community for the first time since finishing college.

Four months into her plan, Whitney realizes that she's fatigued all the time, with a sense of brain fog and decreased interest in what used to spark her attention and fulfil her. She's also constipated and has noticed that her hair has become dull and brittle. She wonders if she needs to cut out gluten. Deciding she must just be overworked, Whitney takes a long weekend to see her two closest college friends. She declines to have a drink with them at night and feels anxious all weekend as her friends eat and relax. Skipping her daily runs and eating out makes her feel grumpy and irritable.

On the last day of their trip, her friends sit her down and ask what's going on. They tell her it looks like she has developed an eating disorder. Whitney is surprised. She defends herself by noting her weight isn't too low, she's not throwing up, and she eats high quality food at every meal. She's just focusing on her health these days.

Background

"Orthorexia" is a term coined by physician Steven Bratman. It does not exist as a formal diagnosis in the DSM-5, but it is a helpful and relevant label. Orthorexia refers to, as Bratman says, "an unhealthy obsession with eating healthy food."[1] Patients spend a large amount of time thinking about and assessing their nutrition, feel impure or excessively guilty when they deviate from whatever set of food rules they have arbitrarily decided on, progressively eliminate nutrients in a quest for health, and may become malnourished, with or without weight loss.

People with orthorexia practice increasingly compulsive or rigid behaviors around food, where their sense of self is wrapped up in adherence to these rules. In addition, orthorexia impairs their social, academic, and professional functioning. Orthorexic food rules differ widely from one person to another, a reminder that there is no single, perfectly healthful way to eat. And of course, orthorexia can lead to anorexia nervosa, as the malnourished brain starts to get "sparky" and progresses from a fixation on quality of food to an additional fixation on quantity of food and body size.

A truly healthy and well-balanced person can enjoy nutrition and movement that satisfies their personal strategy for wellness *and* can comfortably eat the other half of their child's hot dog or celebrate with office birthday party cupcakes. Someone with orthorexia struggles mightily with these deviations.

Health Benefits of Dietary Fat and Carbohydrates

Orthorexia can lead to malnutrition, even when the person's focus has never been on weight loss.[2] Extreme food rules can cause poor physical functioning. Vitamin and mineral deficiencies contribute to poor skin and hair quality. Even when the vitamins are consumed in the food, inadequate dietary fat intake may prevent their absorption. Vitamins A, D, E, and K are fat-soluble, meaning that to be absorbed, there must also be dietary fat present in the intestine.

A rigorous study evaluated absorption of a particular nutrient in salads called carotenoids. Carotenoids are healthful, fat-soluble pigments found in fresh vegetables. In the study, subjects consumed a salad with fat-free, low fat, or full fat dressing, and then blood samples were taken to evaluate absorption of carotenoids. In those who ate fat-free dressing, the levels of carotenoids were undetectable, while individuals consuming low fat dressing had slightly higher levels. Only individuals consuming salad with full fat dressing had significant absorption of carotenoids. Thus, someone eating salad must consume it with full fat dressing just to gain the full health benefits.[3]

Just as people think low fat dressings are good for them, they think a low carbohydrate diet is as well. This is, for the most part, untrue. A very low carbohydrate diet, sometimes called a ketogenic diet, causes the body to break down its own muscle tissue to synthesize glucose. In reality, this type of diet contributes to fatigue, brain fog, and diminished athletic performance.[4] The scientific evidence base thus far has only proven the value of a low carbohydrate diet in individuals, particularly children, with severe epilepsy, or seizure disorder.[5]

By now, you are well aware that I firmly reject diet culture. For those whose watercooler discussions have drummed up enthusiasm for low carbohydrate diets or genetically guided meal plans for weight loss, I point to a recent, highly rigorous study out of Stanford that showed that there was no significant difference in weight change between year-long adherence to a "healthy low fat diet" and a "healthy low carbohydrate diet." Nor was there any effect on matching an individual's expected genetic contribution to carbohydrate or fat metabolism with a particular type of diet.[6] Once again, a Health At Every Size philosophy, described in Chapter 10, serves people better than any diet craze, avoiding weight cycling and offering up a consistent, sound strategy for one's relationship with food and movement.

"Clean Eating," "Cleanses," and Other Nonsense Fads

Not surprisingly, I have some opinions about the whole "clean eating" movement. In a word, it's pseudoscientific. Sure, beautiful, fresh foods are great and ideally comprise a significant portion of what we eat. However, clean eating would have us believe that consuming anything but certain arbitrary "chosen foods" somehow sullies the temple of our body. That's just not true. From a medical perspective, the human body evolved to use an extraordinarily broad variety of nutrients effectively for fuel. Think about the fact that giraffes can pretty much only eat acacia leaves and shoots, or that humpback whales can only eat krill, plankton, and small fish. These complicated mammals must consume a very narrow diet.

By contrast, think about how differently people eat across the world. As long as there is no food shortage, each of these very different cultural food habits appears successfully to turn children into well-nourished, thriving adults. Humans are the ultimate nutritional off-roading machines. I like to tell patients that getting obsessed with clean eating is like getting into peak athletic shape and then never leaving the house for fear of getting muddy.

It's worth mentioning that our society has become truly unscientific in its overvaluation and fear of certain foods and food groups. There's this belief I would find hilarious (were it not so pernicious) that you actually "are what you eat." Apparently, if you want to look like lean protein you have to eat nothing but lean protein. (A vegan diet does not turn us into a vegetable.) This is not, in fact, how the body works. Alleged "super foods" like kale, quinoa, and pomegranates are currently the "it kids" of the nutrition world. And sure, these are tasty (to some) and nutritious. Hamburgers, pizza, and milkshakes have their places too. I like to say that my motto when it comes to how to eat is "moderation in moderation." Even the word "moderation" is too strict for my liking. Sometimes eating immoderately (that is, with abandon) is wonderful.

Individuals engaging in "cleanses" and "detoxes" are using strategies that are among the most pseudoscientific of all the so-called clean eating trends. The idea that the human body is dirty and needs cleaning invokes a biblical view of moral sin. Presently, our society is more interested in defining good, clean living through how we eat rather than through our interpersonal interactions. People believe that if they briefly restrict their calories to some absurd combination of highly limited items (Juice! Tea! Vinegar! Cucumber!), with or without an additional laxative regimen, that this will somehow improve their cognitive ability, "detox" them from gastrointestinal "buildups," or cause weight loss.

Participating in such an experience might engender brief feelings of mental positivity related to thinking one is doing something virtuous. Then crankiness will set in from too little energy intake. Individuals might lose a few pounds from dehydration and from eating so little, but their metabolism will quickly slow due to inadequate calories. As a result, their weight is likely to rebound higher after the cleanse is over.

Unsurprisingly, the weight loss of a cleanse is ephemeral and mostly based on dehydration. As for detoxing the body, this is why we have a liver and kidneys, which are the most spectacular detoxifiers imaginable. The intestines move all solid waste out appropriately. There is no such thing as "intestinal buildup," despite cleanse sellers trying to tell us otherwise. Human evolution has given us everything our bodies need for successful daily functioning.

Ultimately, fasts and detoxes represent a classic marketing scam in which well-meaning people are sold a bill of goods, with promises that they can help their health and/or drop weight quickly. And, of course, the sellers of insecurity are all too happy to then sell the solution to a problem that never existed in the first place.

A Word About Allergies, Celiac Disease, and Food Intolerances

This topic could take up a whole book of its own, but a few key points must be made here. Formal food allergies require a person to avoid certain foods or risk serious health consequences. Those with celiac disease, for instance, cannot eat gluten or they develop abdominal pain, diarrhea, and other medical problems. Gluten refers to the proteins in cereal grains, particularly wheat, that are responsible for the elastic texture of bread dough.

A diagnosis of celiac disease is made when blood antigens—anti-endomysial antibody, anti-tissue transglutaminase antibody, and deamidated gliadin antibody—are positive, or a small bowel biopsy shows characteristic changes called villous atrophy, while patients are still consuming gluten. Someone on a gluten-free diet who has celiac disease will not have positive antibody levels in their blood. One percent of the population worldwide has celiac disease, while far more carry a genetic predisposition.[7] Keep in mind: a genetic predisposition to celiac disease is no reason to restrict gluten intake.

Non-celiac gluten sensitivity (NCGS), however, is increasingly common and experienced by people without celiac disease who believe they feel better physically when not consuming gluten. Those with NCGS represent a diverse group of individuals. Some may primarily have IBS, which can be worsened by gluten consumption.[8] Others may experience intestinal symptoms due to sensitivities to other food groups and could actually eat gluten without incurring trouble if they avoided the other food groups.[9] By far, though, the largest number of people avoid gluten because they believe a gluten-free diet is more healthful, including athletes.[10]

As a physician with expertise in eating disorders, my take on all of this is straightforward: for those without a true allergy, gluten is just a nutrient, no better or worse for a person than any other. Creating health-related rules around its consumption has no scientific basis. However, I cannot deny someone's lived experience if they feel ill when they eat gluten, or any other food group, such as dairy, despite not having a formal allergy. When it comes to patients with eating disorders, I am willing to concede that they not eat gluten if they feel they have NCGS.

However, that doesn't mean they can restrict all carbohydrates. Rice, potatoes, and other grains will be an expected part of their balanced diet. For someone with an eating disorder, where the line can get blurry between food intolerances and the discomfort of a starved digestive system, I set a fairly high standard for being allowed to avoid a whole food group, such as dairy. If patients have no symptoms when off dairy, and consistently have symptoms when consuming dairy, even when they take lactase, then I will concede its omission.

Treatment of Orthorexia

Early identification of orthorexia can be very helpful in minimizing medical and psychological harm. Patients should seek a therapist and a dietitian who has eating disorder expertise. The unfortunate fact is that many medical professionals, complementary medicine practitioners, and non-eating disorder dietitians will actually recommend clean eating-type rules for their patients. Caught up in systems of weight bias, lack of attention to good science, and with multibillion-dollar industries eagerly endorsing these recommendations, practitioners can perpetuate these nutritional myths in harmful ways onto clients. By contrast, eating disorder practitioners will very rarely endorse restrictive eating.

Case Resolution: Whitney

Whitney's friends express their concern compassionately and gently, rather than in an accusing way. They tell her she doesn't look well and that they miss their friend. All weekend, they note, they've watched her struggle with eating foods she used to love. They feel her slipping away from them. One of them has heard of orthorexia before, and she tells Whitney about it. She says that this quest for health can lead to far worse health outcomes. Her friends ask her to find a therapist and a dietitian and get help.

Whitney is shocked. It never occurred to her before that she might be developing an eating disorder or that her food rules could cause harm. She doesn't really believe that there's an issue, but she trusts her friends. She promises at least to have a session or two with experts and explore the possibility. Whitney finds a wonderful dietitian who convincingly educates her about the value of all different food groups and the dangers of an overly restrictive diet. As she tries to incorporate previously forbidden foods back into her diet, she's overwhelmed by the guilt and anxiety she feels and realizes she needs more help, and she connects with a therapist as well.

Over the following year, Whitney returns to a relationship with food not governed by rules. Her energy returns, her digestive system normalizes, her interests in other activities reawaken, and her hair becomes shiny again. Therapy has proven extremely productive in helping her work through issues and gain skills. She again feels vital, grounded, and able to honor and live her values.

Notes

1 www.orthorexia.com Accessed March 4, 2018.
2 Moroze RM, Dunn TM, Craig Holland J, Yager J, Weintraub P. Microthinking about micronutrients: a case of transition from obsessions about healthy eating to near-fatal "orthorexia nervosa" and proposed diagnostic criteria. *Psychosomatics.* 2015 July–August; 56(4):397–403. doi: 10.1016/j.psym.2014.03.003.
3 Brown MJ, Ferruzzi MG, Nguyen ML, Cooper DA, Eldridge AL, Schwartz SJ, White WS. Carotenoid bioavailability is higher from salads ingested with full-fat than with fat-reduced salad dressings as measured with electrochemical detection. *Am J Clin Nutr.* 2004 August; 80(2):396–403. PubMed PMID: 15277161.
4 Wroble KA, Trott MN, Schweitzer GG, Rahman RS, Kelly PV, Weiss EP. Low-carbohydrate, ketogenic diet impairs anaerobic exercise performance in exercise-trained women and men: a randomized-sequence crossover trial. *J Sports Med Phys Fitness.* 2018 April 4. doi: 10.23736/S0022-4707.18.08318-4.
5 Nei M, Ngo L, Sirven JI, Sperling MR. Ketogenic diet in adolescents and adults with epilepsy. *Seizure.* 2014 June; 23(6):439–442. doi: 10.1016/j.seizure.2014.02.015.
6 Gardner CD, Trepanowski JF, Del Gobbo LC, Hauser ME, Rigdon J, Ioannidis JPA, Desai M, King AC. Effect of low-fat vs low-carbohydrate diet on 12-month weight loss in overweight adults and the association with genotype pattern or insulin secretion: the DIETFITS randomized clinical trial. *JAMA.* 2018 February 20; 319(7):667–679. doi: 10.1001/jama.2018.0245.
7 Lebwohl B, Ludvigsson JF, Green PH. Celiac disease and non-celiac gluten sensitivity. *BMJ.* 2015 October 5; 351:h4347. doi: 10.1136/bmj.h4347.

8 Vazquez-Roque MI, Camilleri M, Smyrk T, Murray JA, Marietta E, O'Neill J, Carlson P, Lamsam J, Janzow D, Eckert D, Burton D, Zinsmeister AR. A controlled trial of gluten-free diet in patients with irritable bowel syndrome-diarrhea: effects on bowel frequency and intestinal function. *Gastroenterology*. 2013 May; 144(5):903–911.e3. doi: 10.1053/j.gastro.2013.01.049.

9 Biesiekierski JR, Peters SL, Newnham ED, Rosella O, Muir JG, Gibson PR. No effects of gluten in patients with self-reported non-celiac gluten sensitivity after dietary reduction of fermentable, poorly absorbed, short-chain carbohydrates. *Gastroenterology*. 2013 August; 145(2):320–8.e1–3. doi: 10.1053/j.gastro.2013. 04.051.

10 Lis DM, Stellingwerff T, Shing CM, Ahuja KD, Fell JW. Exploring the popularity, experiences, and beliefs surrounding gluten-free diets in nonceliac athletes. *Int J Sport Nutr Exerc Metab*. 2015 February; 25(1):37–45. doi: 10.1123/ijsnem. 2013-0247.

Chapter 16

Elite Athletes

Case: Rebecca

Rebecca is a 20-year-old cisgender Caucasian female who is a varsity lightweight rower for her university. Making weight for her boat last year as a freshman involved losing seven pounds in eight weeks. She did this through cutting down slightly on her caloric intake as she continued to practice hard, and then in the final week she radically decreased intake of food and liquids, tried to sweat as much as possible, and even used laxatives a few times.

This fall, as a sophomore, she has a little more weight to lose. A couple of her teammates invite her to join them in a 30-day "juice cleanse." The varsity coach is aware of this plan but doesn't discourage participation. Rebecca joins them, and for the first week she feels fine, if a little cranky from hunger. The next three weeks become significantly more uncomfortable. She feels mentally tired, physically weak with worse practice times, constipated, anxious, snappy, and she has trouble sleeping. Her period, which has been somewhat irregular since she first got it at age 14, doesn't come that month. Her weight drops below the required cutoff.

As the cleanse ends, Rebecca has six more weeks before her official season weigh in. She finds herself ravenously consuming large amounts of carb-rich foods in secret, while publicly continuing on the guarded meal plan the rest of her teammates follow at this time of year. She purges by vomiting once after such an episode, but she is so miserable throwing up that she resolves never to do it again. She even tries chewing and then spitting out the food, to enjoy the taste without eating it. Within a week, her weight has rebounded nearly to her pre-cleanse number. Rebecca seeks out her favorite athletic trainer and confesses that she needs help with her nutrition, although she's so mortified that she does not share the full details. The trainer refers her to an excellent eating disorder dietitian in the community who has expertise with elite athletes.

Background

The topic of athletes and disordered eating or eating disorders could fill an entire book of its own. This chapter introduces a few key concepts related to elite athletes, but by no means is it an exhaustive review. Ultimately, athletes with eating disorders are at risk for all the same medical complications you have been reading about in this book. In addition, however, they are also at heightened risk for certain complications relative to their sport, like stress fractures in those who engage in high impact sports and electrolyte disturbances in endurance athletes who train and compete in hot conditions.

Furthermore, athletes are constantly subjected to scrutiny of their body composition and shape. This is particularly true in judged sports, like diving, gymnastics, and figure skating, but it still holds true in refereed sports too. Whether the ideal for a given sport is to be lean and muscular, big and strong, or strong and light, athletes' bodies themselves are being assessed in addition to their performance.

Studies generally show that collegiate athletes are a lower risk for eating disorders than non-athletes.[1] However, athletes of all genders are at risk for presenting with low energy availability, meaning inadequate caloric intake relative to their energy output. Reasons can range from disordered eating behaviors to a simple misunderstanding of how much food to consume or what to eat.[2] Low carbohydrate diets, for instance, have no role in building strong bodies. Sports in which leanness is traditionally an aesthetic focus, such as cross country, swimming, gymnastics, ice skating, diving, and volleyball, appear to foster a higher risk for disordered eating.[3]

Athletes are undaunted by the hard work, pain, and suffering inherent to successful performance. They trust coaching relationships to confer information that may translate well on the field, road, or stage, but which may not serve them well with nutritional advice. Athletes should be encouraged to request that nutrition recommendations come from experts—typically sports or eating disorder nutritionists—rather than coaches, who are well meaning but may not have scientifically sound perspectives or any formal training in sports nutrition. Requesting this expertise isn't being "un-coachable," but rather responsible.

Athletes want what's best for their bodies and are always looking for the "edge" over the competition. Modern society often suggests this can be found through a change in food intake. In reality, the best "edge" is achieved through careful attention to good hydration, consistent sleep and adequate recovery time, sufficient energy intake, and attention to one's mental health and emotional needs.

However, size, shape, leanness, and muscularity are still overvalued in sports. As a result, in trying to honor and optimize performance, athletes are susceptible to applying stringent criteria to their food intake that can actually lead to malnourishment, medical problems, and even mental illness. Sadly and paradoxically, the means by which these athletes attempt to improve their performance may instead impair it.

For athletes in sports that have weight classes, these pressures and resultant behaviors can be even more intense. A calorically restrictive meal plan can lead to bingeing or to chewing and spitting, as the hungry individual's cave person brain becomes ravenous for off-limits food groups and sufficient calories. Many athletes isolate in shame when they engage in such behaviors, telling themselves, "I know better!" even as they cannot resist. As a result, their dietary struggles can be missed by coaches, trainers, teammates, friends, and family.

Relative Energy Deficiency in Sport

The medical complications of energy deficiency in athletes have been elegantly summarized by the concept of "relative energy deficiency in sport" or RED-S (pronounced "reds").[4] This replaces the older "female athlete triad" that only applied to post-pubertal females and solely focused on the interrelationship of low energy availability, menstrual dysfunction, and low bone mineral density. By contrast, RED-S encompasses a broad spectrum of physiological and psychological impairment caused by inadequate energy availability. In essence, these are indistinguishable from the medical complications of dietary restriction that you have learned about throughout this book.

Permission to Play/Compete

A major consideration for athletes is whether they are healthy enough to practice and compete. The outstanding 2014 consensus statement from the Female Athlete Triad Coalition produced a "scorecard" to help make this decision for female athletes. Risk assessment yields a score across a number of factors like energy availability, low BMI, delayed onset of first menstrual period and current menstrual status, low bone mineral density, and presence or type of stress fractures. This score is then used to determine if the athlete qualifies for full clearance, provisional clearance, or restriction from training and competition.[5]

More broadly, the International Olympic Committee (IOC) presents a RED-S-oriented assessment model for sport participation that is relevant to athletes of all genders.[4] Athletes with anorexia nervosa and other serious eating disorders, those with serious medical and psychological problems related to low energy availability, and those engaging in extreme weight loss techniques fall into the "High risk: no start red light" category.

Athletes qualify for the "Moderate risk: caution yellow light" category when they manifest any of a number of concerning symptoms. These include prolonged low body fat, substantial weight loss, cessation of expected growth and development in adolescents, abnormal menstrual cycles in females or abnormal hormonal profile in males, reduced bone mineral density from prior scan or Z-scores less than –1, one or more stress fractures associated with reduced sex hormone production in the context of low energy availability, other psychological or physical complications of low energy availability, disordered eating behaviors affecting other team members, and lack of progress in treatment and/or noncompliance with treatment plans.

It is not uncommon for parents and coaches to be reluctant to pull athletes out of their sport in the setting of an eating disorder, fearful of disrupting a vital scholarship, preventing the potential to qualify for a higher level of competition, or simply removing their loved one's motivation due to love of the sport. However, as the most rigorous current consensus statements make clear, the sequelae of RED-S and eating disorders are serious and must carry commensurate consequences with regards to sport participation. If the athlete truly wants to return to their sport, they can prove that by overcoming the eating disorder's demands and moving consistently toward recovery.

Is It an Eating Disorder or Not?

Beth Hartman McGilley, PhD, FAED, CEDS, is an eating disorder expert who specializes in working with athletes. When an athlete presents to her with eating-related concerns, one way she differentiates between disordered eating due to lack of proper education in sports nutrition, versus development of an eating disorder, is by assessing how they respond to dietary treatment recommendations. Athletes who don't have an eating disorder will follow a dietitian's recommendations, increase calories, increase weight if needed, and rest and heal as advised. They are driven to win and can embrace the concept that proper nutrition is a key to optimal performance. Athletes who have developed an eating disorder may intend to follow the dietary recommendations but quickly find their competitive desire defeated by anxiety. Their drive for thinness, body image disturbance, and/or concerns about weight gain, shape, and further anticipated loss of performance will maintain their eating disorder symptoms. They are driven by fear.

Case Resolution: Rebecca

Rebecca meets with the dietitian and opens up about everything that's been going on. The dietitian understands that making weight for a varsity athlete is a fact of life, even as she carefully screens Rebecca for development of an eating disorder. All Rebecca wants is to get back to her normal life, have a great rowing season, and feel better. She's never been focused on what her body looks like or the number on the scale, except as it related to qualifying as a lightweight rower. She's ready to do whatever the dietitian recommends.

The dietitian helps her develop a balanced meal plan that will nourish her through intense workouts, while coming in calorically somewhat under her baseline metabolic rate, as measured by indirect calorimetry. She notes that the upcoming weeks will show whether Rebecca is safe and ready to compete. She'll be watching for eating disorder behaviors, ability to adhere to the meal plan, resolution of the cleanse-induced symptoms, and emotional state.

Rebecca is ready to be done with fad diets, which she now realizes almost stole her season from her. She feels satisfied and nourished with her meal plan, and her performance improves again. All her symptoms resolve, and she makes the weight cutoff without engaging in any extreme behaviors.

Notes

1 Wollenberg G, Shriver LH, Gates GE. Comparison of disordered eating symptoms and emotion regulation difficulties between female college athletes and non-athletes. *Eat Behav.* 2015 August; 18:1–6. doi: 10.1016/j.eatbeh.2015.03.008.

2 Logue D, Madigan SM, Delahunt E, Heinen M, McDonnell SJ, Corish CA. Low energy availability in athletes: a review of prevalence, dietary patterns, physiological health, and sports performance. *Sports Med.* 2018 January; 48(1):73–96. doi: 10.1007/s40279-017-0790-3.

3 Wells EK, Chin AD, Tacke JA, Bunn JA. Risk of disordered eating among Division I female college athletes. *Int J Exerc Sci.* 2015 July 15; 8(3):256–264. PubMed PMID: 27293502.

4 Mountjoy M, Sundgot-Borgen J, Burke L, Carter S, Constantini N, Lebrun C, Meyer N, Sherman R, Steffen K, Budgett R, Ljungqvist A. The IOC consensus statement: beyond the Female Athlete Triad–Relative Energy Deficiency in Sport (RED-S). *Br J Sports Med.* 2014 April; 48(7):491–497. doi: 10.1136/bjsports-2014-093502.

5 De Souza MJ, Nattiv A, Joy E, Misra M, Williams NI, Mallinson RJ, Gibbs JC, Olmsted M, Goolsby M, Matheson G; Female Athlete Triad Coalition; American College of Sports Medicine; American Medical Society for Sports Medicine; American Bone Health Alliance. 2014 Female Athlete Triad Coalition consensus statement on treatment and return to play of the female athlete triad. *Clin J Sport Med.* 2014 March; 24(2):96–119. doi: 10.1097/JSM.0000000000000085.

Chapter 17

Male Patients

Case: Jorge

Jorge is a 21-year-old cisgender Latino male college wrestler. He's suffered through countless seasons of dropping weight to make his weight class, through team-sanctioned practices that range from significant caloric restriction to laxative abuse to "sweating it out." Each season, he's felt worse about himself and dreads the start of competition and practice. Binge eating has become harder to control. With every binge, he knows how hard it will be to "undo" his action, but he can't help it. This year, he's starting out ten pounds heavier, having grown an inch since last season, but his coach still wants him to compete in the same weight class. One night, Jorge uses a razor to cut shallow lines in his left arm. His overwhelm and feelings of being out of control find relief in the tangible, distracting sting of his cuts.

Case: Martin

Martin is a 21-year-old cisgender African American male who got into bodybuilding a year ago. Working to pay his bills as a server, he was looking for something to give him purpose. Bodybuilding soon took over all his thoughts. The community of tight-knit guys, the structure of his days being clearly outlined by his workouts, and even the discipline of learning exactly how to eat all appealed to him. When not at work, he focuses every other waking moment around lifting. Yet to his surprise, the longer he participates, the smaller and weaker he feels.

He watches some of the other guys at the gym with awe. They seem so much bigger, stronger, and more "cut" than he is. Martin's friends start to tease him that they never see him anymore, and it's no fun to go out with him because he eats such a strict and bizarre diet. Then they stop teasing him and fade away as he stops returning texts or seeing them. Martin feels uncomfortable out in public because his body doesn't fit into standard clothing. People come up to him all the time and comment on how big he is. He never knows how to respond because all he can think about is how inadequate his body actually feels.

Martin's sense of inferiority to the others, even when those same guys reassure and encourage him, is crushing him. A sore throat and fever bring him to a walk-in clinic where the physician's assistant tells him his blood pressure is dangerously high. She comments casually that he should really lose some weight because according to the chart she consults, he's in the "obese" category.

Background

These are just two of countless, diverse experiences males have with disordered eating and eating disorders. I have tried to represent males throughout this book in the case vignettes. Where the lifetime prevalence of anorexia nervosa in females is 0.9 percent, in males it is 0.3 percent.[1] The prevalence of bulimia nervosa in females is 1.3 percent, and in males it is 0.5 percent, as measured among US adolescents.[2] Studies indicate that males who develop an eating disorder may have a stronger genetic predisposition to mental illness in conjunction with more adverse environmental factors than females.[3] BED is far more common than either anorexia or bulimia nervosa, with prevalence rates estimated at 2–3 percent, equal across gender.[4]

A large Swedish study evaluated over 600 male patients who received hospital care for anorexia nervosa over 27 years. Male patients with anorexia nervosa and any other psychiatric comorbidity had a death rate nine times higher than healthy peers. Compared with these healthy peers, males with anorexia nervosa who abused alcohol were more than 11 times as likely to die of natural (disease-associated) causes, and more than 35 times as likely to die of unnatural (accident, overdose, or suicide) causes.[5]

Complex Causes of Eating Disorders in Males

As ever, eating disorders are complicated in their origins and have biological, inherited, and environmental contributions. Popular culture and media certainly play an important role. Seemingly recognizing that the market has been saturated with messages that sell females insecurity in order to compel them to buy a solution, now males are being increasingly targeted. Action figures from the 1970s that had normal body proportions are remade today as steroidal, grotesque versions of the same characters with bulging muscles, zero body fat, and tiny waists.

Even little boys' Halloween costumes unfortunately perpetuate these messages. Preschoolers wear superhero costumes padded with deltoids, biceps, pectoral muscles, and a seemingly obligatory "six pack." Such merchandizing runs the risk of giving our little boys the message that they can't be super or magical unless they have the "right" body for it. Would we accept our girls' princess costumes if they came padded with breasts and hips?

In addition, the current trend of monitoring all measurable human activities via trackers and wearable technology has been shown to worsen eating disorder symptomatology.[6] I always recommend my patients turn off their trackers.

There are differences in eating disorder behaviors and underlying psychopathology between males and females.[7] For a superb book that focuses entirely on males and disordered eating, look no further than *The Adonis complex* by Roberto Olivardia, PhD.[8] While female patients often possess a drive for thinness, male patients more often report a desire to be lean and muscular based on current aesthetics propagated by the media. This drive may lead them to cut out needed food groups, to overexercise, or to purge. Ultimately, malnutrition steals both fat and muscle tissue. Images of males in advertisements are often no more real than images of females, altered with extensive computer enhancement.

Muscle Dysmorphia/"Bigorexia"

A drive for muscularity can cause a subset of bodybuilders and other athletes to develop distortions in their self-perception, called muscle dysmorphia.[9] Some also call this "bigorexia." While by no means universal in the bodybuilding world, this problem causes men to see themselves as smaller and weaker than they are. They develop rigidity and anxiety around food and exercise that look similar to the psychopathology of eating disorders. Indeed, the abnormal food and fluid intake required for bodybuilders, especially around competitions, can cause intense food cravings and a physiologically starved state that heighten the risk of refeeding syndrome. One case described a young man who binged after a bodybuilding competition and subsequently developed such severely low levels of potassium and phosphorus that he temporarily became paralyzed.[10]

Males Arrive for Treatment Just as Sick as Females

Males with anorexia nervosa become equally as medically ill and develop the same medical complications as females.[11] A study showed that males who were admitted to the hospital with severely low body weight due to anorexia nervosa manifested a high incidence of starvation-related abnormal liver function tests, low testosterone levels, low vitamin D levels, and a high incidence of bone density loss.[12] In Chapter 3, I reviewed in detail the topic of bone density loss in male patients. In sum, male patients may develop any eating disorder, although possibly driven by a different set of body preoccupations. They deserve swift diagnosis and expert treatment.

The Failure of the Body Mass Index (BMI) Measurement

Neither the BMI nor the percentage of "ideal body weight" (IBW) are useful individual clinical tools. They should only be used in scientific papers. Even in this setting, cited as benchmarks to compare patients using standardized measures, these calculations are severely limited. One cannot ascertain health status from a patient's height and weight.

Unfortunately, the BMI has become a vital sign in most medical practices due to health insurance requirements. Shame and anxiety about BMI keep patients away from medical care.[13] Insurance reviews of patients with eating disorders in higher levels of care often focus on the BMI, and ongoing authorization for care can hinge upon weight. Lamentably, this further reinforces patients' focus on weight and invalidation if their eating disorder doesn't happen to involve emaciation.

Male patients are particularly poorly served by the BMI, which measures the weight in kilograms per meter of height squared. The BMI does not take into account gender differences in muscularity or build. Thus, the BMI measurement would have us believe that a man and a woman who are both 5′9″ and weigh the same have the same type of body. We know intuitively, however, that the man in this situation has a lower weight for height than the woman. Similarly, muscularity can make the BMI appear quite high, which is only a problem in a society that has decided to pathologize higher body weight.

The Hamwi equation for so-called IBW is an academic benchmark for target weight, used in journal articles and treatment programs as a universal, if flawed, assessment of weight for height.[14] It was appropriated from literature about diabetic patients from the middle of the last century.[15] Unlike the BMI, it at least gives males a higher denominator by which to benchmark their weight in cases of underweight. The difference between the BMI and the IBW is relevant for males seeking a higher level of care for eating disorder treatment.

A given residential eating disorder program might be equipped to care for individuals with a BMI of $15 \, \text{kg}/\text{m}^2$ or higher. Anything lower, and the program recognizes there may be medical and psychological comorbidities that cannot be managed in their setting. A 5′3″ female patient with a BMI of $15 \, \text{kg}/\text{m}^2$ has an IBW by Hamwi of 74 percent. However, a 6′0″ male patient with the same BMI of $15 \, \text{kg}/\text{m}^2$ has an IBW of only 62 percent. He thus may have more medical complications related to a more substantial degree of underweight than predicted by the BMI. IBW is a better benchmark than BMI for males in the narrow context of assessing underweight and the potential for concurrent medical complications. A male patient may be accepted into a residential program on the basis of his BMI only to be too medically compromised to receive appropriate care.

Many male patients feel isolated in higher levels of eating disorder care programming. Being surrounded by a mostly female population, where some are processing male-instigated traumas, can feel stigmatizing and unhelpful. That said, there are a number of programs in the country that focus exclusively on the care of male patients. Others do a good job of creating tracks that allow male patients to share their unique experiences and fears and receive individualized care.

Families and care providers should have a high index of suspicion for an eating disorder if a boy stalls out on his growth curves, becomes highly focused on the nutritional content or "healthiness" of food, or escalates physical activity toward the end of changing his body appearance. Adolescent boys with a burgeoning eating disorder may withdraw from social food encounters, demonstrate escalating body dissatisfaction in conversations or on social media, or be found using supplements (illegal or legal) that promise weight loss or greater muscularity.

Families are advised to resist expressing concern over higher body weights at various stages of their sons' growth. Similarly, praising boys for weight loss or commenting on the appearance of their bodies (positively or negatively) potentially sets up a focus on appearance over actual health. This type of appearance-focused commentary within a family runs the risk of losing the sacred space of home as a place where the body is safe. Boys and men will be exposed to endless body discussion and judgment outside of their homes. A shift toward HAES-informed support of nutrition and movement combined with commentary on what bodies can *do*, rather than what they look like, will equip boys with resilience against the temptations of disordered eating.

In a society of extreme workout regimens, pseudoscientific notions of healthy eating, and ever present size stigma, adult men can also fall into disordered eating patterns that risk turning into full blown eating disorders. Moreover, rigid eating and workout habits will be watched carefully by their children and peers. Men concerned with promoting good health in their children will be most successful if they are able to demonstrate flexible, moderate eating habits, resist the temptation to comment on theirs or anyone else's bodies, and engage in joyful rather than compensatory movement.

Case Resolution: Jorge and Martin

The resolution for both Jorge and Martin involves improved recognition of males with disordered eating and eating disorders and the medical and psychological issues that accompany them. Medical providers, families, coaches, teammates, and friends can all be more watchful when someone in their life radically changes the way he eats, exercises, or experiences his body. As ever, eating disorders are not fads or choices, but mental illnesses. Early identification of risky behaviors, referral to an expert team, and close monitoring and support through the treatment process are key.

Notes

1 Hudson JI, Hiripi E, Pope HG Jr., Kessler RC. The prevalence and correlates of eating disorders in the National Comorbidity Survey Replication. *Biol Psychiatry.* 2007 February 1; 61(3):348–358. PubMed PMID: 16815322.

2 Swanson SA, Crow SJ, Le Grange D, Swendsen J, Merikangas KR. Prevalence and correlates of eating disorders in adolescents. Results from the national comorbidity survey replication adolescent supplement. *Arch Gen Psychiatry.* 2011 July; 68(7):714–723. doi: 10.1001/archgenpsychiatry.2011.22.

3 Raevuori A, Hoek HW, Susser E, Kaprio J, Rissanen A, Keski-Rahkonen A. Epidemiology of anorexia nervosa in men: a nationwide study of Finnish twins. *PLoS One.* 2009; 4(2):e4402. doi: 10.1371/journal.pone.0004402.

4 Hudson JI, Coit CE, Lalonde JK, Pope HG Jr. By how much will the proposed new DSM-5 criteria increase the prevalence of binge eating disorder? *Int J Eat Disord.* 2012 January; 45(1):139–141. doi: 10.1002/eat.20890.

5 Kask J, Ramklint M, Kolia N, Panagiotakos D, Ekbom A, Ekselius L, Papadopoulos FC. Anorexia nervosa in males: excess mortality and psychiatric co-morbidity in 609 Swedish in-patients. *Psychol Med.* 2017 June; 47(8):1489–1499. doi: 10. 1017/S0033291717000034.

6 Levinson CA, Fewell L, Brosof LC. My Fitness Pal calorie tracker usage in the eating disorders. *Eat Behav.* 2017 December; 27:14–16. doi: 10.1016/j.eatbeh. 2017.08.003.

7 Valente S, Di Girolamo G, Forlani M, Biondini A, Scudellari P, De Ronchi D, Atti AR. Sex-specific issues in eating disorders: a clinical and psychopathological investigation. *Eat Weight Disord.* 2017 December; 22(4):707–715. doi: 10. 1007/s40519-017-0432-7.

8 Pope H, Phillips KA, Olivardia, R. (2000). *The Adonis complex: the secret crisis of male body obsession.* New York: Free Press.

9 Olivardia R, Pope HG Jr., Hudson JI. Muscle dysmorphia in male weightlifters: a case-control study. *Am J Psychiatry.* 2000 August; 157(8):1291–1296. PubMed PMID: 10910793.

10 Lee TW, Bae E, Hwang K, Chang HN, Park HJ, Jeon DH, Cho HS, Chang SH, Park DJ. Severe hypokalemic paralysis and rhabdomyolysis occurring after binge eating in a young bodybuilder: case report. *Medicine (Baltimore).* 2017 October; 96(40):e8251. doi: 10.1097/MD.0000000000008251.

11 Skolnick A, Schulman RC, Galindo RJ, Mechanick JI. The endocrinopathies of male anorexia nervosa: case series. *AACE Clin Case Rep.* 2016 Fall; 2(4): e351–e357. doi: 10.4158/EP15945.CR.

12 Sabel AL, Rosen E, Mehler PS. Severe anorexia nervosa in males: clinical presentations and medical treatment. *Eat Disord.* 2014; 22(3):209–220. doi: 10.1080/ 10640266.2014.890459.

13 Mensinger JL, Tylka TL, Calamari ME. Mechanisms underlying weight status and healthcare avoidance in women: a study of weight stigma, body-related shame and guilt, and healthcare stress. *Body Image.* 2018 March 22; 25:139–147. doi: 10.1016/j.bodyim.2018.03.001.

14 The Hamwi method for calculating ideal body weight varies by sex. In females, it is calculated as 100 pounds for the first five feet in height, then five pounds for every inch in height thereafter. In males, it is calculated as 106 pounds for the first five feet in height, then six pounds for every inch thereafter.

15 Danowski TS, Hamwi GJ, Fajans SS, Sussman KE, American Diabetes Association. (1964). *Diabetes mellitus: diagnosis and treatment* (Vol. 1). New York, NY: American Diabetes Association.

Chapter 18

Gender and Sexual Minorities

Case: Derek

Derek is a 19-year-old cisgender African American male who just graduated from high school. Bullied throughout school for being effeminate, he's also experienced racism since he was a child. He's known since middle school that he was gay, but it was not safe to come out either at school or at home. He will be heading off to New York this fall to attend college on a music scholarship, and he's desperate to establish a new life that's congruent with who he actually is. From a small town, Derek doesn't know any other gay men who are out. His online world has become increasingly more real to him than his actual life, as he absorbs messages about gay culture and tries to figure out how to remake himself to fit into his new, imagined identity in college.

Derek decides his body doesn't match the gay man's ideal of lean and muscular, at least as he's imagined it based on online research and popular culture. He goes on a diet, starts working out, and orders diet pills off the internet. He imagines himself arriving at college and immediately fitting in, being welcomed and not questioned either for his race or his sexuality.

Case: TJ

TJ is a 26-year-old Caucasian individual assigned female at birth and for the last year identifying as gender non-binary, using the singular pronouns they and them. They knew early on that something felt wrong in their body. The dresses, typical gender roles, and concept of being a girl felt inappropriate for as long as TJ can remember. By the same token, while some of the aspects of boyhood appealed to TJ, including the greater freedoms and emphasis on independence and capability, they didn't feel quite like a boy either. As a child, TJ ultimately chose to self-express as a tomboy.

Middle school was difficult because adolescence started to bring body changes with which TJ felt deeply at odds. They didn't identify with developing breasts or drawing the male gaze. TJ quietly started eating less, hoping that decreased calories would delay the outward signs of puberty. However, the restrictive food rules that quickly became mandatory also triggered late-night binges. Famished, TJ would practically empty the pantry of snack foods and then lie awake miserably imagining body changes happening right then and there. TJ's weight rose rapidly through middle school, increasing their sense of isolation and difference from peers.

TJ came out as bisexual in high school and joined the LGBTQ student organization, which offered a harbor for queer folks. The student group was a lifesaver, overseen by a gay teacher and a lesbian school counselor. It provided a safe space for conversations about gender, sexuality, discrimination, community, and self-expression. TJ had a good college experience, and their restrictive eating and binges diminished considerably as a supportive community normalized body diversity. However, an ongoing sense of dissonance in their body—neither feeling female, nor particularly connected with the idea of being a trans man—was a daily distraction. Drinking with friends numbed this constant inner dialogue, and TJ was soon drinking heavily most nights.

It wasn't until the last few months of social work school that TJ connected with the concept of being gender non-binary. They dropped their female pronouns, adopted the initials TJ as their legal name, and found a therapist in the community who specialized in LGBTQ clients.

Background

Sex, gender identity, gender presentation, and sexuality are all separate concepts, and the terms are worthy of clarification. The acronym Lesbian Gay Bisexual Transgender Queer/Questioning (LGBTQ) broadly encompasses a highly diverse group of individuals.

Sex refers to the combination of genes and gene expression that leads doctors and families to identify a baby as male or female at birth. While most babies with XX chromosomes appear to have female genitalia, and most babies with XY chromosomes appear to have male genitalia, there are genetic variations that cause this not to be the case. Some babies' genitalia is not clearly male or female. Male, female, and intersex are the three main labels that apply to sex.

Gender identity refers to one's sense of self. As you have read throughout this book, cisgender means that one identifies with one's sex assigned at birth, while transgender means one's gender identity differs from that conventionally associated with the sex they were assigned at birth. Gender non-binary signifies individuals who neither identify entirely with their sex assigned at birth nor with another sex.

Gender presentation refers to the way that one chooses to self-represent in society. Our current understanding of gender has moved away from the binary. We no longer see gender identity as either man or woman, or even as somewhere on a spectrum between man and woman, because that continues to enforce the binary of man and woman as polar ends of a grayscale spectrum. It is common, but inappropriate, for medical forms to query "Gender: M/F." The question on medical forms should be phrased "Sex: M/F/intersex" and, if gender is queried, left blank for the person to fill in.

Sexuality refers to the way a person might experience or express themselves sexually and/or romantically. We know that sexual attraction and expression comprise only one aspect of one's self. Romantic, emotional, aesthetic, and physical/sensual attraction and expression are all relevant as well. Sexuality isn't binary either. Heterosexual, homosexual, bisexual, pansexual, and asexual orientations, among others, are all words used to describe an individual's sexual and romantic attraction.

Sexual Minorities and Eating Disorders

Current statistics estimate that at least 5–7 percent of American adolescents identify as LGBTQ.[1] The American Association of Pediatrics (AAP) Committee on Adolescence notes that, despite many challenges, most LGBTQ youth emerge as healthy adults. "Isms" (e.g., heterosexism and cissexism) and phobias all contribute to outcome disparities in mental and physical health. The AAP emphasizes that transgender adolescents need to be supported, affirmed, and educated about seeking hormone treatments only from a licensed doctor.[2] Gay men and lesbian women have a sobering fourfold increase in suicide attempts compared with straight peers.[3] Healthcare providers must create an environment free of marginalization, social stigma, and heteronormative bias for individuals of all ages.[4]

Sexual minority youth are particularly vulnerable to eating disorders, as borne out in multiple studies. All the risk factors that make adolescence a time of particular vulnerability to the advent of eating disorders are heightened by the emergence of sexual and gender identity around that same time.[5] Most studies indicate that gay boys and men are more likely to engage in dieting, bingeing, and diet pill use than their heterosexual counterparts.[6] This may have to do with the media's greater influence and focus on appearance in gay men's culture. Data are mixed on lesbian girls and women, with some studies suggesting they are more satisfied with their bodies and thus less likely to engage in eating disorder behaviors, and other studies showing that they too engage in more purging and diet pill use than their straight peers.[7]

In a study that examined almost 300,000 college students, self-reported eating disorder behaviors (excluding BED) were highest among transgender students and lowest among cisgender heterosexual men. By comparison with cisgender heterosexual women—in whom 1 percent were diagnosed with a formal eating disorder in the prior year, 3 percent had deliberately vomited or used laxatives in the past month, and 3.5 percent had used diet pills in the last month—transgender students were two to four times more likely to use eating disorder behaviors, while cisgender heterosexual men were about a third as likely. Gay men had 1.5 times the formal eating disorder diagnoses as straight women did, while lesbians had similar rates of eating disorders as straight women.[8]

While desiring to change one's appearance might be responsible for some of the heightened prevalence of eating disorders in sexual minorities, social justice themes may be even more important. "Minority stress" is the technical term that refers to the excess stress experienced by individuals in stigmatized social categories. This can refer to gender, racial, religious, sexual, and other minority statuses. Violence, discrimination, bullying, loneliness, internalized stigma, and pressure by family, school, religious, and social communities to conceal one's identity all have a major impact on mental health. Eating disorders can numb these emotional stressors, even as the evanescent lure of changing one's body in an attempt to change one's happiness continues to emanate from a fat phobic and body shaming culture.

Gender Minorities

Gender dysphoria is the appropriate term for the dissonance that transgender individuals feel with their sex as assigned at birth. It is medically necessary, evidence based, and well established that doctors should work with patients and their families to affirm gender identity in a stepwise process throughout adolescence, if patients present before adulthood.[9] Clear treatment algorithms have also been developed for transgender adults. It is clear that gender confirmation—through familial acceptance, name and pronoun changes, school support, and eventually medical care through hormones and possibly surgeries—improves quality of life and mental and medical outcomes for gender minorities.

The Endocrine Society prepares clinical practice guidelines on medical topics. Their guideline on gender dysphoric individuals highlights that gender affirmation requires a multidisciplinary team. Part of the team's work involves early medical interventions that aim to suppress the sex hormone production determined by the person's genetic sex, and then later to maintain sex hormone levels within the normal range for the person's affirmed gender. They recommend treating gender dysphoric adolescents who have entered at least the second stage of puberty, the earliest visible sign of puberty, with sex hormone suppression via gonadotropin-releasing hormone agonists.

These gonadotropin-releasing hormone agonists are not sex hormones but rather serve to halt further secondary sexual trait development. For an adolescent transgender patient assigned female at birth, for instance, this plays the vital role of halting breast development. After a few years of sex hormone blockade, proactive sex hormones that affirm the gender can be initiated. In general, the Society notes that adolescents are able to consistently express their wishes and consent for gender-affirming sex hormones by age 16, although in some cases consent can be granted earlier. According to the guidelines, neither sex hormone blockade nor sex hormones should be started in pre-pubertal children. The Society suggests that individuals undergoing gender-affirming hormone treatments be offered fertility preservation (sperm or egg preservation), should they desire to have genetic offspring in the future.[10]

Unfortunately, the medical insurance system in the United States lags behind the evidence base. Transgender individuals continue to face significant barriers in accessing appropriate hormone therapy, much less gender confirmation surgeries. In one study, fewer than a third of transgender adolescents had their hormone therapy covered by insurance.[11] Stressors such as these may contribute to the distress and potentially injurious coping mechanisms experienced by gender minorities.

Gender Minorities and Eating Disorders

Studies have shown that people with gender dysphoria have high rates of eating disorders and disordered eating. Accordingly, patients receiving gender-affirming treatment should be assessed on an ongoing basis for eating disorders.[12] Much more research is still needed to assess prevalence, prevention measures, and optimal treatment strategies specifically for sexual minority patients with disordered eating. The existing studies on LGBTQ patients and eating disorders must cover a remarkably diverse group of patients, often without the statistical power to investigate transgender patients specifically.

One study that did evaluate exclusively gender minority patients assessed 452 transgender adults in Massachusetts.[13] In this particular group, 31 percent were assigned female at birth and gender non-conforming/non-binary, 31 percent were trans men, 9 percent were assigned male at birth and gender non-conforming, and 28 percent were trans women. By far, the group comprised of assigned female at birth, gender non-conforming, had the highest rate of self-reported and formally diagnosed eating disorders in their lifetime, at 7.4 percent. In fact, subjects were three times likelier to have had an eating disorder if they identified as non-binary, compared with trans binary (that is, trans man or trans woman). The lowest level of eating disorders was found in the trans women.

The study went on to postulate some reasons for these findings. One hypothesis is that sexual minorities with lower visual conformity (that is, who defy a quick visual label as "male" or "female") are more vulnerable to societal mistreatment. The same may hold for binary individuals who are less visually gender conforming, for instance a trans woman who still possesses male features. In both cases, the "otherness" can contribute to minority stress through discrimination, isolation, and violence. Eating disorders offer a strategy of avoidant coping, as can substance abuse.

In addition, eating disorders can offer sexual minorities the opportunity to change their gendered features. Given the pressures on women to be thin, a trans woman may diet or develop an eating disorder in the service of achieving a thin body that "passes" or looks like the stereotypical construct associated with women. Trans men may act upon a drive for a less feminine body shape.[14] The authors hypothesized that perhaps the individuals assigned female at birth, identifying as gender non-binary, who have the highest rate of eating disorders, may be striving to alter gendered features or may be burdened by a particularly intense body dissatisfaction.

Since body dissatisfaction often plays such an important role in the development and maintenance of eating disorders in sexual minorities, one might expect that appropriate gender dysphoria treatment through medical gender affirmation would improve body image. Indeed, this turns out to be the case.[15] A study from a national transgender health service showed that people not on gender-affirming hormone treatment reported higher levels of eating psychopathology than people on hormones. This finding was linked to high body dissatisfaction, perfectionism, anxiety, and low self-esteem. That is, the hormones themselves did not magically reduce eating disorder symptoms but instead ameliorated the risk factors that promoted eating disorder behaviors.[16]

Unique Medical Considerations

One interesting and important finding about the medical risk for refeeding syndrome in trans women was reported from an eating disorder program. A trans woman patient had remarkably persistent low serum phosphorus levels that lasted several months into nutritional rehabilitation. It turns out that high dose estrogen supplementation causes the kidneys to excrete phosphorus in the urine. As a result of this individual taking high dose estrogen, her blood levels of phosphorus remained persistently low, requiring greater than average phosphorus supplementation over a much longer period of time.[17]

This case report potentially changes management of trans women in treatment for eating disorders in two ways. One, an estradiol level should be checked to be sure that the estrogen dose is correct and not too high. Two, trans women should have phosphorus levels checked intermittently during nutritional rehabilitation for far longer than one would typically do with other patients, to ensure low levels aren't being missed.

I also advise providers caring for transgender patients to consider another topic where eating disorder care and gender dysphoria overlap. Patients assigned female at birth and who have gender dysphoria with an eating disorder may lose their periods due to malnutrition. This may be very important psychologically for the patient because getting a period is a reminder of a gender with which they don't align. Providers must be compassionate and sensitive to this reality.

One of the biggest fears associated with weight restoration might be resumption of the period. If a gender dysphoric adolescent is on continuous birth control to suppress periods, this should not be stopped just because the clinical team "wants to see the period return as a marker of medical health." Additionally, in gender dysphoric patients who have not committed to hormone therapy and who do not want birth control pills, offering someone a progesterone-releasing IUD can suppress the period for up to five years. These IUDs are considered safe and are commonly used for a wide variety of indications. By taking away the stress of a monthly menstrual cycle, the provider may be removing a driver of body dissatisfaction and thus may make recovery work easier.

Finally, I have many times been asked how to calculate an "ideal body weight" or target weight range for transgender patients who are recovering from anorexia nervosa. This may be used to assess "how sick" patients are (by comparison with a healthy weight) or as a goal for nutritional rehabilitation. Clinicians wonder if they should use the calculations and trajectory of the individual's sex assigned at birth or affirmed gender? My answer is, "Neither. Let's move away from rigidly defined weight goals, please. Let's individualize and consider the whole person."

When using weight to help determine level of illness, the concept of weight suppression may be more valuable than some gendered so-called ideal body weight baseline. As I noted in Chapter 1, weight suppression is calculated as the highest recent body weight minus the current body weight, divided by the highest recent body weight. When considering at what body weight range an individual will have achieved stability and health, once again HAES precepts can guide us. There is no unifying calculation, gendered or not. I think that transgender individuals with anorexia nervosa have achieved a practical weight range when they consistently consume adequate nutrition, can move for joy, are medically stable, and when the weight range is reasonably acceptable both to patient and treatment team.

Case Resolution: Derek

Derek arrives at college anxious, exhausted, and overwhelmed. His intention over the summer to diet and lift weights to fit in spiraled into a full fledged eating disorder. He realizes he needs help and thus seeks out the student counseling center. Sitting in the waiting room, he sees posters and brochures that celebrate diversity on campus and introduce students to the wide array of student organizations available. Empowered, he asks the counseling center if he can see a therapist who is also African American and who has expertise in LGBTQ clients. They are able to comply. Over the coming months, Derek and his therapist explore a wide array of topics, ranging well beyond body image and encompassing racism, stigma, sexuality, and identity. Derek loves school, and he deliberately seeks out organizations that foster a sense of community and belonging. His eating normalizes, and he develops a stronger connection with body acceptance.

Case Resolution: TJ

TJ and their therapist discuss a broad range of topics over the subsequent year, from social justice, to gender, to self-esteem, to sexuality, to alcohol use, to food and body image. Additionally, TJ finds a doctor who comes highly referred from some friends in the LGBTQ community. The doctor's paperwork uses the terms "sex" and "gender" properly, the office has comfortable furniture made for a diversity of body sizes, and the printed materials in the office espouse a HAES approach. The nurse assures TJ that they will never be weighed in this office, as weight isn't a measure of health. The doctor appropriately inquires about TJ's pronouns and invites TJ to describe how this medical clinic might be most helpful to them. TJ has no interest in gender-affirming hormones, as their gender identity is non-binary. There isn't a medical solution for their gender dysphoria. TJ mostly wants a safe place to stop by if a sore throat or fever crops up, and they want to check in on their alcohol use from time to time. The drinking has decreased significantly since starting therapy. The doctor and TJ part with an open-ended agreement to meet if any medical needs arise.

Notes

1 Gates GJ. Demographics and LGBT health. *J Health Soc Behav.* 2013 March; 54(1):72–74. doi: 10.1177/0022146512474429.
2 Committee On Adolescence. Office-based care for lesbian, gay, bisexual, transgender, and questioning youth. *Pediatrics.* 2013 July; 132(1):198–203. PubMed PMID: 23796746.
3 Haas AP, Lane A. Working group for postmortem identification of SO/GI. Collecting sexual orientation and gender identity data in suicide and other violent deaths: a step towards identifying and addressing LGBT mortality disparities. *LGBT Health.* 2015 March; 2(1):84–87. doi: 10.1089/lgbt.2014.0083.
4 Mead, DR. Dana, RC. Carson, CA. The primary care approach to lesbian, gay, bisexual, transgender, and queer/questioning populations. *Consultant.* 2017; 57(2):1–4.
5 McClain Z, Peebles R. Body image and eating disorders among lesbian, gay, bisexual, and transgender youth. *Pediatr Clin North Am.* 2016 December; 63(6):1079–1090. doi: 10.1016/j.pcl.2016.07.008.
6 Austin SB, Ziyadeh N, Kahn JA, Camargo CA Jr., Colditz GA, Field AE. Sexual orientation, weight concerns, and eating-disordered behaviors in adolescent girls and boys. *J Am Acad Child Adolesc Psychiatry.* 2004 September; 43(9):1115–1123. PubMed PMID: 15322415.
7 Austin SB, Nelson LA, Birkett MA, Calzo JP, Everett B. Eating disorder symptoms and obesity at the intersections of gender, ethnicity, and sexual

orientation in US high school students. *Am J Public Health.* 2013 February; 103(2):e16–22. doi: 10.2105/AJPH.2012.301150.

8 Diemer EW, Grant JD, Munn-Chernoff MA, Patterson DA, Duncan AE. Gender identity, sexual orientation, and eating-related pathology in a national sample of college students. *J Adolesc Health.* 2015 August; 57(2):144–149. doi: 10.1016/j. jadohealth.2015.03.003.

9 World Professional Association for Transgender Health (WPATH). Standards of Care, Version 7. Standards of care for the health of transsexual, transgender, and gender nonconforming people. https://s3.amazonaws.com/amo_hub_content/Association140/files/WPATH-Position-on-Medical-Necessity-12-21-2016.pdf Accessed February 13, 2018.

10 Hembree WC, Cohen-Kettenis PT, Gooren L, Hannema SE, Meyer WJ, Murad MH, Rosenthal SM, Safer JD, Tangpricha V, T'Sjoen GG. Endocrine treatment of gender-dysphoric/gender-incongruent persons: an endocrine society clinical practice guideline. *J Clin Endocrinol Metab.* 2017 November 1; 102(11):3869–3903. doi: 10.1210/jc.2017-01658.

11 Nahata L, Quinn GP, Caltabellotta NM, Tishelman AC. Mental health concerns and insurance denials among transgender adolescents. *LGBT Health.* 2017 June; 4(3):188–193. doi: 10.1089/lgbt.2016.0151.

12 Feder S, Isserlin L, Seale E, Hammond N, Norris ML. Exploring the association between eating disorders and gender dysphoria in youth. *Eat Disord.* 2017 July–September; 25(4):310–317. doi: 10.1080/10640266.2017.1297112.

13 Diemer EW, White Hughto JM, Gordon AR, Guss C, Austin SB, Reisner SL. Beyond the binary: differences in eating disorder prevalence by gender identity in a transgender sample. *Transgend Health.* 2018 January 1; 3(1):17–23. doi: 10. 1089/trgh.2017.0043.

14 Strandjord SE, Ng H, Rome ES. Effects of treating gender dysphoria and anorexia nervosa in a transgender adolescent: lessons learned. *Int J Eat Disord.* 2015 November; 48(7):942–945. doi: 10.1002/eat.22438.

15 Jones BA, Haycraft E, Murjan S, Arcelus J. Body dissatisfaction and disordered eating in trans people: a systematic review of the literature. *Int Rev Psychiatry.* 2016; 28(1):81–94. doi: 10.3109/09540261.2015.1089217.

16 Jones BA, Haycraft E, Bouman WP, Brewin N, Claes L, Arcelus J. Risk factors for eating disorder psychopathology within the treatment seeking transgender population: the role of cross-sex hormone treatment. *Eur Eat Disord Rev.* 2018 March; 26(2):120–128. doi: 10.1002/erv.2576.

17 Beaty L, Trees N, Mehler P. Recurrent persistent hypophosphatemia in a male-to-female transgender patient with anorexia nervosa: case report. *Int J Eat Disord.* 2017 May; 50(5):606–608. doi: 10.1002/eat.22707.

Chapter 19

Women's Sexual and Reproductive Health

Case: Angela

Angela is a 32-year-old cisgender South Asian female who had restrictive anorexia nervosa for two years when she was a teenager. She feels she has been recovered for years, although she is still quite strict in her food and exercise rules, monitors her weight daily, and lives on the low side of a safe weight range. Her menstrual periods, regular for years on the Pill, now come every few months off the Pill, at unpredictable times.

Angela and her husband want to get pregnant. They have been trying for the past six months without success, so they go to see her gynecologist to consider fertility assistance. At the appointment, the doctor takes the time to ask thoughtful questions. In the course of this conversation, Angela reveals that intercourse has always been painful for her, although lubrication helps. The doctor also inquires about Angela's eating, exercise, weight, and history of anorexia. She examines Angela and sends off some routine lab work.

Background

This chapter reviews the relationship between eating disorders, fertility, and pregnancy. Unfortunately, many patients with eating disorders have been threatened at some point by someone saying, "If you keep this up, you'll never be able to have kids." First of all, such a threat is unkind and scientifically inaccurate. The feminist in me bristles at the tendency for women to be shamed, blamed, and frightened within the medical system. Second of all, many of my patients were told this when they were teenagers who weren't even contemplating their future fertility. Nonetheless, the comment sticks and lingers. Broadly speaking, given that many women who have never had an eating disorder struggle with fertility, full recovery should give women as good a chance of getting pregnant as any woman has.

The data on this topic emerge from two main sources: eating disorder centers and the general population. Not surprisingly, studies from eating disorder centers represent patients with a history of higher acuity or longer lasting disease than studies that draw from the general population. Thus, some research shows significant differences in fertility and pregnancy outcomes in those with eating disorders compared with healthy controls, while other research shows fewer differences. On the whole, the more severe or prolonged the eating disorder, and the more disordered the woman is at the time of trying to get pregnant or sustain a pregnancy, the more significant the medical, gynecological, and obstetrical complications.[1]

Sex

Let's start by talking about sex. As one might imagine, individuals with a mental illness that radically distorts body image can have higher rates of poor sexual function.[2,3] Most studies show that among patients with eating disorders, those with anorexia nervosa have the lowest levels of libido, highest avoidance of sexual relationships, and worst anxiety, correlated with BMI. In one study, patients with bulimia nervosa did not have different sexual function compared with controls unless they had significant depression.[4] Another study showed that women with BED in larger bodies have higher sexual dysfunction compared with women in larger bodies who do not have BED.[5]

Some individuals dissociate during sexual experiences. Dissociation is a psychological reaction in which an individual may feel absent, out-of-body, and unaware of what they are doing, with little or no memory of what happened while dissociated. A study showed that women who both dissociate and have a tendency toward binge eating have an actual measurable stress response, with elevated blood cortisol levels, during sexual stimuli.[6]

Pain during penetrative intercourse is quite common in females with malnutrition. First of all, malnourished tissues become more fragile, so intercourse can physically damage the vagina. Second, a low estrogen state will also contribute to vaginal dryness and fragility, as well as to decreased lubrication. Pelvic floor dysfunction, discussed in Chapter 11, can also exacerbate pelvic pain and vaginal discomfort. Sometimes a short course of vaginal estrogen cream is useful while working toward weight restoration and before sex hormone production has resumed. In most cases, use of a good quality lubricant during intercourse will help reduce pain, as will pelvic floor therapy. Open communication, attention to foreplay, patience, and compassion are all key elements in maintaining or resuming sexual activity.

How Do Eating Disorders Affect Fertility?

For many women, unrealistic body ideals and societal overvaluation of thinness make pregnancy and early motherhood an anxiety-provoking time with regards to body image. Photos of celebrities who "got their body back" (or didn't, whatever these concepts mean) after pregnancy abound. For some reason, possessing a pregnant belly is read as an invitation to body commentary and even touching by complete strangers. Where women all too often participate in or have judgmental body commentary foisted upon them on any given day, pregnancy appears to magnify this tendency.

What do we know about how eating disorders affect fertility? A large study in the Netherlands evaluated almost 9000 women living in the city of Rotterdam. This was a population study, rather than one emerging from an eating disorder program.[7] Women with bulimia nervosa had more than double the odds of having undergone fertility treatment relative to women without a psychiatric disorder.

A large Swedish study of patients who had had at least one inpatient eating disorder admission evaluated pregnancy outcomes over 15 years. Patients with anorexia nervosa were less than half as likely to become pregnant during the study period as control subjects without an eating disorder history. Across all the eating disorders, pregnancy and childbirth rates were lower than those of controls.[8]

Another study in a private infertility clinic showed that a remarkable 20 percent of women presenting for their first intervention met criteria for a current or past eating disorder. None of these patients had disclosed the eating disorder history to their reproductive endocrinologist.[9] These data show how many women have an active eating disorder or disordered eating that is going undetected and untreated. They may then struggle to get pregnant because ongoing psychological and nutritional stressors contribute to decreased ovulation and impaired fertility.

The flip side of the fertility clinic coin is unexpected pregnancy. All patients with an eating disorder history in the Rotterdam study had higher incidences of unexpected pregnancy than those without an eating disorder. The highest rates were found in patients with anorexia nervosa in the year prior to pregnancy, in whom 55 percent of their pregnancies were a surprise. Other studies have confirmed that those with a history of anorexia nervosa may have up to double the unexpected pregnancy rate of the general population. Because patients with eating disorders may not have regular periods, they may think they are protected from getting pregnant. This is a mistake. As I mentioned in Chapter 3, I like to remind my patients that "eggs happen." That is, even if a woman hasn't had a period in months and might be in the depths of eating disorder behaviors, this is no guarantee she won't get pregnant. Anyone who is sexually active in a heterosexual relationship, and who doesn't currently desire pregnancy, should use birth control consistently.

Many doctors lack training in this arena. Eighty-four percent of clinicians in Australian and New Zealand fertility clinics agreed that it is important to screen for eating disorders, but only 35 percent routinely did so and only 9 percent said their clinics had practice guidelines for management of eating disorders. Fully 92 percent of interviewed clinicians felt they needed further education and clinical guidelines, given that fewer than 40 percent felt they could even recognize an eating disorder.[10] Gynecologists generally feel their training in eating disorders was inadequate.[11]

How Do Eating Disorders Influence Pregnancy Outcomes?

Let's consider how eating disorders affect pregnancy and birth. The aforementioned Swedish study in patients previously admitted for their eating disorder showed that the highest rates of induced abortion (that is, not miscarriage but termination of a pregnancy) were in those with bulimia nervosa. Fully 23 percent of pregnancies in those with bulimia nervosa ended in termination. The highest rates of miscarriage were in those with BED. Forty-seven percent of those with BED experienced a miscarriage, as opposed to 17 percent of controls. Infertility treatment was sought by 7.2 percent of patients with a history of eating disorders, as compared with 4.5 percent of controls.

Patients with BED have been found to have higher birthweight babies compared with patients without eating disorders.[12] This can potentially make delivery more complicated. The risk for delivering a baby who is unusually small at birth, called intrauterine growth retardation (IUGR), is well established in patients with anorexia nervosa. This risk appears to disappear when patients gain adequate weight during pregnancy. Twins births are more prevalent in patients with all types of eating disorders, which is likely related to assisted fertility.[7] Other childbirth outcomes show mixed data. Typically, patients who needed a higher level of care due to their eating disorder or are sick while pregnant are found to have more complications, such as higher C-section rates or premature delivery.

How Does Pregnancy Influence Eating Disorders?

What if we flip the question and ask how pregnancy affects eating disorder outcomes? The Norwegian Mother and Child Cohort Study was the first large scale population study to evaluate the peripartum (meaning before and after birth) effect on eating disorders. It collected information on pregnant women in society. Patients were considered to have an eating disorder if they endorsed typical symptoms and behaviors within at least six months of becoming pregnant. The study found that compared with controls, women with an eating disorder gained more weight during pregnancy, worried more about their size and shape, and had higher rates of postpartum depression.

Most often, eating disorder symptoms dramatically improve during pregnancy, as patients are able to resist behaviors for the sake of their babies. This is certainly good news, but it can also mislead patients into thinking their eating disorder has resolved and thus they can stop therapy and nutrition monitoring. In fact, the Norwegian study showed that 18 months after delivery, only 50 percent of those with anorexia and 39 percent of patients with bulimia remained in recovery. At 36 months after delivery—that is, with a three year old running around—41 percent of patients with anorexia and 70 percent of patients with bulimia had relapsed.[13]

Another large Swedish study evaluated 5200 women who had ever been admitted during their lives for anorexia nervosa. These patients would be expected to have more severe eating disorders than those in a population study. The 63 percent of women who never got pregnant accounted for 86 percent of the deaths in the cohort. Childbearing actually decreased mortality by over 60 percent. It's not that pregnancy saves lives. Rather, it stands as a physiologic and emotional marker for a certain level of recovery.[14]

Case Resolution: Angela

Angela's new doctor sees her in follow-up. Her estradiol levels are low. An ultrasound of her uterus shows that her uterus is small as well. The doctor explains that Angela's rigid eating patterns, inadequate caloric intake, exercise regimen, and low body weight are all contributing to her infertility. Her body essentially thinks it's in a starved and stressful environment. Accordingly, she has shut off sex hormone production in order to spare calories and prevent pregnancy. The doctor explains that this physiology—secondary amenorrhea due to hypothalamic hypogonadism—is the same as she would have experienced during her years with anorexia nervosa. The doctor advises her to ease up on food rules, gain some weight, cut back on intense exercise, and keep trying for pregnancy naturally. She also advises Angela to use a good quality lubricant during intercourse so that it's less painful.

Angela is shocked. She had truly thought she was living in a healthy way in anticipation of pregnancy. She thinks she's okay with following her doctor's advice because her top priority is starting a family. However, she seeks out a therapist to have guidance and support just in case the process turns out to be more of a challenge than she had anticipated. At first, it feels alien, uncomfortable, and even unsafe to eat more and rest her body. When her clothing starts feeling tight, she really struggles. Her therapist urges her to buy appropriately sized clothing and keep pushing forward.

Within two months, sex is less painful. Angela feels better than she has in years. She feels free from rules she now realizes had dominated her life. She's started a productive stretch of work with her therapist and realizes she needed this final chapter of recovery before she became pregnant. She plans to continue to see her therapist, at least through the first few months of parenthood, and then see how things go. Three months later, her pregnancy test is positive.

Notes

1 Kimmel MC, Ferguson EH, Zerwas S, Bulik CM, Meltzer-Brody S. Obstetric and gynecologic problems associated with eating disorders. *Int J Eat Disord.* 2016 March; 49(3):260–275. doi: 10.1002/eat.22483.

2 Castellini G, Lelli L, Lo Sauro C, Fioravanti G, Vignozzi L, Maggi M, Faravelli C, Ricca V. Anorectic and bulimic patients suffer from relevant sexual dysfunctions. *J Sex Med.* 2012 October; 9(10):2590–2599. doi: 10.1111/j.1743-6109. 2012.02888.x.

3 Pinheiro AP, Raney TJ, Thornton LM, Fichter MM, Berrettini WH, Goldman D, Halmi KA, Kaplan AS, Strober M, Treasure J, Woodside DB, Kaye WH, Bulik CM. Sexual functioning in women with eating disorders. *Int J Eat Disord.* 2010 March; 43(2):123–129. doi: 10.1002/eat.20671.

4 Gonidakis F, Kravvariti V, Varsou E. Sexual function of women suffering from anorexia nervosa and bulimia nervosa. *J Sex Marital Ther.* 2015; 41(4):368–378. doi: 10.1080/0092623X.2014.915904.

5 Castellini G, Mannucci E, Mazzei C, Lo Sauro C, Faravelli C, Rotella CM, Maggi M, Ricca V. Sexual function in obese women with and without binge eating disorder. *J Sex Med.* 2010 December; 7(12):3969–3978. doi: 10.1111/j.1743-6109. 2010.01990.x.

6 Castellini G, Lo Sauro C, Ricca V, Rellini AH. Body esteem as a common factor of a tendency toward binge eating and sexual dissatisfaction among women: the role of dissociation and stress response during sex. *J Sex Med.* 2017 August; 14(8):1036–1045. doi: 10.1016/j.jsxm.2017.06.001.

7 Micali N, dos-Santos-Silva I, De Stavola B, Steenweg-de Graaff J, Jaddoe V, Hofman A, Verhulst FC, Steegers E, Tiemeier H. Fertility treatment, twin births, and unplanned pregnancies in women with eating disorders: findings from a population-based birth cohort. *BJOG.* 2014 March; 121(4):408–416. doi: 10.1111/1471-0528.12503.

8 Linna MS, Raevuori A, Haukka J, Suvisaari JM, Suokas JT, Gissler M. Reproductive health outcomes in eating disorders. *Int J Eat Disord.* 2013 December; 46(8):826–833. doi: 10.1002/eat.22179.

9 Freizinger M, Franko DL, Dacey M, Okun B, Domar AD. The prevalence of eating disorders in infertile women. *Fertil Steril.* 2010 January; 93(1):72–78. doi: 10.1016/j.fertnstert.2008.09.055.

10 Rodino IS, Byrne SM, Sanders KA. Eating disorders in the context of preconception care: fertility specialists' knowledge, attitudes, and clinical practices. *Fertil Steril.* 2017 February; 107(2):494–501. doi: 10.1016/j.fertnstert.2016. 10.036.

11 Leddy MA, Jones C, Morgan MA, Schulkin J. Eating disorders and obstetric-gynecologic care. *J Womens Health (Larchmt).* 2009 September; 18(9):1395–1401. doi: 10.1089/jwh.2008.1183.

12 Linna MS, Raevuori A, Haukka J, Suvisaari JM, Suokas JT, Gissler M. Pregnancy, obstetric, and perinatal health outcomes in eating disorders. *Am J Obstet Gynecol.* 2014 October; 211(4):392.e1–8. doi: 10.1016/j.ajog.2014.03.067.

13 Knoph C, Von Holle A, Zerwas S, Torgersen L, Tambs K, Stoltenberg C, Bulik CM, Reichborn-Kjennerud T. Course and predictors of maternal eating disorders in the postpartum period. *Int J Eat Disord.* 2013 May; 46(4):355–368. doi: 10.1002/eat.22088.

14 Papadopoulos FC, Karamanis G, Brandt L, Ekbom A, Ekselius L. Childbearing and mortality among women with anorexia nervosa. *Int J Eat Disord.* 2013 March; 46(2):164–170. doi: 10.1002/eat.22051.

Chapter 20

Older Patients

Case: Patricia

Patricia is a 53-year-old cisgender Caucasian female who developed anorexia nervosa, restricting subtype, when she was 15 years old. A single admission to what passed back then for an eating disorder program was a terrible experience. She managed to get through high school and college, living a fairly isolated and rule-bound life. In her 20s, she married and started a career. For a time, she was healthier. She was able to get pregnant after a year of trying, and her son was born when she was 34. Eating then started to become a struggle again. She completed a second residential treatment program when her son was in third grade. It was better than the first treatment experience but still hard for her. While in treatment, she missed her family, felt ashamed as a woman "still" struggling in her 40s, and experienced social isolation while surrounded by younger patients. She ultimately was able to hold on to a decent recovery for a while after this treatment episode. Despite years of therapy, Patricia always focused on everyone else's needs before her own and had a hard time resting and recharging. That "to do" checklist always loomed in her brain.

At age 52, she and her husband divorced just as her son was finishing high school. Faced with losing the two people she'd spent her adulthood taking care of, and worried about how she'd support herself financially, Patricia's anorexia came roaring back. Her friends watched helplessly as she retreated and lost weight.

Case: Joe

Joe is a 48-year-old cisgender African American male who has felt isolated much of his life due to his larger body. As a child, he was teased about his size, and a coach first recommended a diet when he was nine years old. Joe remembers sneaking into the kitchen at night and devouring foods he craved after a day of deprivation. Every few years, Joe tried some new diet and exercise plan. He'd follow it intensively for a month or so, tracking his weight obsessively several times a day as it decreased, then he would either get injured or exhausted. Every time he burned out, Joe's weight invariably rose higher than it had been before.

Joe now mostly restricts during the day at work, waking up each morning determined to lose the weight. By evening, he's so ravenous that he picks up a large quantity of fast food after work and eats it by the time he arrives home. He feels isolated and ashamed. He hasn't seen a doctor since college, knowing the doctor will lecture him about his weight. He's worried about diabetes, and he feels exhausted all the time and wonders if he has sleep apnea. Despite his fears about his health, Joe's shame about his weight and prior negative experiences with doctors keep him from seeking medical attention. He wishes he just had more willpower.

Background

Eating disorders are not just diseases that affect teenagers. Studies highlight how commonly eating disorders occur in middle-aged and older adults, too.[1] The Gender and Body Image Study confirmed the high prevalence of chronic use of weight loss strategies, body dysmorphias, and the close connection between emotional distress and body perceptions in women over 50 years old.[2] A comprehensive review of patients over 40 years old showed that eating disorder prevalence in women is around 3 percent and in males is 1–2 percent.

The most common diagnoses are BED and OSFED.[3] That is, these patients most often do not live in emaciated bodies that raise the alarm in the doctor's office or for the patients themselves. In fact, most of these older patients are not in treatment. Life transitions, such as divorce, children leaving home, and menopause are considered important triggers for the worsening of eating disorder severity.

Most older adults with eating disorders have had some sort of eating or body pathology since adolescence.[4] Studies have generally focused on the psychological aspects of eating disorders in older adults, with fewer looking at medical outcomes. Ten-year mortality rates are generally felt to be worse in patients over 40.[5] One study reported that patients over 50 years old with anorexia nervosa experience high levels of shame, difficulties accessing resources, and discrimination by clinicians.[6]

Medical Outcomes

One study evaluated patients with severe anorexia nervosa admitted to the hospital for medical stabilization. It found that 46 percent of patients were 30 years old or more, while almost a quarter of the patients were over 40 years old, with a median age of 48 years. This is not what many people imagine when they think of the population who needs the highest level of care in the country for an eating disorder. The older patients in this study presented just as medically compromised as the younger patients, and they had equally good outcomes and similar lengths of stay during their medical stabilization.[7]

Medical treatment of older adults with eating disorders involves all the same concepts you have been reading about in this book: a non-assumptive approach that starts with inviting patients to name their individual goals and values, a multidisciplinary team, and an effort to ameliorate symptoms from both measurable and unmeasurable medical problems. Anyone of any age with an eating disorder should feel that full recovery is possible. I remind patients all the time that they cannot control the thoughts and feelings of their eating disorder, but they can control the way they respond to those thoughts and feelings. It might take longer, there might be more wear and tear on the body that can't be fully reversed, and it might be really hard work, but recovery is absolutely possible.

We must also face the reality, though, that some older patients with eating disorders find that lasting change is out of reach. They want to survive and live their lives, but the duration of the eating disorder, challenging life events, or comorbid psychiatric illnesses make sustained recovery work exceptionally difficult. Many of these patients decline recommended treatment, causing worry and distress for their family and team. Chapter 22 reviews when it is and is not appropriate to mandate treatment against a patient's will.

"Trying Recovery"

With my older patients with anorexia nervosa and those who have been ill from their eating disorder for a long time, I often introduce the idea of "trying recovery." Even when these patients feel motivated to make changes, the very idea of who they would be without their eating disorder can be overwhelming. Every day, minute-to-minute, a battle is waging inside them. If they complete a meal, their anorexic self is disappointed. If they restrict or use behaviors around a meal, their recovery-oriented self is disappointed. Most of my patients are so sensitive that causing disappointment is a particularly painful experience. However, as a result of this constant internal struggle within them, they feel like a disappointment all the time, and it's exhausting. Who has the emotional energy to engage in productive therapeutic work when all their focus is on the fight between the recovery voice and the eating disorder voice?

I invite these patients to "try recovery." Sometimes fully committing to a recovered life, while in the depths of an eating disorder, is almost unimaginable. I ask,

> What if, instead, you agreed to *try* recovery for, say, a 6-month period? Pick a calendar date, 6 months from now, that's meaningful to you. Tell your eating disorder that during those 6 months you're trying recovery, and fiercely resist the eating disorder voice during

that time. Then when the meal comes, of course you eat it. And you don't purge it. And you don't excessively exercise. Because you are trying recovery.

This can ward off the eating disorder voice just long enough to make meaningful progress.

Trying recovery could also be called a "time-limited trial of care" because the patient doesn't have to commit to what seems like a daunting process forever, just for a certain period of time. During that protected time, though, they give it their all. It's not the time for doubting and resisting. At the end of the time-limited trial, the patient assesses if they feel better. If so, what a valuable win. If not, they do have the option to return to their eating disorder. At least they will make an informed decision knowing what life in recovery is actually like, rather than anxiously imagining the worst and then not even trying it.

Yes, the six months will still be really hard. And yes, I openly admit I hope that once they're nourished, rested, and supported in great therapy for a period of time, they will realize that recovery is a much better place than illness. Mainly, a time-limited trial can feel like a less intimidating way to start. This is a somewhat controversial strategy. I've met therapists who feel like this isn't rigorous enough or is risky. But the fact is, the patients I recommend this to are struggling to engage at all and feel hopeless. Trying recovery is thus a far better approach than giving up from the outset.

Case Resolution: Patricia

Patricia's two closest friends stage an intervention. They gather at her home one evening and tell her how terribly worried they are about her anorexia relapse. Patricia is startled. She had thought she was fine and that no one had noticed. She tries to wave them off, and she feels embarrassed by the attention. However, her friends don't let up. They tell her how much they care about her. They remind her how many years they've known her, and they point out that their funny, smart, caring friend has been absent now for a while. They remind Patricia that even with her son off to college, he still needs his mom and has lots of life milestones ahead that she needs to be present for.

Patricia's friends have brought some resources along. They found a list of eating disorder therapists and dietitians in their community online, and they ask her at least to reach out and have an initial session. Patricia is torn: on the one hand, all she really wants to do is sink deeper into her disorder and get even sicker so that her body matches the pain in her soul. She feels so overwhelmed that all she wants to do is disappear. On the other hand, her friends' message is compelling. After some hesitation, she books herself a first appointment with a therapist and a dietitian.

Case Resolution: Joe

Joe's sister, who herself is recovered from an eating disorder, has connected with a body positivity group online that promotes HAES. She calls him for their monthly chat, and Joe confesses that he feels really unwell and isn't sure what to do. His sister says what she's been saying for years: she feels Joe has an eating disorder rather than a lack of willpower. Joe had always resisted that idea because he thought eating disorders only affected women. However, he feels so unwell that he asks her what she recommends.

His sister has been waiting for this moment. She gives him the name of a doctor who adheres to the HAES philosophy and urges him to start there. Joe reluctantly makes an appointment. The doctor is kind, the furniture, blood pressure cuff, and gown all fit his body, and the nurse makes a point of not checking his weight.

The doctor listens carefully to Joe's history with food as well as to his current medical concerns. She concludes that he meets the criteria for BED. She shares with him details about HAES and notes that if he's looking for a weight loss doctor, he's definitely come to the wrong place. The doctor invites Joe to share his goals and values. She then outlines that recovery will focus on helping him to make values-based decisions and move toward his goals without any focus on weight. She encourages him to start work with a HAES-informed therapist and dietitian, to which Joe somewhat reluctantly agrees.

In the meantime, his doctor assures him that based on his bloodwork, he doesn't have diabetes, although his blood pressure is high. They begin treatment for this. She refers him to an evaluation for sleep apnea, requesting in her referral that the referring clinic not bring up weight or weight loss. While this is no guarantee, she tells Joe she'll always try to advocate for him when he's in the medical system outside of her clinic. Joe feels supported, empowered, and hopeful.

Notes

1 Mangweth-Matzek B, Hoek HW, Rupp CI, Lackner-Seifert K, Frey N, Whitworth AB, Pope HG, Kinzl J. Prevalence of eating disorders in middle-aged women. *Int J Eat Disord.* 2014 April; 47(3):320–324. doi: 10.1002/eat.22232.

2 Gagne DA, Von Holle A, Brownley KA, Runfola CD, Hofmeier S, Branch KE, Bulik CM. Eating disorder symptoms and weight and shape concerns in a large web-based convenience sample of women ages 50 and above: results of the Gender and Body Image (GABI) study. *Int J Eat Disord.* 2012 November; 45(7): 832–844. doi: 10.1002/eat.22030.

3 Mangweth-Matzek B, Hoek HW. Epidemiology and treatment of eating disorders in men and women of middle and older age. *Curr Opin Psychiatry.* 2017 November; 30(6):446–451. doi: 10.1097/YCO.0000000000000356.

4 Huas C, Caille A, Godart N, Foulon C, Pham-Scottez A, Divac S, Dechartres A, Lavoisy G, Guelfi JD, Rouillon F, Falissard B. Factors predictive of ten-year mortality in severe anorexia nervosa patients. *Acta Psychiatr Scand.* 2011 January; 123(1):62–70. doi: 10.1111/j.1600-0447.2010.01627.x.

5 Suokas JT, Suvisaari JM, Gissler M, Löfman R, Linna MS, Raevuori A, Haukka J. Mortality in eating disorders: a follow-up study of adult eating disorder patients

treated in tertiary care, 1995–2010. *Psychiatry Res.* 2013 December 30; 210(3): 1101–1106. doi: 10.1016/j.psychres.2013.07.042.

6 Scholtz S, Hill LS, Lacey H. Eating disorders in older women: does late onset anorexia nervosa exist? *Int J Eat Disord.* 2010 July; 43(5):393–397. doi: 10.1002/eat.20704.

7 Gaudiani JL, Brinton JT, Sabel AL, Rylander M, Catanach B, Mehler PS. Medical outcomes for adults hospitalized with severe anorexia nervosa: an analysis by age group. *Int J Eat Disord.* 2016 April; 49(4):378–385. doi: 10.1002/eat.22437.

Chapter 21

Substance Use Disorder

Case: Shelley

Shelley is a 32-year-old cisgender Caucasian female who has struggled with anorexia nervosa purging subtype and substance abuse for years. Her parents remember her as a feisty, daring little girl who loved to put on performances for anyone who would watch. They also recollect that she constantly seemed to be in conflict with one or more of her friends at any given time. Popular and charismatic, she was also extremely sensitive. Her bewildered parents would frequently observe their stormy daughter returning home after school in floods of tears because of an argument or perceived insult from one of her friends. They would try to comfort her with variable success. They watched Shelley struggle to self-soothe and have a hard time distinguishing between big conflicts and small conflicts; all affected her equally strongly.

Shelley remembers her childhood mostly fondly but always felt her parents didn't understand her and never showed up for her the way she needed them to. She started drinking and smoking cigarettes with her friends at age 13, and she started smoking pot when she was 14. She had sex for the first time while high that same year. Shelley's eating disorder started when she was 15, when she started to diet along with her group of friends. Her determination to be the best at whatever she did drove her to restrict harder than the others. However, she was so famished that she started to binge. Deciding this was unacceptable, she soon started to purge after her binges. She flew under the radar, seeming like a successful, popular, thin, beautiful young woman throughout high school.

In college, Shelley would often restrict calories all day in order to go out partying with her sorority sisters at night and not worry about the calories. Her enjoyment of college and constant social support started to stabilize her eating disorder behaviors. However, she started using cocaine regularly. She didn't feel concerned as her grades were fine and she was using less cocaine than many of her peers.

After graduation from college, Shelley crashed. Suddenly on her own and facing expectations that she get a job, she felt isolated and overwhelmed at the prospect of the adult life ahead of her. Shelly responded by diving into restriction, purging, and alcohol. Over the next few years, her parents supported her through various substance use and eating disorder treatment programs. However, she was never fully abstinent either from substances or from her eating disorder while in programming. As time went on, she increasingly left treatment against medical advice. Shelley stabilized somewhat in her late 20s. A friend's death then sent her into a full blown relapse in order to numb the pain of her grief. Now drinking heavily, intermittently using cocaine, underweight and with several emergency department visits for passing out and abnormal electrolytes, Shelley realizes she needs more definitive help.

Background

Eating disorders and substance use disorders co-occur with a remarkably high frequency. Up to half of patients with eating disorders abuse drugs or alcohol. In patients with substance use disorder, more than 35 percent also report an eating disorder.[1] We know that this is vastly higher than the 1–4 percent of eating disorders in the general population. In adolescents with eating disordered behaviors, rates of substance use and abuse are 20–40 percent higher than peers without eating disorders.[2]

A large study of women with anorexia nervosa subdivided patients into different behavior groups, including a group with restrictive anorexia nervosa (called "RAN") and a group with lifetime history of anorexia nervosa and bulimia nervosa (called "ANBN"). Among the whole sample, 20 percent met criteria for a lifetime history of alcohol abuse or dependence. The prevalence was highest in the ANBN group at 35 percent and lowest in the RAN group at 13.7 percent.

The risk for drug abuse or dependence was 6.25 times higher in the ANBN group, with a prevalence of 32 percent, compared with the RAN group. Cannabis was the most commonly used drug overall. However, patients with ANBN were also 6.55 times more likely to use stimulants, 5.89 times more likely to use cocaine, and 4.72 times more likely to use sedatives than patients with RAN. Patients in the group who ever purged were 1.83 times more likely to abuse alcohol and 3.79 times more likely to abuse drugs than patients who purely restricted.[3]

Another study followed patients over ten years who had been hospitalized for their anorexia nervosa. It found that patients who reported binge eating while underweight were six times likelier to have substance use disorder than those who purely restricted. This risk was also associated with a higher incidence of alcohol use disorder among first degree relatives.[4] In addition, women with an eating disorder, particularly if they engaged in any purging behaviors, were more likely to smoke cigarettes, and smoked more frequently to control weight, than healthy controls.[5]

Patients who restrict calories or purge to avoid weight gain from drinking alcohol are said to have "drunkorexia," an informal term that nonetheless captures the spirit of the problem. A study showed that individuals engaging in "drunkorexia" are at risk for future formal diagnoses of eating and substance use disorders.[6]

Food is Not an Addiction

Does this mean that we should regard eating disorders as food or starvation addictions and by extension that these patients are simply at higher risk for other addictions? Absolutely not. I firmly reject the proposition that food or sugar addiction exists. The notion of sugar addiction is another example of modern day pseudoscience. A study extensively reviewed the literature and neuroscience on so-called "processed food and sugar addiction" in animals and humans. It found little evidence to support sugar addiction in humans. In animals, addiction-like behaviors such as bingeing only occurred when animals had intermittent, rather than routine, access to sugar.[7]

Once again, we find that restriction causes bingeing, not the palatability of the food itself. If a person deprives themselves of sufficient food or a certain type of food (a.k.a. "being on a diet"), they set up cravings and are more likely to binge. By contrast, consistent, moderate consumption of unrestricted foods doesn't set the deprivation-binge pendulum in motion. Another study reframed the concept of food addiction as an "unnecessary medicalization," identifying that our basic reward system for eating or even overeating food shouldn't be pathologized as a disease.[8]

Why Do Eating Disorders and Substance Abuse Co-Occur?

What are the reasons for this high rate of comorbidity between eating disorders and substance use disorder? Most agree that a biopsychosocial model best fits this problem. Biological features like inherited risk for addiction or temperamental traits, personality factors like impulsivity, novelty seeking,[9] and mood dysregulation, comorbid psychological illness, and environmental exposures all play a part.[10] One study demonstrated, perhaps not surprisingly, that patients with BED and comorbid mood disorders, personality disorder features, and substance use disorder had more severe eating disorder symptoms.[11]

Alcohol and drugs can play three key roles for patients with eating disorders. One, alcohol and drugs satisfy the novelty seeker's quest "to have a good time." Two, using substances can serve as self-medication. If an individual is anxious, depressed, overwhelmed, or has other psychiatric diagnoses like bipolar disorder that haven't been adequately addressed by medications, alcohol and drugs can provide welcome relief, or at least an escape. Three, some substances carry the side effect of weight loss. Ranging from legal to illegal, tobacco, caffeine, cocaine, heroin, and amphetamines all can be used to suppress appetite and body weight. Given that alcohol and drugs serve clear purposes for patients, it is important to remember that sobriety work must offer ways to satisfy or redirect these needs in other ways.

Outcomes and Treatment

Despite the impact that substance use disorder has on health and lives, only 6 percent of individuals with substance use disorder seek treatment. Among this minutely small proportion, over half never complete treatment.[12] In patients with eating disorders, substance abuse results in worse outcomes than those with eating disorders alone. Similarly, those with substance use disorder who also have an eating disorder show more severe substance abuse and worse functional outcomes. These comorbid diagnoses contribute to increased medical complications, worse psychopathology, longer time to recovery, and higher relapse rates.[13]

One of the challenges patients with comorbid eating disorders and substance use disorder face is the high prevalence of early treatment termination. While reasons may range from inability to tolerate a sober and nourished life to frustration with care systems that are often inadequate for managing both conditions, studies have shown that individuals with both diagnoses have a much higher rate of stopping treatment.

One study of patients in a residential substance use facility found that about 7 percent of patients likely had an eating disorder, and about 65 percent of patients likely had an alcohol use disorder. Seventeen percent of patients left against medical advice. A regression analysis controlled for age, years of education, depression symptoms, alcohol use, and drug abuse. It found that eating disorder symptoms were significantly associated with the decision to leave treatment against medical advice.[14]

Similarly, in a study of young adult men in residential substance use treatment who were assessed for binge/purge and binge eating symptoms, treatment rejection was associated with eating disorder symptoms after controlling for multiple other factors. The authors concluded that impulsivity, distress intolerance, and challenges with emotional regulation were particularly high among the men with disordered eating symptoms.[15]

Treatment for patients with comorbid eating disorders and substance use disorder should take place in settings that have expertise in both. For instance, when patients enter substance use treatment, their eating disorder symptoms often spiral out of control as they confront sobriety. Many substance use programs simply lack the staffing and protocols to help create appropriate meal plans, observe patients at the table, monitor bathrooms for purging, and therapeutically support eating disorder recovery. Similarly, many patients who enter day treatment for eating disorder symptoms find their substance abuse escalating. As one numbing strategy is taken away, the patient can be inexorably drawn to the other.

My clinical experience is that top residential eating disorder programs are probably best for those with comorbid substance use disorders. These programs can consistently nourish and support patients through their eating disorder, while by virtue of being residential, they are also oases for sobriety. However, if patients' drug or alcohol abuse is severe enough, they may need to start their treatment in a medical hospital for detoxification. Ideally, this would occur in a medical hospital with eating disorder expertise so that no time is wasted. Detoxing someone from heroin or alcohol for a week while they are still restricting food or purging in the hospital doesn't prepare them sufficiently to enter a mental health residential program.

Case Resolution: Shelley

Shelley's readiness to change prompts her parents to call a highly regarded residential eating disorder program. During the intake, the program recommends that Shelley start her recovery work at a specialized medical hospital that can oversee detoxification from alcohol as well as begin nutritional rehabilitation. Shelley admits to the medical hospital with a high blood alcohol level, noting that she had a "last hurrah" en route to the hospital. The first week of hospitalization is a challenge. Her alcohol withdrawal is severe, requiring intensive monitoring and medical management. Getting her to eat is hard while she withdraws from alcohol, and she accepts a nasojejunal (NJ) tube to get through this stage.

By the time she emerges from the hospital, Shelley is fully detoxified from alcohol, has gained a few pounds, and is tolerating a high calorie nutritional rehabilitation meal plan by mouth. She feels vastly better. She feels so much better, in fact, that it's hard to convince her to proceed as planned to the residential eating disorder program. She is convinced that she's "fine" and will be able to sustain this at home. Only with intensive family support and the hospital team's efforts does she agree to try admission to the eating disorder program.

Over the next eight weeks in residential, with a nourished, sober brain, Shelley makes therapeutic progress that had always eluded her in the past. When it comes time to transition to day treatment, she again resists because she feels so confident that she can manage on her own. Once again, her family and the team convince her to give it a go. Within the first week, she gets drunk with her roommate in the program's apartments. This serves as a wake up call, and she redoubles her efforts in treatment. By the time she leaves the program several months later, having completed all levels of available care, she has a great team in place, plans to attend AA meetings, and knows not to discount the power of her substance use disorder or her eating disorder.

Notes

1 The National Center on Addiction and Substance Abuse (CASA) at Columbia University, Food for Thought: Substance Abuse and Eating Disorders. 2003. The National Center on Addiction and Substance Abuse at Columbia University, New York.
2 Denoth F, Siciliano V, Iozzo P, Fortunato L, Molinaro S. The association between overweight and illegal drug consumption in adolescents: is there an

underlying influence of the sociocultural environment? *PLoS One.* 2011; 6(11):e27358. doi: 10.1371/journal.pone.0027358.

3 Root TL, Pinheiro AP, Thornton L, Strober M, Fernández-Aranda F, Brandt H, Crawford S, Fichter MM, Halmi KA, Johnson C, Kaplan AS, Klump KL, La Via M, Mitchell J, Woodside DB, Rotondo A, Berrettini WH, Kaye WH, Bulik CM. Substance use disorders in women with anorexia nervosa. *Int J Eat Disord.* 2010 January; 43(1):14–21. doi: 10.1002/eat.20670.

4 Strober M, Freeman R, Bower S, Rigali J. Binge eating in anorexia nervosa predicts later onset of substance use disorder: A ten-year prospective, longitudinal follow-up of 95 adolescents. *J Youth Adol* 1996; 25(4):519–532.

5 Krug I, Treasure J, Anderluh M, Bellodi L, Cellini E, di Bernardo M, Granero R, Karwautz A, Nacmias B, Penelo E, Ricca V, Sorbi S, Tchanturia K, Wagner G, Collier D, Fernández-Aranda F. Present and lifetime comorbidity of tobacco, alcohol and drug use in eating disorders: a European multicenter study. *Drug Alcohol Depend.* 2008 September 1; 97(1–2):169–179. doi: 10.1016/j.drugalcdep. 2008.04.015.

6 Hunt TK, Forbush KT. Is "drunkorexia" an eating disorder, substance use disorder, or both? *Eat Behav.* 2016 August; 22:40–45. doi: 10.1016/j.eatbeh.2016. 03.034.

7 Westwater ML, Fletcher PC, Ziauddeen H. Sugar addiction: the state of the science. *Eur J Nutr.* 2016 November; 55(Suppl. 2):55–69. doi: 10.1007/s00394-016-1229-6.

8 Finlayson G. Food addiction and obesity: unnecessary medicalization of hedonic overeating. *Nat Rev Endocrinol.* 2017 August; 13(8):493–498. doi: 10. 1038/nrendo.2017.61.

9 Krug I, Pinheiro AP, Bulik C, Jiménez-Murcia S, Granero R, Penelo E, Masuet C, Agüera Z, Fernández-Aranda F. Lifetime substance abuse, family history of alcohol abuse/dependence and novelty seeking in eating disorders: comparison study of eating disorder subgroups. *Psychiatry Clin Neurosci.* 2009 February; 63(1):82–87. doi: 10.1111/j.1440-1819.2008.01908.x.

10 Gregorowski C, Seedat S, Jordaan GP. A clinical approach to the assessment and management of co-morbid eating disorders and substance use disorders. *BMC Psychiatry.* 2013 November 7; 13:289. doi: 10.1186/1471-244X-13-289.

11 Becker DF, Grilo CM. Comorbidity of mood and substance use disorders in patients with binge-eating disorder: associations with personality disorder and eating disorder pathology. *J Psychosom Res.* 2015 August; 79(2):159–164. doi: 10.1016/j.jpsychores.2015.01.016.

12 Doumas DM, Blasey CM, Thacker CL. Attrition from alcohol and drug outpatient treatment: psychological distress and interpersonal problems as indicators. *Alcohol Treat Q.* 2005; 23(4):55–67.

13 Courbasson CM, Smith PD, Cleland PA. Substance use disorders, anorexia, bulimia, and concurrent disorders. *Can J Public Health.* 2005 March–April; 96(2):102–106. PubMed PMID: 15850027.

14 Elmquist J, Shorey RC, Anderson S, Stuart GL. Eating disorder symptoms and length of stay in residential treatment for substance use: a brief report. *J Dual Diagn.* 2015; 11(3–4):233–237. doi: 10.1080/15504263.2015.1104480.

15 Elmquist J, Shorey RC, Anderson SE, Temple JR, Stuart GL. The relationship between eating disorder symptoms and treatment rejection among young adult men in residential substance use treatment. *Subst Abuse.* 2016 May 22; 10:39–44. doi: 10.4137/SART.S33396.

Chapter 22

Caring for the Patient Who Declines Treatment

The Spectrum from Mandated Treatment to Hospice Care

Case: Elana

Elana is a 38-year-old cisgender Caucasian female with a history of anorexia nervosa, restricting subtype, since she was 11 years old. Elana has been to countless eating disorder treatment programs over the years, fully weight restoring each time only to relapse almost immediately upon discharge. Despite the severity of her mental illness, she finished college over six years. However, she has never been able to keep a job.

Elana lives with her parents and has watched her siblings marry and have kids. She adores her nieces and nephews and feels sad that her eating disorder has robbed her of the opportunity of having a spouse and children. Elana's team (which consists of a therapist, dietitian, internist, and psychiatrist) has been with her for the past five years. She sees them regularly when she's not in treatment, and they are dedicated to her and communicate regularly with each other.

For the last few years, every time Elana relapses, she gets sick faster than ever. She emerges from several months of residential care feeling like she's coming out of her skin with distress about the weight restoration process. Even she is startled by how fast her weight drops after treatment. She has tried virtually every psychotropic medication and intervention, and they all either didn't work or gave her intolerable side effects.

A year ago, Elana's parents threatened to disown her unless she went back to treatment, and they insisted she look into experimental brain interventions in university studies. None of these studies would take her because of the chronicity of her disease and comorbidities. At that time, Elana did go back into treatment at an outstanding program out of respect for her parents, but despite being "a good patient" and fully weight restoring, she just didn't feel better. The voice never faded.

Elana loves her family and lives for her dog. She doesn't want to die from her eating disorder and has always doubted she would ever get sick enough for this to happen, despite having been warned about it countless times. However, she finds it essentially impossible to do what's necessary to live. The eating disorder voice is always deafening in her head. Elana's main desire, at this point, is to stay outpatient because she feels higher levels of care don't work, are expensive, and make her feel unbearably homesick when she's away. In addition, she is adamant about not gaining weight.

Elana's team does everything they can to honor her request. Having watched her fail to tolerate full weight restoration so many times before, they encourage her to find a harm reduction point where she can live underweight but not dangerously cachectic. She agrees this is a good idea, but her weight falls right through the agreed-upon range. The team members' calls with each other escalate. They wonder how they can keep her safe in the community. They have her sign against medical advice (AMA) forms when she refuses to go to the hospital or a treatment program. They wonder if they need to fire her. She begs them to stand by her and keep helping her find a tolerable middle ground, even as her anxiety, rigidity, and uncomfortable physical symptoms escalate with her malnutrition.

Elana's parents feel anguished. They see their beautiful, smart, funny daughter wasting away. The idea of her dying of anorexia nervosa is unacceptable to them, but they have seen that treatment hasn't worked. They aren't sure what to do now.

Background

Many patients with eating disorders and their families are forced to confront difficult situations where necessary treatment is rejected with potentially life-threatening consequences, usually due to a high degree of malnutrition or purging. Eating disorders resist diagnosis and treatment by their very nature. They are what's called ego syntonic, meaning the disorders are in harmony with the person's sense of self. Someone with cancer rarely if ever embraces their diagnosis as enhancing their purpose and uniqueness, soothing their demons, and promising salvation from all woes. This is, however, what many people feel about their eating disorder. A starved brain becomes especially resistant and rigid, such that feeling hopeless about recovery is common. So how do we know when to force someone into treatment against their will, and how do we know when it's time to stop forcing them and imagine that they might in fact die from their disease?

Resistance to treatment can encompass everything from declining a higher level of care, to declining to recover at a rate or to a weight range desired by the outpatient team, to refusing care altogether. Both options— treating someone against their will or agreeing not to do so—should be considered with gravity. Our society strongly believes in the right of self-determination. That is, we don't take the decision of taking away adults' rights to act independently lightly, and that's as it should be. We don't, for instance, mandate that all adults make good medical choices. That would result in a totalitarian state. We permit patients to decline care against medical advice as long as they understand the consequences of their choice. Thus, taking away that right and mandating treatment is a serious issue.

On the other hand, the idea that some patients might not be able to get better from their eating disorder is an emotional and even controversial topic for many. Concepts like "never giving up" and "fighting this to the end," whether in eating disorders or in any medical situation, emerge from people's personal, cultural, familial, and religious roots. Since medical school, I have been keenly interested in the notion of appropriate goals of care at end of life. Some of my most meaningful, heart-filling conversations as a physician have taken place in the context of a general medicine patient's impending death. For many, this is unthinkable. However, anyone who's done hospice or palliative care work knows that there can be something infinitely tender, powerful, and privileged in bearing witness to a person's final days or even minutes. As with birth or marriage, at the time of death one is aware of a vast, important moment transpiring in a life, one that affects not just the individual but also their entire family.

This chapter mostly draws upon the literature of those with anorexia nervosa and underweight. The main reason for this is that these patients who decline recommended care have an obvious, proximate mechanism for death by starvation: cardiac arrest from a blood glucose that drops or low potassium due to purging, in the context of minimal electrolyte stores in their body. There are many patients with severe eating disorders and extreme restriction and purging behaviors who occupy larger bodies. As ever, this patient population is often overlooked. More attention is needed on this topic for such individuals. And for all with mental illness, the risk of suicide remains a potential mechanism for death that must always be assessed.

Overview of Strategy

The flow chart in Figure 22.1 summarizes my thought process, based on current literature, when it comes to the patient who declines treatment. This flow chart represents a very simplified summary of the concepts and terms that I will review subsequently.

Motivating Voluntary Engagement

As always, it's worthwhile to start by inviting patients to share their values and goals with me. Ones I've heard many times include, "Return to school," "Stay alive for my child," and "Do a good job with my work." My overarching strategy is to keep working to motivate a patient's voluntary acceptance of treatment at whatever level of care is appropriate. When it comes to eating disorders, these patients need clinicians who have real eating disorder expertise. Expert clinicians will be dedicated to a multidisciplinary, highly communicative team approach. Each one will bring

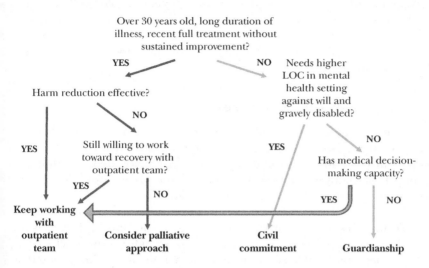

Figure 22.1 Flow Chart for the Patient Declining Recommended Treatment.

their unique skills to try and motivate a patient refusing treatment. Most of us carry a fierce, burning optimism that anyone can fully recover from an eating disorder.

Younger Patients Who Decline Care

If efforts to motivate the patient do not work, and they continue to refuse recommended treatment, the first questions to ask are whether they are over 30, have been ill a long time, and have recently experienced a full course of high quality eating disorder treatment.[1] The idea behind these criteria is that a person younger than 30 may yet mature into a more recovery-focused set of values, developing from "all I want is not to gain weight" to "there are more important things in my life than staying sick and malnourished." Most patients experience meaningful improvement in their eating disorder distortions following full weight restoration.

Children up to the age of 18 can almost always have their protestations overridden by their parents in medical and psychiatric settings. Many parents face the terrifying challenge of their 17-year-old with an eating disorder arriving at their eighteenth birthday and then declining treatment, demanding to head off to college, and insisting that they are adults now and it's time to honor their autonomy and independence. This must be anticipated and prepared for.

A unified treatment team can respectfully point out that if going to college or enjoying independence are important to the patient, as they often are, an eating disorder is one of the most likely barriers to both.

No patient with an eating disorder is truly independent, controlled as they are by arbitrary and cruel food and exercise rules as well as ruminative thoughts that crowd out all other interests and relationships. Progressive medical illness is likely to pull young adults out of school and disrupt academic and athletic goals.

Leverage: Parental Resources

There may come a point, however, where parents must assert whatever leverage they possess to mandate that appropriate treatment—whether outpatient or residential—be accepted by their newly fledged adult offspring. That might mean a refusal to continue to pay school tuition or to support their child's lifestyle. The message can be,

> We want more than anything to have a relationship with you as an adult where you show you are capable of caring for yourself. However, it's unacceptable that you insist upon remaining ill and imagining that you can have both your eating disorder and the privilege of school and a life we support financially. We're adults too. And we choose not to enable your illness.

I've had many parents express worry to me that this will steal their child's motivation and hope. I can assure them: whatever manipulations the eating disorder is employing to stay in its abusive relationship with their child, getting the child into appropriate treatment is far more likely to result in recovery than holding out rewards and letting the brain stay starved for weeks and months more. Many of my patients in their 30s and 40s reflect on how they wish their parents had been more insistent on recovery earlier. They ultimately interpreted their parents' giving in and allowing them to continue their eating disordered life as a sign that they weren't sick enough.

Guardianship

If this kind of leverage isn't enough, or in situations where parents or partners have exhausted all possible influence without prompting acceptance of treatment, there are next steps. Some parents begin seeking preemptive guardianship over their 17-year-old child who has an eating disorder in anticipation of the upcoming eighteenth birthday.

The same policies that protect adult autonomy broadly in our society can prove immensely frustrating to loved ones of patients with eating disorders who refuse treatment. Depending on one's state of residence, it can be nearly impossible to obtain guardianship because some state laws so strongly favor autonomy over saving lives. The court might see an impeccably groomed, brilliant, articulate young adult and have a hard time granting guardianship to their desperate parents. Guardianship is a legal process that is typically pursued when individuals have been proven not to be able to take care of themselves in fundamental ways and lack medical decision making capacity.

A quarter of psychiatric consultations in hospitals, performed by doctors or psychologists, address decision making capacity.[2] There are four key questions to be answered in a capacity evaluation. Does the patient have the ability to make a choice? Can they understand information? Do they have the ability to understand the consequences of a choice? And finally, can they manipulate information rationally, understanding the proposed treatments, risks, benefits, and alternatives?

For instance, a 20 year old, who has been medically hospitalized for severe anorexia nervosa and has a very low blood glucose might demand to leave against medical advice when presented with a juice. The doctor might ask her, "What would happen if you left right now?" With her hypoglycemic brain and anorexia denial, she might say, "Nothing. I'll be fine." The doctor would follow up, "What are the alternatives to hospitalization and this juice you are refusing?" The patient might reply irritably, "I'd just go back to my life." This is a patient who lacks capacity due to a medical cause, and she would not be allowed to leave against medical advice. A proxy would be established to sign off on medical decisions, and then this could be converted to guardianship in the court if treatment refusal and lack of decision making capacity persisted.

Civil Commitment

In Colorado, where my clinic is located, guardians can mandate care in a medical setting, but they cannot require admission to inpatient psychiatric care against the patient's wishes. Colorado has tended to favor saving lives over autonomy, with some of the strongest mental health laws fostering patient survival in the United States. These have proven immensely helpful for saving the lives of patients with eating disorders receiving care in this state.

So, if a guardian cannot mandate admission to a mental health facility, as may be needed when a patient with an eating disorder needs but refuses a higher level of care, what's the alternative? Civil commitment is the alternative to guardianship. Civil commitment means that a judge orders a patient into mandatory treatment, going above even the authority of guardianship. In Colorado, only a civil commitment (called a short term certification) can require a patient to enter mental health inpatient care against their will.

Unlike the guardianship process, which is pursued through a medical model that evaluates decision making capacity, the civil commitment process usually runs through a mental health pathway. In the case of severe mental illness, the individual is assessed for grave disability and imminent harm. If the fairly stringent criteria are met, the patient can be placed on a mental health hold that is converted to a short term certification in court. While almost no patient calmly accepts a civil commitment, most patients I have cared for who have needed one have eventually thanked their treatment team for advocating for needed care that the eating disorder adamantly rejected.

There are a few key limitations here. One, there are many states that will not even allow commitments for patients with eating disorders. Two, a commitment is only active in the state in which it was issued, and not all states possess an eating disorder facility that can accept and contain a committed patient. However, in states where it is both permissible and where there are inpatient resources to provide excellent care, like Colorado, commitments can be a life-saving option.

There are many ethical gray zones on this topic. It's all well and good to say that someone who needs good eating disorder treatment must receive it, but what about when there's no payer source? What if the patient is uninsured or has a governmental insurer not accepted by programs and their family has no financial resources? Or has a limited insurance plan with no out of network benefits or without mental health residential coverage? When I lay out the evidence base that relates to patients who decline treatment, outlining when to push forward with mandated treatment versus support a palliative approach, I realize I am doing so in a "perfect world" of resource neutrality that doesn't exist in real life. It makes a complicated topic even more so.

Older Patients Who Decline Treatment

Let's turn to the patient population that is older, has been sick a long time, has not experienced relief of psychiatric symptoms despite recently completing highly expert eating disorder programming and taking medications, feels that they will not benefit from a return to a higher level of care despite progressive illness, *and* no longer wishes to pursue full recovery. Expert clinical consensus holds that forcing such patients into treatment against their will proves futile.[3]

It is unlikely that repeated exposures to the treatment that failed to work in the recent past will suddenly bring about a different result. Life may be prolonged briefly, during enforced treatment, but this specific population of patients relapses rapidly after the enforcement period is over. In addition, these patients often suffer greatly in the process of mandated treatment. I want to make clear that any patient who does wish to pursue full recovery, no matter what their age, how long they have been ill, or how sick they are in the present moment, should be supported and encouraged to do so.

A body of literature addresses patients with severe and enduring eating disorders (SEED), or more specifically severe and enduring anorexia nervosa (SE-AN). Definitions vary, but SE-AN generally refers to patients with seven or more years of consecutive illness. This diverse group of patients ranges in age from 20–62, usually characterized by duration of their illness.[4,5] In a recent study on adults with SE-AN, younger age, shorter duration of illness, and better social adjustment predicted improved outcomes.[6] As many as a fifth of patients diagnosed with anorexia nervosa will go on to live with SE-AN, neither fully recovered nor fully in their disorder.[7] Given the breadth of patients who meet criteria, we cannot use the broad definition of SE-AN to guide decisions of mandated treatment or palliative care.

Harm Reduction

In patients older than 30 who have recently completed gold standard of care but relapse and decline to return to a higher level of care, the outpatient team might proceed with offering a harm reduction strategy. This means setting treatment goals below those for full recovery, for instance a reduced weight goal. These goals ideally are more palatable and less overwhelming to the patient, while still allowing a quality of life that is acceptable. It's harder to achieve harm reduction in purging behaviors because it's nearly impossible to gauge how much vomiting or laxative abuse might be safe as far as electrolyte levels are concerned. What is "safe" one week might cause dangerously low potassium the next week.

If a patient can sustain a harm reduction strategy, they can keep working with their team productively. There always remains the chance that a very slow pace of recovery work will earn trust and improve eating disorder symptomatology such that the patient accepts a more complete recovery over time.

Palliative Care and Hospice: Defining Terms

For some patients, a harm reduction strategy does not work. There is no "sub-basement" level of illness at which the eating disorder is satisfied. Many people think that palliative care and hospice care are one and the same or that both equate to "giving up." This is incorrect. Palliative care is its own medical specialty, dedicated to easing physical and emotional symptoms and avoiding aggressive treatments that are unlikely to improve a person's outcome. Quality of life and symptom management are key.

People may receive palliative care alongside ongoing active treatment— be that for their cancer, emphysema, or eating disorder—for a long period of time. In fact, palliative care has been shown to prolong life in patients with cancer, compared with those receiving medical care alone.[8] Not surprisingly, attending to the whole person's wellbeing—psychological, spiritual, and physical—yields better outcomes than focusing on medical issues alone.

Hospice care is provided at the end of life, typically in the last few weeks to months, aiming to ameliorate symptoms while fostering comfort and dignity. No measures are ever taken to hasten the dying process. However, hospice care also helps avoid treatments that would prolong the process, like intravenous fluids in someone who is comatose.

Palliative Care in Severe Persistent Mental Illness

Severe persistent mental illness (SPMI) describes psychiatric illnesses that have multiple comorbidities, chronic courses, frequent relapses, and higher than average death rates. The Swiss Academy of Medical Sciences guidelines on SPMI notes that a palliative approach aims to ameliorate symptoms and disability, improve quality of life, and reduce suicide rates. It can be offered in conjunction with active treatment. They specifically name three diseases that may benefit: therapy-refractory depression, severe schizophrenia, and severe anorexia nervosa.[9] Palliative psychiatry is its own specialty that provides support in coping with and accepting distressing mental symptoms. It affirms life but acknowledges that SPMI may be incurable. A team approach integrates the physical psychological, social, and spiritual aspects of patient care, offering a support system for patients and families.

There is no magical number that qualifies a person for palliative care, no number of times hospitalized, age, years with the disorder, medications tried, nor expected prognosis. Ultimately, it's the whole story of each patient that helps guide clinicians. Palliative care in anorexia nervosa might specifically involve ongoing supportive therapy and medical care to mitigate physical and psychological symptoms. The team agrees not to mandate a higher level of care against the patient's will. They might help family members move from policing and strategizing roles into accepting and supporting roles, spending as much good time together as possible.

Hospice

Palliative care efforts can go on for years. If and when a patient becomes sufficiently nutritionally compromised that they are unable to care for themselves independently, a move toward hospice services can be made. In my experience with patients, it can be very hard to predict when someone will die from an eating disorder. As we have seen, humans are remarkably resilient to starvation. Medical equipment can be brought into the home, if desired, and assistance with skin care, activities of daily living, and symptom management can be offered by professionals, along with ongoing family support.

No patient with this stage of an eating disorder should be asked, "So you want to die?" However, this question remains all too common. Imagine a woman with Stage 4 breast cancer who has tried all the available treatments, whose cancer has tragically returned. The cancer is now causing intolerable symptoms. The experimental treatments available have no guarantee of success and may make symptoms even worse. Additionally, engaging in further treatment would keep the patient out of her home and away from her family. When such a patient, after extensive conversations with her medical team and loved ones, elects not to pursue further experimental treatments, but rather to live out her days at home, absolutely no one would shame and demean her by demanding, "Oh, so you want to die?"

The fact that nearly all my chronically ill older patients who decline further treatment have had this question asked of them shows the inherent biases still held by doctors and society at large about eating disorders and mental illness. Doctors have been trained that mental illness isn't a choice. Yet in that frustrated question, they reveal that they too, deep down, believe that the solution is to "just eat." Collectively, we must recognize that suffering of the mind, in ways we cannot measure, might be just as real and painful as that of the physical body.

One branch of medical ethics literature declines to accept the concept of futility in anorexia nervosa. My answer to that is that I have worked with, truly gotten to know, and deeply cared about some of the most chronically ill and medically compromised patients in the United States. These are people whose suffering is so immense due to their eating disorder and psychiatric comorbidities, without relief from standard and even experimental treatments, that it is clearly inhumane to require them to suffer further. This topic isn't theoretical to my patients; it's real, personal, and urgent.

One large study of patient outcomes concluded that patients should not be offered palliative care. This Massachusetts General Hospital study started in 1987 and tracked eating disorder patients who had been admitted with anorexia or bulimia. They assessed patients at nine and then 20–25 years after discharge. At the 9-year follow-up, 31 percent of patients with anorexia and 68 percent of patients with bulimia had recovered. At the 22-year follow-up, 63 percent of patients with anorexia and 68 percent of those with bulimia had recovered. The authors pointed out that half of those with anorexia who had not recovered by nine years had achieved recovery at 22 years.

My response is that this leaves 36 percent of patients with anorexia nervosa who had not recovered after *22 years* of trying! Some of those might still be seeking active, full recovery, which is wonderful and should be fully supported. But for those who are suffering deeply, and whose families are anguished, trying to figure out what next, they deserve to have a voice in electing less aggressive care should they desire.

Case Resolution: Elana

Elana, her team, and her parents meet. The conversation is a lengthy and emotional one. Elana is clear that she never wants to return to a higher level of care. Her parents are clear that they cannot bear to see her die while living under their roof, and they note that her siblings feel increasingly uncomfortable having such a visibly malnourished family member around their children. However, they promise that they will never again send her to treatment against her will.

Now that she does not have the threat of forced treatment hanging over her head, causing stress and overwhelm, Elana agrees to try harm reduction once again. She and her team agree on a certain weight range that she will slowly but steadily try to achieve. She knows the process will be very challenging, but with her team's support, family's promise, and her own commitment not to put her parents in a situation they can't bear, she feels some renewed hope.

Notes

1 Lopez A, Yager J, Feinstein RE. Medical futility and psychiatry: palliative care and hospice care as a last resort in the treatment of refractory anorexia nervosa. *Int J Eat Disord.* 2010 May; 43(4):372–377. doi: 10.1002/eat.20701.

2 Leo RJ. Competency and the capacity to make treatment decisions: a primer for primary care physicians. *Prim Care Companion J Clin Psychiatry.* 1999 October; 1(5):131–141. PubMed PMID: 15014674.

3 Strober M. Managing the chronic, treatment-resistant patient with anorexia nervosa. *Int J Eat Disord.* 2004 November; 36(3):245–255. PubMed PMID: 15478130.

4 Bamford B, Barras C, Sly R, Stiles-Shields C, Touyz S, Le Grange D, Hay P, Crosby R, Lacey H. Eating disorder symptoms and quality of life: where should clinicians place their focus in severe and enduring anorexia nervosa? *Int J Eat Disord.* 2015 January; 48(1):133–138. doi: 10.1002/eat.22327.

5 Abd Elbaky GB, Hay PJ, le Grange D, Lacey H, Crosby RD, Touyz S. Pre-treatment predictors of attrition in a randomised controlled trial of psychological therapy for severe and enduring anorexia nervosa. *BMC Psychiatry.* 2014 March 7; 14:69. doi: 10.1186/1471-244X-14-69.

6 Le Grange D, Fitzsimmons-Craft EE, Crosby RD, Hay P, Lacey H, Bamford B, Stiles-Shields C, Touyz S. Predictors and moderators of outcome for severe and enduring anorexia nervosa. *Behav Res Ther.* 2014 May; 56:91–98. doi: 10.1016/j.brat.2014.03.006.

7 Touyz S., et al. (2016) *Managing severe and enduring anorexia nervosa.* New York, NY: Routledge.

8 Temel JS, Greer JA, Muzikansky A, Gallagher ER, Admane S, Jackson VA, Dahlin CM, Blinderman CD, Jacobsen J, Pirl WF, Billings JA, Lynch TJ. Early palliative care for patients with metastatic non-small-cell lung cancer. *N Engl J Med.* 2010 August 19; 363(8):733–742. doi: 10.1056/NEJMoa1000678.

9 Trachsel M, Wild V, Biller-Andorno N, Krones T. Compulsory treatment in chronic anorexia nervosa by all means? Searching for a middle ground between a curative and a palliative approach. *Am J Bioeth.* 2015; 15(7):55–56. doi: 10.1080/15265161.2015.1039730.

Conclusion
How We Can Each Make a Positive Contribution

I've been asked countless times, either at work or at dinner parties when people find out about my profession, "Do you have any thoughts about what I can do to protect my kids from eating disorders?" The person asking might be the parent of a toddler, hoping to prevent future problems. They might want to help their teenager manage the pressures of social media. Or they might be someone with an eating disorder who wants to avoid creating another link in a generational chain of body image problems, or who would like to share these ideas with their families to create positive changes in the home. I will wrap up the book by offering my thoughts on this important topic.

The reality of eating disorders is that they are complex, multifaceted disorders, and prevention can't be reduced to a simple formula. While there is no guarantee that doing (or not doing) any one thing can prevent an eating disorder, these suggestions feel like a good place to start as they, at the very least, teach people how to stop contributing to social body image "pollution" in an already "smoggy" world.

Don't Talk about Your Body

My first recommendation is to stop talking about your body. No comments, either positive or negative. This is because a focus on body appearance, especially when a narrow set of ideals are applied to concepts like beauty, acceptance, or health, is unscientific, nurtures internalized size stigma, and may induce shame or body dissatisfaction. Your children (especially if you have emotionally attuned, sensitive children) are watching you like little hawks, learning to follow your cues. Don't celebrate if you lost weight, and don't complain about any aspect of your shape or size. Don't criticize your body when out clothes shopping, and don't decline to get in the pool because you're ashamed of how you look.

Your child loves you and almost certainly loves your body because it belongs to you. If that knowledge isn't enough, or if you find yourself in a dynamic where your child is reassuring you that your body is just fine, it may be time for therapy. No child should have the burden of reassuring their parent that they are acceptable. Being exposed to a parent's self-criticism clouds a child's beautiful, innocent wisdom by the growing awareness that if their beloved parent dislikes their own body, then the child's body might be unacceptable as well.

Women in particular tend, for many of the reasons discussed in this book and many that are beyond its scope, to openly criticize their bodies. This has become an acceptable social topic: how much weight you gained over vacation, what diet you'll try next, how healthy you feel after a cleanse. To a certain extent, women are taught by society not to act too full of themselves, not to come across as overly confident. So, upon receiving a compliment, women may immediately come back with a self-deprecating reply like, "Oh, well, these jeans are just flattering. You should see me in a bathing suit." Stop. How can we say we're trying to raise confident, body-positive children when their idols are tearing themselves down? Answer a compliment with a smile and a simple "thanks." Teach by example.

Don't Talk about Other People's Bodies

Equally important is not commenting on other people's bodies. This applies to your friends, distant cousins at family reunions, people on TV, and certainly your children. No good comes from comments like, "Wow, she's gained weight" or "I wish I were skinny like her/ripped like him" or "You look great!" (often meaning: you've lost weight). Home is the first place children develop a sense of self. Their joyful, carefree relationship with their bodies—running around half naked in the sprinkler in the summer, playing dress-up—risks becoming more self-conscious the more they learn that some bodies are deemed acceptable and desirable and some aren't. Refuse to contribute to this fall from grace.

It's not uncommon for parents, wanting to promote an awareness of health but filtering this desire through their own internalized size bias, to point out well-known athletes or media figures as role models of looking fit and healthy. Most of us will never have the body appearance of such individuals because we are mere mortals who don't have time to cultivate such an appearance, even if it were genetically possible. We can, however, be strong and healthy (if these are our values) without having a body that looks like theirs. We must consciously unhook health outcomes from appearance. It's great to celebrate someone's strength or achievement— just don't comment on their body size or shape.

Create a Family Food Culture

Induct your children into your family's food culture. There are infinite different ways to raise and nourish children successfully. One of the great joys of parenting is to introduce your child to your family's values. In my family, for instance, we love the outdoors, good food with special cooking traditions on holidays, the theater, travel, board games, music, and reading. It's a joy to watch my daughters engage in these values and develop their own opinions and preferences.

One of my jobs as a parent is to teach my children our family's food values, equip them with nutritional education that matches our family's belief structures, and, given my profession, keep them as safe as possible from disordered eating. To that end, there are no "good" and "bad" foods in our house. Children are very concrete. "Bad" means something serious to them.

My kids are equally picky in totally different ways (one loves meats, fish, beans, and carbs but dislikes most fruits and vegetables, while the other has never met a fruit or vegetable she doesn't love but is a little iffy about proteins). And yet, their palates are slowly expanding. They enjoy foods now that they didn't a few years ago. As a family, we follow the same "moderation in moderation" message that I discuss with my patients. There are no off-limits foods.

Whenever possible, we eat together as a family. Except for the occasional meltdown over what's being served for family dinner, when I may throw together a quesadilla for one of them, we eat the same food. When they feel full, they stop eating. The "clean plate club"—requiring children to finish their meal no matter what—disconnects kids from their intuitions about satiety.

It's hard on kids when a parent never eats with the family, eats something completely different, or never orders an ice cream cone during a weekend excursion. By eating balanced meals together and practicing moderation, without any comments on body size and food, families teach their kids life lessons about how to honor intuitive hunger and fullness cues.

Exercise without Reference to Body Size and Shape

For as long as I can remember, when my daughters asked me why I wanted to go for a walk or exercise, I'd reply, "So Mommy can stay strong to play with you." Avoid linking exercise and body appearance. This gives your children, whose main exercise may be play or who may be serious athletes at a young age, permission to occupy their diverse bodies without judgment. If you comment on anything related to their bodies and exercise, make the comment a functional one: "I can see how much faster you're running now!" or "Your balance has really improved," or "Wow, you looked strong out there."

Answer Questions with Questions

When your four year old gleefully observes "Mommy's big tummy!" while cuddling or your eight year old asks you the question, "Mom, am I fat?" or "Dad, are you fat?" first take a deep breath. The adult brain may jump to all sorts of conclusions learned from years of citizenship in a biased society. Common parental answers to these interactions include, "My belly isn't that big!" or "It's big because I had to carry you," or "No, honey, you're beautiful," or "Yeah, but I'm trying to lose weight." These well-meaning answers assume the child equates larger body size or fatness with negativity, lack of beauty, or something shameful that requires eating differently. It's very possible the child thought none of these things (but now they do). Don't jump to reassure.

Instead, keep the tone light, and in the first scenario, remember how much bigger an adult truly looks to a child. Regardless of where your body falls on the size spectrum, shower your little one with kisses and agree, "Yep, Mommy's tummy is a lot bigger than your tummy!" In the second scenario, ask a few follow-up questions. "What does fat mean to you? Who's been talking about fatness? Tell me more." Allow your child to share what's on their mind so that you can be responsive to the question without imposing your own biases.

Ultimately, these interactions offer wonderful opportunities to start teaching your child about body diversity, tuned for their age and maturity level. Depending on what your child says about why they asked the question, you can explain, "Everybody's body is different, and we celebrate uniqueness in this family." If the question relates to having observed teasing, you can respond, "I'm sorry to hear that kids in your school were bullying someone because they were bigger. That's mean and unkind. We don't believe in that in our family." If the question pertains to fears about health or personal safety, you can reply,

> In our family, we know you can't just look at someone and tell if they are healthy or unhealthy by the size of their body. I'm doing what I'm able to in order to play with you and have fun together.

When you consider how much your own parents' opinions on weight and size still stick with you to this day (for better or worse), you realize how these positive messages can really make a difference.

"I Just Want My Kids to be Healthy and Not Get Teased"

Many parents, in their quest for non-GMO, organic, healthful, preservative-free, locally sourced foods, are guided by a genuine desire for their children to grow up healthy, fit, and accepted socially. Parents, in particular, can experience a pang of remorse when their child's snack of Oreos and Goldfish are subjected to nervous-to-horrified reactions by another parent who prepared heirloom orange wedges in perfectly chemical-free containers for their little one. The fact is that most parents truly just want to do right by their child.

What many parents don't consider is the invisible cost of strict (bordering on orthorexic) food rules, followed in the name of health. That cost is a perpetual haze of food anxiety that swirls through the home. This anxiety isn't healthy for anyone, much less the kids who exist on the far side of the perfectionistic/achieving/intense side of the bell curve. Plus, such food rules are often arbitrary and can change by the month. For instance, coconut oil has recently been thought to possess special benefits, leading some health-focused families to insist upon its use over traditional cooking oils. However, coconut oil turns out to have more than twice the saturated fat as lard, and the American Heart Association recently recommended against consuming it.[1] So, if you happen to love coconut oil, great, consume it in moderation. But don't seek it out as a health food. Strict family food rules that might contribute to the development of an eating disorder risk exchanging theoretical food-related health benefits for a potentially deadly mental illness that is proven to cause serious harm.

What about parents who think their child should lose weight in order to be healthy? This is complicated by well-meaning pediatricians who have actually recommended weight loss. Multiple studies have shown that dieting among adolescents leads to greater weight gain.[2] Adolescents who engage in secretive eating, possibly in reaction to being on a diet, show more disordered eating-related psychopathology and dieting behaviors as well as loss-of-control eating than those who do not eat secretly.[3] This makes sense now that you have read this book.

Children come in all shapes and sizes, go through growth spurts and body changes, and progress through adolescence into adulthood in their own unique ways. Making negative comments about your child's body is likelier to sow seeds of body dissatisfaction than it is to promote healthy behaviors. And body dissatisfaction has been found to be the number one predictor of early onset eating disorders.[4] Rather than hope their bodies conform to a narrowly defined, thin, white ideal, teach your children to celebrate who they are and honor themselves independent of their size and shape. Focus on emotional health, fun movement, and balanced meals together, not body weight.

"I've Been Doing it All Wrong. How Do I Change?"

One of the most influential acts a powerful person can perform—and no one is more powerful to a child than a parent—is to admit that they were doing something wrong and talk about how they plan to change. Let's imagine that you have a loved one with an eating disorder, or you have been a victim of diet culture for years (or your family has for generations), or you have just finished reading this book, and you reflect on your home culture around bodies and food. Maybe there have been conversations or habits that you now realize you'd like to change going forward. What now?

If your kids are young enough, you can make these changes right now, and the main conversations will take place with your partner if present, extended family, or friend group. You can let them know that you aren't going to engage in diet or weight talk anymore because you've learned these topics are toxic, and while some people might be able to have such conversations safely, you never know who might be harmed by such subjects.

If your kids are older, it's fair to have an open conversation with them. What kid doesn't love it when their parents are wrong? You can say,

> I realize I've been talking about my body and other people's bodies in a way that hasn't been that great. I'm sorry. I really want to start over and set a new tone in this house. Could we have a conversation about how to change this?

If your partner or extended family insists upon continuing to criticize or admire bodies and talk about food in a non-productive way despite the respectful but clear boundaries that you set, all you can do is try and stay out of it yourself and not participate. This will still give your kids a haven of safety in their own bodies when they are alone with you, with opportunities to process your own perspective on the topic, by comparison with others', in an open, inquisitive, and thoughtful manner.

How Should I Approach a Friend Who Seems to Have a Problem?

I often get asked how to address a friend or colleague (or parent in the carpool line, or fellow gym member) who seems to have developed an eating disorder. Usually, this refers to someone who has lost a lot of weight or looks dangerously thin. On the whole, we have to remember that assumptions can be misleading. While someone working out for hours likely doesn't have a medical condition causing their visible malnutrition, another person might have cancer or another chronic disease. That said, many patients have stayed in their eating disorder longer because no one mentioned anything, contributing to the misconception that they must be "fine."

It's best to reserve these conversations for someone you know well, not a stranger. Rather than start by jumping to conclusions, you might pick a safe, private moment and share your observations.

> I have noticed that you seem to have lost a lot of weight lately, and that I never see you eat socially anymore. I hear you talking a lot about food, bodies, healthy eating, and how often you are working out. I'd like to share with you that these observations make me worry you've developed an eating disorder.

If the person seems open to this discussion, you can warmly assure them of your support and ask if they'd like help finding experts who can help, like a therapist, dietitian, and doctor. If they shut it down and assure you that they are fine, you can at least encourage them to make a doctor's appointment, because in your experience, people who are truly "fine" don't discount a friend's concerns and persist in certain behaviors. Remember: your role isn't to fix your friend, it's to share your observations and encourage them to seek expert help.

Creating a Safe Refuge for All Bodies

In the final analysis, we can't shelter our kids completely from a world that is hostile to body diversity and bombards them with pseudoscientific messages about nutrition. I do recommend delaying access to social media as long as possible, given the portrayal of superficial, falsely perfected lives and the comparison culture fostered on these platforms. What we can do—with our kids, our friends, and our loved ones—is to make a positive contribution by making sure that our homes are a safe refuge for all bodies. Within our walls, those who enter can find sanctuary from the outside world.

We can carry this power to make a positive contribution outside the walls of our homes, too. At work, with friends, anywhere we go, we can resist contributing to a culture of body dissatisfaction and narrowly defined standards of beauty or health. Those who need to process distress and seek support around themes of nutrition and body image, even without an eating disorder, ideally should seek a good therapist rather than engage in self-deprecating language in daily life. It's also important to use a critical lens when viewing how diverse bodies are portrayed and treated in society. In so doing, we can then help our children cultivate their own critical thinking habits. Professionally speaking, eating disorder clinicians in all specialties have a responsibility to provide considerate and scientifically sound care to people of all shapes and sizes.

Be gentle and compassionate with yourself. Model the caring, vulnerable, thoughtful coping strategies you hope the next generation will someday use when they have to deal with disappointment, failure, or fatigue. And take with you the recognition that if you have an eating disorder or disordered eating, in this very moment you are sick enough to seek help and work toward recovery.

Notes

1 Sacks FM, Lichtenstein AH, Wu JHY, Appel LJ, Creager MA, Kris-Etherton PM, Miller M, Rimm EB, Rudel LL, Robinson JG, Stone NJ, Van Horn LV; American Heart Association. Dietary fats and cardiovascular disease: a presidential advisory from the American Heart Association. *Circulation*. 2017 July 18; 136(3):e1–e23. doi: 10.1161/CIR.0000000000000510.

2 Goldschmidt AB, Wall MM, Choo TJ, Evans EW, Jelalian E, Larson N, Neumark-Sztainer D. Fifteen-year weight and disordered eating patterns among community-based adolescents. *Am J Prev Med*. 2018 January; 54(1):e21–e29. doi: 10.1016/j.amepre.2017.09.005.

3 Kass AE, Wilfley DE, Eddy KT, Boutelle KN, Zucker N, Peterson CB, Le Grange D, Celio-Doyle A, Goldschmidt AB. Secretive eating among youth with overweight or obesity. *Appetite*. 2017 July 1; 114:275–281. doi: 10.1016/j.appet.2017.03.042.

4 Rohde P, Stice E, Marti CN. Development and predictive effects of eating disorder risk factors during adolescence: implications for prevention efforts. *Int J Eat Disord*. 2015 March; 48(2):187–198. doi: 10.1002/eat.22270.

Acknowledgments

I have many people to acknowledge with gratitude. First and foremost, I love and appreciate my husband Bryan and daughters, Sydney and Skye. They make life so much fun and inspire me to hold boundaries in order to enjoy my time with them mindfully and whole-heartedly. Bryan, Sydney, and Skye patiently and supportively hung in there over the many months that I went to bed early to wake up early and write.

My team at the Gaudiani Clinic makes every day a joy, and I love them dearly: Meghan Eliopulos reviewed multiple drafts of the book, and Sue Bennett was also a primary editor. Aimee Becker expertly reviewed my chapter on Gender and Sexual Minorities. Abby Brockman and Elissa Rosen complete the team.

Other expert reviewers to whom I owe great thanks for their direction and guidance on specific chapters include Carmen Cool, Lisa DuBreuil, Kate McCrann, Kate Ackerman, Lindo Bacon, Beth Hartman McGilley, and Margo Maine. Desiree Adaway contributed vital education. Ginger Broadus provided invaluable insights.

Friends both personal and professional have given me the gift of their support, interest, and enthusiasm over the years. I thank Roy Erlichman for his generous and wise coaching as I made the leap to start my own clinic. Carolyn Costin helped immensely with getting the book-writing process started and with many subsequent questions. Steven Parisi helped bring to life an early cover design.

Alyssa Jarvis has for years kept all the vital elements of home and hearth running smoothly and happily.

My darling sisters, Caroline and Alexandra Gaudiani, inspire and encourage me, make me laugh, and keep me from taking myself too seriously. Danica Griffith, Brook Griese, and Julia Archambault are the sisters of my soul who recharge me with their love, encouragement, and wisdom.

My parents, Candace and Vince Gaudiani, have provided every kind of support it is possible to provide, for which I am immensely grateful.

I salute the movie *Wonder Woman* and Gal Gadot for inspiring me to launch this project when I did.

And to my patients: thank you for being the best teachers. I promise to keep listening and learning.

Index

Made in the USA
Monee, IL
02 July 2024

61089440R00154